CW00519305

ISBN-10:1907934100
ISBN-13: 978-1907934100

CONTENTS

Preface

The topics covered in this book are aimed at business students who need an introduction to solving problems in business. Primary aims are to equip learners with the knowledge and skills needed to cope with the vast array of data and information available to managers. Basic practical quantitative skills introduced here include spreadsheets and data representations.

Case studies and scenarios are used to highlight different solving approaches.

On successful completion of material in this book, the learner will have acquired the following:

- knowledge – to be able to identify different types of organisational problems, understand techniques for problem solving in organisations and analyse quantitative data.
- intellectual/transferrable skills – to be able to conduct quantitative analysis using Information technology for problem solving.

Worked examples, all drawn from real business situations, are included throughout to reinforce the essential ideas underlying each topic.

The author gratefully acknowledges business colleagues based at the *Universidad Metropolitana de Educacion, Ciencia y Tecnologia*, Panama and John Dwyer in the Business School at the *University of Roehampton*, United Kingdom.

Thanks also to John's colleagues who advised on various topics, including business problem solving (Rob Manderson, Premkanth Puwanenthiren), employee issues (Tim Hill), quantitative methods (Souad Slyman), survey design (Haytham Siala), financial problems (Katerina Ipatova), overall structure (Teresa Waring) and publishing issues (Julie Dwyer).

Ella Verméz

Panama City
August 2016

About the Author

Ella Verméz specialises in consulting and educational services for small businesses and she divides her time between Panama and the United Kingdom.

Multilingual in Spanish, English and Italian, Ella was born in Panama and set up her own consulting enterprise after graduating from *Universidad Metropolitana de Educacion, Ciencia y Tecnologia* in Panama.

As an educational consultant, Ella assists authors of prospective brochures, books and promotional materials.

As a keen enthusiast of landscaping and horticulture, Ella is the Managing Director of specialist designers *Natures Gardens*.

Ella would welcome suggestions for improvement and inclusions to this edition of *An Introduction to Analysing Business Data & Information*.

Please communicate in the first instance via email to:

vermeze@naturesgardens.co.uk

1. INTRODUCTION

In this text, we are primarily concerned with:

- analysis
- data
- information
- problem solving

all within a business context.

Business Analysis

The business world is surrounded by the need for analysis. Although there are different role definitions, depending upon the organization, there does seem to be an area of common ground where most business analysts work. The responsibilities include:

- To investigate business systems, taking a holistic view of the situation. This may include examining elements of the organisation structures and staff development issues as well as current processes and IT systems.

- To evaluate actions to improve the operation of a business system. Again, this may require an examination of organisational structure and staff development needs, to ensure that they are in line with any proposed process redesign and system development.

- To document the business requirements for the IT system support using appropriate documentation standards.

At every level of business, ranging from an sole trader enterprise to an established corporation, analysis of many aspects of the business activities are crucial to success. Understanding the business models involved, anticipating the pitfalls to watch out for and recognising the potential for growth are everyday issues for every successful manager.

Business Data & Information

Business data surrounds every organisation. In some cases it simply sits there untouched. In other cases, it is turned into meaningful information which managers can use to make informed decisions. Certainly, every organisation is surrounded by massive quantities of data.

Data is frequently measured, collected, reported and analysed, whereupon it can be visualized using graphs, images or other analysis tools. Data as a general concept refers to the fact that some existing information or knowledge is represented or coded in some form suitable for better usage or processing. Raw data is a collection of numbers or characters in a form before transformation by researchers into useful information.

Business Problem Solving

Business data surrounds every organisation. In some cases it simply remains untouched. In other cases, it is turned into meaningful information which managers can use to make informed decisions.

Of course, there are general problem solving skills that can be applied in business situations. Breaking down complex problems into simpler, more manageable problems and negotiating with customers and employers are just two examples.

In the following sections, we will look variously at analysing business data and information, with a problem-solving approach.

2. BUSINESS DATA & INFORMATION

Some people believe that the terms 'data' and 'information' are interchangeable and mean the same thing. However, there is a distinct difference between the two. Data can be any character, text, words, number, pictures, sound, or video and, if not put into context, means little or nothing to a human. However, information is useful and usually formatted in a manner that allows it to be reasoned about by a human. The *DIKW Pyramid* (see figure 2.1), also known variously as the *DIKW Hierarchy* or the *Knowledge Pyramid*, is a way of visualising the difference. It refers to a class of models for representing data, information, knowledge and wisdom. Typically, information is defined in terms of data, knowledge in terms of information and wisdom in terms of knowledge.

Figure 2.1 The WKID pyramid.

Computers typically read or input data but it is not necessarily something that a computer actually *understands*. Through the use of formulae, programming scripts or software applications, a computer can turn data into information that a human can start to understand. Consider the following examples of the data and information for a similar situation:

Example of Data
John Smith 19 BUS SW15 5SL 2016

Example of Information
Name: John Smith
Age: 19
Degree: Business Management
Address:
University of Roehampton
LONDON
SW15 5SL
Year of entry: 2016

As we can see in the above example, if we looked only at the data, it might be possible to understand some of the text on the line but it isn't really useful or clear. That same information, when broken out into readable text and slightly formatted, becomes much more useful and allows us to identify that it is contact information for student John Smith. In this example, the data could be a CSV file that can be converted into an Excel spreadsheet or database to make it usable information. Other file format common in business are word-processed files (e.g. Word), graphics files (e.g. Jpeg), statistics files (e.g. SPSS) and more.

A Manager's View of Data

Businesses are surrounded by so much data nowadays. A few decades ago, small word-processing files or small spreadsheet files were the business norm. Before that paper-based files were the preferred means of storage for many businesses. Nowadays, the volumes of data available to even a small business are enormous. In fact, entire industries have sprung up surrounding customer profiling, intelligent marketing and data mining. These have become so critical to a business that failing to properly analyse the data it holds can ultimately lead to collapse.

Thankfully there are some basic guidelines that managers can follow in order to deal with this situation:

Find out what data the business has

The first step to overhauling data governance in a business organisation is to conduct an audit of all the information it holds. A manager needs to figure out how much information being kept, should be kept and how much is unnecessary 'data noise' clogging up spreadsheets and databases. Indeed, there are often legal requirements on how long data should be stored.

Make sure data is properly labelled

The 'very basis' of a good data policy lies in knowing if a document should be designated as an important 'record'. Organisations need clear, consistent guidelines to help staff separate these records from routine documents, since classifying every bit of data as a record is expensive and unnecessary. Clear, unambiguous labelling is essential.

Train all staff

It has been estimated that about eighty percent of data breaches stem from human error, so any business needs to train all staff on how to avoid data breaches and understand threats. In many countries, there are prevailing fines of up to five percent of turnover for breaking data regulations and strict rules on reporting breaches, so a manager needs to decide who is in charge of reporting. Regular, effective staff training is therefore essential.

Make some employees 'data owners'

An astute manager should not be afraid to assign ownership of data to individual senior managers. There may be too much data in the organisation for one person to handle every type of information but it is vital to have clarity regarding responsibility for managing data across different teams.

Keep policies and systems up-to-date

Old data policies were often written before the age of Web and social media, so they need to be updated regularly as technology evolves. Staying ahead of the game protects companies from breaches and turns records into assets. Nowadays, claiming ignorance of prevailing data policies is no defence.

An Individual's View of Data

Individuals are also surrounded by so much data these days. A few decades ago small disk or perhaps a modest external drive was perfectly adequate for storing all of our work and personal files. Before that, paper-based files and filo-faxes were a preferred means of storage for many. Nowadays, we need to catalogue and store data files which can sometimes be very large, including pictures, videos and more, filling several computers.

Of course, at work we have to be acutely aware of rules and regulation governing data storage. It might well apply that certain files have to go in specific places, some publicly accessible, some privately protected. Thankfully there are some basic guidelines that we can each follow in order to deal with this situation:

Organise and structure data files

Choosing a logical and consistent way to organise and name our data files and folders allows us (and others when necessary) to locate and use them. We need to think about how to name and structure data at the start of a project. Organising data files carefully saves time and frustration and prevents duplication or errors.

Use logical folders

Applying a logical structure to files within folders relating to projects or issues keeps things in the same place, making them easy to find. Leaving files unsorted simply creates problems. We should structure folders hierarchically, a design hierarchy comprising higher level broader topics, with more specific folders within these. We should also apply good folder naming, e.g. folders named after projects and research issues with clear meaning, as opposed to seemingly-random numbers or codes.

Review what we have

Keeping multiple copies of data is pointless. We need to consider carefully what we should retain, for how long, and what can (and cannot) be destroyed or deleted. Consider this at intervals and at the end of a project. Don't name folders or store data in relation to the names of individuals e.g. 'Julie's files'. What happens when they leave? Who knows what is there?

Organise email

It is easy to neglect the organisation and management of email. The value of email should be considered in terms of content, the associated attachments and also as a means to describe processes, decisions and communications. As with all recorded information held by a business organisation or university, emails are covered by Data Protection and Freedom of Information legislation and so can be requested under these laws. This means they need to be managed effectively. One tip is to delete emails we don't need. Another tip is to store attachments to a folder in locations where they need to be.

Analysis of Data

Analysis of data involves processes of inspecting, cleaning, transforming and modelling with the goals of discovering useful information, suggesting conclusions and supporting decision making. Needless to say, successfully extracting useful, focussed information from raw data does not happen easily (see figure 2.2).

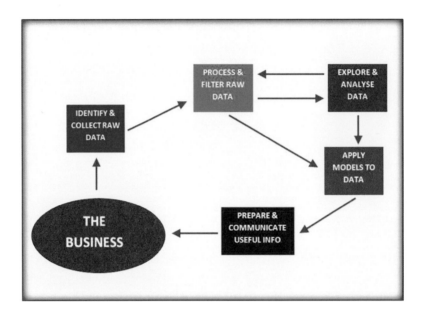

Figure 2.2 Generic processes relating to data and information in business.

Identifying and Collecting Raw Data

Raw data is data that has not yet been processed into meaningful business information. Identifying raw data for the business, e.g. customer spending data, might be relatively straightforward but collecting it together much more challenging. For instance, raw data might be found in a multiple of computer file formats or stored in a multiple of physical locations.

There are several dos and don'ts to bear in mind when dealing with customers. First and foremost, we should not harass customers for data. Endless form filling is enough to put any consumer off a purchase. Data collection has to be either unobtrusive or incentivised. We should collect it bit by bit to build up a fuller picture of our customers gradually and in a non-annoying way.

From customer orders, we can obtain contact details and name from orders and begin building a transaction history, whether on or offline (although online makes things even easier as data can automatically be entered into a database). We can add in a birth date as optional. If the transaction is happening online, we can add in an optional section requesting more information. It is preferable to phrase it in a way that appeals to the customer, such as: "So that we can learn more about you and provide you with a service more suited to your personal needs, please fill in...." We can also use this technique if a customer has to register an account with us at any future point. Other types of direct customer data are shown in figure 2.3.

Collecting direct customer data

Name and contact details: Allows a business to market directly to customers. This also lets us make communications personalised. We might also need to contact them if an order is running late.

Transaction history: Indicates user preferences - which products they're most inclined to buy, when and how often. Reveals how valuable a customer they are: how much they spend and how often.

Communications from you to customers and any response they make: We need to keep records of this to make sure our communications are spaced out correctly (i.e. not too often). It also lets us monitor the effectiveness of different types of communication and those to which customers best respond. If we compare the transaction history with the communications record, we may find one method of communication encourages customers to buy more than others.

Profiling (age, gender, profession, income, hobbies, etc): This information is harder to obtain but can be useful for more advanced marketing strategies. Once we have the info for a number of customers, we can build up clearer picture of the precise target customer. It allows us to better focus advertising and marketing efforts, as well as affiliate opportunities and sponsorships. For example, knowing that our target customer goes to the gym several times each week, opens up a new place to advertise, a new line of gym-related products and an opportunity to do a deal with the local gym to offer discounted membership if they shop with you several times. Knowing their age and profession (and so an idea of their income) helps with pricing strategy. The better and more detailed picture you have of our target customer, the more we can tailor and develop products to satisfy them.

Spending habits: It is important to know how our customers shop, such as impulse buying, considered purchasing, comparing the prices from different businesses and so on. We can display goods and structure deals around consumers' spending habits.

Birthdays:
Sending out a birthday text or card can add a personal touch and make a customer feel valued.

Whether or not they pay on time: This is obviously important for cash-flow reasons rather than marketing ones but it is worth adding to the list anyway if we are thinking about data collection.

Figure 2.3 Collecting direct customer data in a small business.

Data obtained from surveys is less direct since it often contains opinions and other subjective information. From surveys, we can obtain a significant amount of information by asking details about their profile (gender, age, etc.). While some respondents may be reluctant to give their name, some will. For those that don't, you get a clearer picture of your overall target customer anyway, which is the aim here.

When marketing, we can run a competition asking for email address and a couple of other details. Customers will normally be more inclined to share personal data when they have something to gain from it.

Online behaviour can help us track spending habits and user preferences, though you may only be able to get an overall picture of your target customer rather than profiles of specific users - use Google Analytics. From research, we can use statistics and research already out there to build a more detailed picture of our target customer (though of course they won't provide information on individuals). We can look at demographic-related reports and spot trends since there are almost certainly others targeting the same demographic.

Processing and Filtering Raw Data

Filtering out duplication or redundancy from data can lead to problems, if not carried out carefully. Occasionally we might keep data that we don't really need. On the other hand, we might discard data that we need, now or in the near future. Of course, our data needs to be stored carefully (see figure 2.4).

How to store customer data

Initially, we can store data in Excel or similar spreadsheet software. But as our data becomes more detailed, we will need specific database software to manage customer data.

Therefore, we can investigate available customer relationship management (CRM) software which would be suitable for the needs of the business, both present and future. In this regard, it is important to judge the right level of complexity. We don't want to end up with something either far too complicated or far too basic for our needs.

We can also make sure our data collection spans all different departments and members of staff in our business. Everyone should be contributing to the same document in similar formats and we can use CRM software to manage this.

Guidance and the law on storing customer data. There are complex laws surrounding business' collection of data and these vary from country to country.

There are several principles of data protection in the UK and anyone processing personal data must comply with them. These state that data must be:

- fairly and lawfully processed
- used for limited purposes
- adequate, relevant, not excessive
- accurate
- not kept longer than necessary
- processed in accordance with the data subject's (eg the customer) rights
- secure
- not transferred to countries without adequate protection

(Reference: http://www.legislation.gov.uk/ukpga/1998/29/contents)

We should also make sure to ask customers' preferences when taking their contact details. Allowing them to opt out of receiving marketing material, for instance, will show respect and consideration. This in turn can be reciprocated with a good customer!

Figure 2.4 How to store customer data

Exploring and Analysing Data

The process of analysing raw data might well involve several iterations before we can start modelling. Categorising the customer data into variable headings such as spending, gender, age, time, frequency and location is often a necessary first step. Depending on legal requirements, it is often necessary to anonymise a business' data before processing further.

Applying Models to Data

Modelling is a means of processing data to identify causations, relationships and forecasts. The resulting information is then checked for its relevance to the business. The specific models to be used might emanate from past business experiences or from a need for projections into the future. Simulations and statistical analysis are two types of model widely used. For example, simulating consumer demand for a new product or service can assist managers in deciding production volumes and staffing.

As with human errors in business decision making, computer and mathematical modelling bring with them errors and approximations. It is important to understand these before making critical decisions. For instance, if a computer model predicts an increase in sales next year of twenty percent (with error of plus or minus thirty per cent), we might actually end up next year with a decrease in sales. In this case, the percentage error is just too large to make business decisions.

Preparing and Communicating Useful Information

Data visualisation is often used to help managers understand the results of a data analysis. Once the data has been analysed, it may be reported in many formats to the users of the analysis to support their requirements. The users may have feedback, which results in additional analysis, since much of the analytical cycle is iterative.

When determining how to communicate the results, an analyst may consider data visualisation techniques to help clearly and efficiently communicate the message to the audience. Data visualisation uses information displays such as tables and charts to help communicate key messages contained in the data. Tables are helpful to a user who might lookup specific numbers, while charts (e.g. bar charts, line charts or scatterplots) may help to convey the quantitative messages contained in the data.

As an example, the auditor of a public company must arrive at a formal opinion on whether financial statements of publicly traded corporations are "fairly stated, in all material respects." This requires extensive analysis of factual data and evidence to support their opinion. When making the leap from facts to opinions, there is always the possibility that the opinion is erroneous.

Customer Data - Retail

We all know supermarkets use information about our shopping habits to target us with personalised vouchers and offers but how would you feel about sitting down to watch a movie and being confronted with adverts based on what was in your shopping trolley at Sainsbury's a few hours earlier? Or what would you think about Tesco using its Clubcard database to check what you are eating and possibly offering vouchers for salad and fruit if your basket is usually groaning with unhealthy items? These are just two of the ways the supermarket giants are planning to make use of the data they gather on us. For every loyalty point or coupon that supermarkets give out, they gobble up a huge amount of information about our shopping habits. We are all familiar with targeted offers linked to loyalty cards but it might seem be surprising just how much data the big retailers collect on all of their shoppers – and even potential customers – and what they do with it.

Anyone opting out of taking out a loyalty card because they don't want others to know the contents of their shopping basket needs to think again. Supermarkets also track debit and credit card payment data and till receipts. So someone, somewhere probably knows about that bottle of wine bought yesterday.

So how do the supermarkets use this data? If a customer has a loyalty card or shops online, supermarkets will build up a demographic profile and collect data about customer loyalty, what they buy and how much they spend. The supermarket can then change what the customer sees logging in to make it easier to find the products of interest (and that their data suggests the customer will buy). In-store they will use their data to make decisions about what they sell and influence us with vouchers given on our last visit. In the UK, Waitrose and Asda freely admit to analysing aggregated payment card data to monitor "customer shopping patterns" (for example, items purchased) over time. Both insist this is common practice in the retail industry and that card numbers are not connected to an individual or an address. Sainsbury's and Tesco claim that they do not track or monitor their customers' payment cards.

Using Business Data to Make Strategic Decisions

Every business can benefit from becoming more analytical across the board - understanding its customers, performing its operations, and making its decisions. But even the most analytically-oriented company needs to target its analytical efforts where they will do the most good, because resources, especially talent, are always constrained. And all business opportunities aren't created equal. Few confer breakthroughs in performance or differentiation in the marketplace.

For companies just embarking on the analytical journey, a specific business problem may be a good initial target. Perhaps customers are complaining about service or quality, or performance benchmarks show that a business process is wasting resources, or a competitor has raised the bar and the business needs analytics to determine and execute a response.

As analytical experience and success grow, so targets become broader and more strategic: to optimise key business processes over time, and to innovate and operate in ways that differentiate the business in the eyes and experience of its customers. If they haven't already done so, companies should be analysing their data and targeting their analytical investments at their distinctive capabilities. Regardless of personal opinions, if the data suggests a particular business product or service is one of their best, this should influence strategic decisions.

A good target is so important to the business and so full of opportunity that it can engage top management commitment and create momentum. It focuses on generating insight rather than merely information, and is both ambitious and approachable: ambitious in that it impacts the business and approachable in that it has access to the resources and capabilities to succeed.

SMART Analysis helps a business to ensure that its progress towards achieving its objectives can be measured:

Specific - so that everyone knows precisely what is to be achieved

Measurable - sets out the levels and values to be achieved

Agreed - relevant staff are involved in setting objectives and committed to keeping them

Relevant - to the organisation's overall purpose

Time-framed - to ensure that it will fit within the organisation's overall plans

Case Studies – Business Data & Information

Case Study: *Data Integrity - How Tesco brought loyalty to its stores in Malaysia.*

Tesco has over 660 million customers that pull in over US$500 billion worth of retail spending. As an international retailer, it has half a million employees working in twelve countries, serving about 75 million customers each week. In Malaysia, there are currently 50 Tesco retail stores and seven stores on the grocery home-shopping front and 1.2 million customers each week. In 2006, Tesco also launched the Clubcard in Malaysia. With Clubcard, it has 1.7 million customers who are active and swiping the card each day. Online shopping is also a new arena the company ventured into last year for seven of its stores.

Tesco used data from Nielsen and other researchers focusing on customer satisfaction studies to receive information on about marketer trends, consumer behaviour and combined it with the data from the Clubcard. This helped the retailer to put the customer into the centre of its decisions. Tesco also wanted to go further and understand how consumers' minds worked and how to be a priority brand in their purchase choices. Simply understanding purchasing habits is important – but it is just one channel. Understanding customers and how they shop is just the start, he added.

For more information, refer to the full case study.

Questions for Discussion:

1. Explain the terms data integrity, loyalty and channel used in this case study.
2. In what ways would you expect customer loyalty to vary between Malaysia and the UK?
3. Explain some of the deficiencies of the "old" email approach.
4. Research and list the names of loyalty cards used by some of Tesco's major competitors.

Case Study: *NATS - Effective strategies for long-term growth.*

Air travel has become a regular part of life for many people, but managing the processes surrounding it is far from simple. During the summer of 2012 the UK welcomed around 200,000 more air passengers through Heathrow and Gatwick airports than in a non-Olympic year. Over 3,000 extra flight slots were needed for the visitors and athletes for the London Olympic Games. Making sure all flights have a safe landing and take-off is part of the responsibilities of NATS.

NATS (formerly National Air Traffic Services), is the main air navigation service provider in the United Kingdom. is a global air navigation provider. The organisation was originally established in 1962 as a government body but in 2001 became a Public/Private Partnership (PPP). The PPP model of ownership meant that private funding could be invested into NATS services and infrastructure. Over £123 million has been invested since the PPP was set up. NATS manages the world's busiest section of airspace as well as the busiest single and dual runway airports in Europe and the Middle East. Its systems and people manage over 6,000 flights a day through UK airspace – over 2 million a year – safely and efficiently. NATS-managed flights experienced delays of just 7.3 seconds per flight in 2011, around 1/10 of the European average. The majority of delays to flights in and out of the UK are caused by factors outside NATS' control.

NATS has grown phenomenally in the last year. Its strategies have taken it from operating in just UK and Gibraltar to offering the full range of its services in 28 countries, with contracts of different sizes and values. NATS offers and operates a range of services. A main function is to manage runways and airspace through Air Traffic Control (ATC). Other roles include providing consultancy and developing solutions for operational, economic and environmental issues, engineering infrastructure and software, defence services and training. Its customers include airports, airlines and aviation authorities. For more information, refer to the full case study.

Questions for Discussion:

1. Explain the terms 'vision' and 'aims'. Give examples related to NATS and a business of your choice.
2. What is a SMART objective? Explain one benefit for NATS of setting SMART objectives.
3. Analyse how having clear, long-term strategies supports NATS' vision for global expansion.
4. To what extent can having a clear vision, strategies, aims and objectives guarantee a business' success? Use the case study to support your ideas.

Exercises – Business Data & Information

1. {multiple choice – choose the most appropriate answer (a), (b), (c) or (d)}

A visual way of representing the difference between data and information is called the:

   (a) WKID pyramid   b) KIWD triangle   (c) IWKD tetrahedron   (d) WIKD circle

2. {multiple choice – choose the most appropriate answer (a), (b), (c) or (d)}

Data that has not yet been processed into useful business information is called:

   (a) Clean data   (b) Raw data   (c) Unformatted data   (d) Metadata

3. {multiple choice – choose the most appropriate answer (a), (b), (c) or (d)}

Collecting data based upon a specific customer with regard to personal details and spending habits is called:

   (a) Profiling   (b) Tracking   (c) Marketing   (d) Selling

4. {multiple choice – choose the most appropriate answer (a), (b), (c) or (d)}

Managing relationships between businesses and customers can be assisted by which type of business software?

   (a) B2B software   (b) Unix software   (c) CRM software   (d) Spyware

5. {multiple choice – choose the most appropriate answer (a), (b), (c) or (d)}

What is the name of the loyalty card currently used by Tesco supermarket?

   (a) Nectar card   (b) Tastecard   (c) Pluscard   (d) Clubcard

6.   Information from Data

Suggest suitable business information interpretations relating to the following basic alphanumeric character data:

(Note: any logical suggestion will suffice)

(i)   B2BB2C
(ii) SUSANJONES19ECONSW155SL201607794675555
(iii) RBSLLOYBARC
(iv) INCVATCGT

7.   Types of Files

Research the following types of data files used in business and state the software packages with which each is associated (e.g. Jpeg, Photoshop):

(i)   xls
(ii) dbs
(iii) docx
(iv) sav
(v)   ppt

8.   Breaches of the UK Data

Research and briefly summarise the following breaches of data protection in the UK:

(i)   Nationwide Building Society (2006)
(ii)   HM Revenue & Customs (2007)
(iii) T-Mobile (2009)
(iv)   Brighton and Sussex University Hospitals NHS Trust (2010)
(v)   Sony PlayStation Network (2011)
(vi)   Morrison's supermarket (2014)
(vii) Staffordshire University (2014)
(viii) Mumsnet (2014)
(ix)   Think W3 Limited (2014)
(x)   Moonpig (2015)
(xi)   TalkTalk (2014/2015)

9.   Wordsearch

```
                            ┌──────────────────────┐
────────────────────────────│        DATA          │────────────────────────────
                            └──────────────────────┘
```

```
T  R  A  W  D  A  T  A  N  M  G  D  L  Z  V  W  H  J  Y  F  S  D  K
I  E  M  O  D  E  L  L  I  N  G  J  E  O  K  G  C  M  O  Y  L  D  A
A  C  T  Y  D  I  O  Z  K  V  Y  S  Z  O  Y  P  E  C  O  B  J  T  O
C  D  S  E  G  G  Q  R  V  I  L  M  C  C  J  A  D  R  M  K  X  Z  C
R  D  R  E  U  S  L  U  A  Z  C  A  L  I  U  Z  L  C  C  P  I  A  J
M  R  C  Z  P  D  E  Z  C  E  Y  R  O  F  M  S  R  T  N  B  W  I  I
S  O  E  L  R  I  R  S  D  A  J  T  B  I  H  B  T  P  Y  K  N  W  B
O  C  K  K  O  M  D  A  T  A  F  O  L  D  E  R  E  O  M  C  I  P  Z
F  E  X  E  F  A  A  V  X  H  H  N  G  H  Y  Q  I  K  M  G  A  T  V
T  R  B  I  I  R  V  I  S  U  A  L  I  S  A  T  I  O  N  E  W  R  Y
W  C  E  J  L  Y  D  A  T  A  L  A  B  E  L  Y  W  N  V  V  R  S  D
A  A  U  P  I  P  U  W  Y  R  T  I  N  F  O  R  M  A  T  I  O  N  B
R  I  C  W  N  D  O  U  J  E  L  I  F  V  S  C  Q  F  U  D  D  N  C
E  B  D  I  G  I  Y  W  T  T  H  N  O  I  T  C  A  S  N  A  R  T  J
P  F  F  J  E  K  W  G  Q  P  A  Q  H  R  E  T  A  I  L  Z  A  Q  Z
W  G  O  G  D  W  A  V  O  B  R  E  T  U  P  M  O  C  O  Z  U  M  N
```

Find the following words in the puzzle.
Words are hidden ↑ ↓ → ← and ↘ .

COMPUTER	INFORMATION	RETAIL
CRMSOFTWARE	LOYALTYCARD	SMART
CSVFILE	MODELLING	TRANSACTION
CUSTOMER	PROFILING	VISUALISATION
DATAFOLDER	RAWDATA	WKIDPYRAMID
DATALABEL	RECORD	

3. PROBLEM SOLVING IN BUSINESS ORGANISATIONS

Information systems and organisations have significant influences on one another. Information systems are built by managers to serve the interests of the business. At the same time, the organisation must be aware of and open to the influences of information systems in order to benefit from new technologies. The interaction between information technology and organisations is complex and is influenced by many factors, including the organisation's structure, business processes, politics, culture, surrounding environment, and management decisions (see figure 3.1).

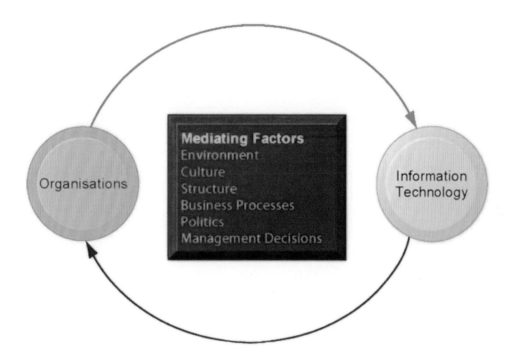

Figure 3.1 Factors in the relationship between organisations and information technology.

Managers need to understand how information systems can change social and work life in the business. It is simply not possible to design new systems or understand existing systems without understanding one's own business organisation.

This complex two-way relationship is mediated by many factors, not the least of which is the set of decisions made (or not made) by managers. Other factors include the organisational culture, structure, politics, business processes and environment.

A manager will be the one to decide which systems will be built, what they will do, and how they will be implemented. Indeed, it may not be possible to anticipate all of the consequences of these decisions. Some of the changes that occur in businesses because of new information technology (IT) investments cannot always be foreseen and have results that may or may not meet expectations. Who would have foreseen twenty years ago, for instance, that e-mail and messaging would become a dominant form of business communication and that many managers would be inundated with more than a hundred e-mail messages each day?

What is an Organisation?

An organisation is a stable, formal social structure that takes resources from the environment and processes them to produce outputs. This technical definition focuses on three elements of an organisation. Capital and labour are primary production factors provided by the environment. The organisation transforms these inputs into products and services. The products and services are then consumed by environments. An organisation is more stable than an informal group (such as a focus group that meets occasionally) in terms of longevity and continuity.

Organisations are formal legal entities with internal rules and procedures that must abide by laws. Organisations are also social structures because they are a collection of social elements. This definition of an organisation is powerful and simple, but it is not very descriptive or even predictive of real-world organisations. A more realistic behavioural definition of an organisation is that it is a collection of rights, privileges, obligations, and responsibilities that are delicately balanced over a period of time, through conflict and conflict resolution (see Figure 3.2).

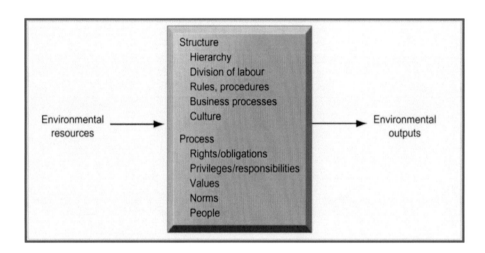

Figure 3.2 Formal business organisation structures and processes.

In this behavioural view of the firm, people who work in organisations develop customary ways of working, they gain attachments to existing relationships and they make arrangements with subordinates and superiors about how work will be done, the amount of work that will be done, and under what conditions work will be done. The behavioural view of organisations emphasises group relationships, values, and structures. Therefore, we should ask how these definitions of organisations relate to information systems technology. A technical view of organisations allows us to focus on how inputs are combined to create outputs when technology changes are introduced. The business is often seen as infinitely malleable, with capital and labour substituting for each other quite easily. But the more realistic behavioural definition of an organisation suggests that building new information systems or rebuilding old ones, involves much more than a technical rearrangement of machines or workers. Some information systems change the organisational balance of rights, privileges, obligations, responsibilities, and feelings that have been established over a long period of time.

Changing the balance can take a long time, be very disruptive and requires more resources to support training and learning. For instance, the length of time required to implement effectively a new information system is often much longer than usually anticipated simply because there is a lag between implementing a technical system and teaching employees and managers how to use the system.

Technological change requires deciding:

- who owns and controls information
- who has the right to access and update that information
- who makes decisions about whom, when, and how

The technical and behavioural definitions of organisations are not contradictory. Indeed, they complement each other. The technical definition tells us how thousands of businesses in competitive markets combine capital, labour and information technology, whereas the behavioural model takes us inside the individual business to see how that technology affects the organisation's inner workings.

Features of Business Organisations

All modern organisations have certain characteristics. They are bureaucracies with clear-cut divisions of labour and specialisation. Organisations arrange specialists in a hierarchy of authority in which everyone is accountable to someone and authority is limited to specific actions governed by abstract rules or procedures. These rules create a system of impartial and universal decision making. Organisations generally try to hire and promote employees on the basis of technical qualifications and professionalism – not personal connections – although, a cynic might say that 'it's who you know, not what you know' that influences hiring and promoting in many organisations. Most business organisations are devoted to the principle of efficiency in maximising output using limited inputs. Other features include their business cultures, environments, processes, ethics, politics and structures. All of these affect the kinds of information systems used by business.

Business Cultures

All organisations have assumptions that define their goals and products. Organisational culture encompasses this set of assumptions about what products the organisation should produce, how it should produce them, where, and for whom. Generally, these cultural assumptions are taken totally for granted and are rarely publicly announced or spoken about. Business processes – the actual way business firms produce value - are usually ensconced in the organisation's culture. Organisational culture is a powerful unifying force that restrains political conflict and promotes common understanding, agreement on procedures, and common practices. If we all share the same basic cultural assumptions, agreement on other matters is more likely. At the same time, organisational culture is a powerful constraint on change, especially technological change. Some organisations will do almost anything to avoid making changes in basic assumptions. Any technological change that threatens commonly held cultural assumptions usually meets a great deal of resistance. However, there are times when the only sensible way for a firm to move forward is to embrace a new technology.

Business Environments

Organisations often reside in environments from which they draw resources and to which they supply goods and services. Organisations and environments have a reciprocal relationship. On the one hand, organisations are open to, and dependent on, the social and physical environment that surrounds them. Without financial and human resources (people willing to work reliably and consistently for a set wage or revenue from customers) organisations could not exist.

Organisations must respond to legislative and other requirements imposed by government, as well as the actions of customers and competitors. On the other hand, organisations can influence their environments. For example, businesses form alliances with other businesses to influence the political process. They advertise to influence customer acceptance of their products.

Environments generally change much faster than organisations. New technologies, new products, and changing public tastes and values (many of which result in new government regulations) put strains on any organisation's culture, politics, and people. Most organisations are unable to adapt to a rapidly changing environment.

Sometimes a technology and resulting business innovation comes along to radically change the business landscape and environment. These innovations are loosely called 'disruptive.' Therefore, what makes a technology disruptive? In some cases, disruptive technologies are substitute products that perform as well or better (often much better) than anything currently produced. In the name of progress, there have been many well-known substitutions:

- the car substituted for the horse-drawn carriage
- the word processor for the typewriter
- the Apple iPod for the portable CD player
- the digital photograph for process film photograph

In these cases, entire industries can be put out of business. In other cases, disruptive technologies simply extend the market, usually with less functionality and much less cost, than existing products. Eventually they turn into low-cost competitors for whatever was sold before. Some firms are able to create these technologies and ride the wave to profits. Others learn quickly and adapt their business and others are obliterated because their products, services and business models become obsolete. They might be said to be very efficient at doing what no longer needs to be done!

There are also cases where no businesses benefit and virtually all the gains go to consumers. Figure 3.3 describes just a few disruptive technologies from the past.

TECHNOLOGY	DESCRIPTION	WINNERS AND LOSERS
Microprocessor chips (1971)	Thousands of transistors on a silicon chip	Microprocessor companies win (Intel, Texas Instruments) while transistor firms (GE) decline
Personal computers (1975)	Small, inexpensive, but fully functional desktop computers	PC manufacturers (HP, Apple, IBM) win, while mainframes (IBM) and minicomputers (DEC) lose
PC word processing (1979)	Inexpensive, limited but functional text editing software	PC and software manufacturers (Microsoft, HP, Apple) win, while typewriters disappear.
World Wide Web (1989)	A global database of digital files and "pages"	Owners of online content and news benefit, while traditional publishers (newspapers) lose
Internet music services (1998)	Repositories of downloadable high quality music	Owners of online music collections (MP3.com, iTunes) win, while record labels (Tower) lose
PageRank algorithm (2000)	A method for ranking Web pages in terms of popularity	Google is the winner (they own the patent), while traditional key word engines (Alta Vista) lose
Software as Web service (2003)	Using the Internet to provide remote access to software	Online software services companies win, while "boxed" software companies (SAP, Oracle) lose

Figure 3.3 A table showing technology winners and losers.

Businesses that invent disruptive technologies as "first movers" do not always benefit if they lack the resources to exploit the technology or fail to see the opportunity. The MITS Altair 8800 is widely regarded as the first personal computer but its inventors did not take advantage of their first-mover status. Second movers, so-called "fast followers" such as IBM and Microsoft, reaped the rewards. Citibank's ATMs revolutionized retail banking, but they were copied by other banks. Now virtually all banks use ATMs, with the benefits going mostly to the consumers.

Google was not a first mover in search engines but an innovative follower that was able to maintain rights to a powerful new search algorithm called PageRank. So far it has been able to hold onto its lead while most other search engines have faded down to small market share.

Business Processes

Most business organisations become very efficient over time because individuals in the business develop routines for producing goods and services. Routines - sometimes called standard operating procedures - are precise rules, procedures, and practices that have been developed to cope with virtually all expected situations. As employees learn these routines, they become highly productive and efficient, and the firm is able to reduce its costs over time as efficiency increases. For instance, when you visit a medical practice, receptionists have a well-developed set of routines for gathering basic information from you. Nurses have a different set of routines for preparing you for a consultation with the doctor. Additionally, the doctor has a well-developed set of routines for diagnosing you.

Business processes are collections of such routines. Indeed, an entire business can in turn be seen as a collection of business processes.

Business Ethics

Business ethics are moral principles that guide the way a business behaves. The same principles that determine individual actions also apply to business. Acting in an ethical way involves distinguishing between 'right' and 'wrong' and then making the 'right' choice. It is relatively easy to identify unethical business practices. For example, companies should not use child labour. They should not unlawfully use copyrighted materials and processes. They should not engage in bribery.

However, it is not always easy to create similar hard-and-fast definitions of good ethical practice. A company must make a competitive return for its shareholders and treat its employees fairly. A company also has wider responsibilities. It should minimise any harm to the environment and work in ways that do not damage the communities in which it operates. This is known as corporate social responsibility (CSR).

Various codes of behaviour are critical for businesses wishing to be considered ethical. The law is the key starting point for any business. Most leading businesses also have their own statement of *Codes of Conduct* which set out their core values and standards. A business should also follow relevant codes of practice that cover its sector. Many companies have created voluntary codes of practice that regulate practices in their industrial sector. These are often drawn up in consultation with governments, employees, local communities and other stakeholders. All companies need to make a profit. However, ethical businesses recognise that this objective must take account of ethics as shown in its statement on CSR.

Business Politics

People in organisations occupy different positions with different specialties, concerns, and perspectives. As a result, they naturally have divergent viewpoints about how resources, rewards and punishments should be distributed. These differences matter to both managers and employees, and they result in political struggle for resources, competition and conflict within every organisation. Political resistance is one of the great difficulties of bringing about organisational change - especially the development of new information systems.

Virtually all large information systems investments that bring about significant changes in strategy, business objectives, business processes and procedures become politically charged events. Managers that know how to work with the politics of an organisation will be more successful than less-skilled managers in implementing new information systems. There are many historical examples of where internal politics defeated the best-laid plans for an information system.

Business Structures

Business organisations generally all have a structure or shape. The table shown in figure 3.4 identifies five basic kinds of organisational structure.

TYPE	DESCRIPTION	EXAMPLES
Entrepreneurial	Young, small firm in a fast-changing environment. It has a simple structure and is managed by an entrepreneur serving as its single CEO	Small start-up businesses
Machine bureaucracy	Large bureaucracy existing in a slowly changing environment, producing standard products, dominated by centralised management and decision making	Midsize manufacturers
Divisionalised bureaucracy	Combination of multiple machine bureaucracies, each producing a different product or service, all topped by one central headquarters	Fortune 500 firms
Professional bureaucracy	Organisation where goods and services depend on the expertise of professionals, dominated by department heads with weak centralised authority	Law firms, hospitals
Adhocracy	Task force organisation that can respond to rapidly changing environments. Consists of large groups of specialists organised into multidisciplinary teams	Consulting firms

Figure 3.4 Types of organisational structure suggested by Mintzberg (1979).

The kind of information systems we find in a business often reflects the type of organisational structure. For instance, in a professional bureaucracy, such as a hospital, it is not unusual to find parallel patient record systems operated by the administration, another by doctors, and another by other professional staff such as nurses and social workers. In small entrepreneurial firms, we will often find poorly designed systems developed in a rush that often outgrows their usefulness quickly. In huge multidivisional firms operating in hundreds of locations, we will often find there is not a single integrating information system but instead each locale or each division has its set of information systems.

Impact of Information Systems on Business Organisations

Information systems have become integral, online, interactive tools deeply involved in the minute-to-minute operations and decision making of large organisations. Over the last decade, information systems have fundamentally altered the economics of organisations and greatly increased the possibilities for organising work. Theories and concepts from economics and sociology help us understand the changes brought about by IT.

Economic Impacts

From the point of view of economics, IT changes both the relative costs of capital and the costs of information. Information systems technology can be viewed as a factor of production that can be substituted for traditional capital and labour. As the cost of information technology decreases, it is substituted for labour, which historically has been a rising cost. Hence, the impact of information technology should result in a decline in the number of middle managers and clerical workers as information technology substitutes for their labour.

As the cost of information technology decreases, it also substitutes for other forms of capital such as buildings and machinery, which remain relatively expensive. Hence, over time we should expect managers to increase their investments in IT because of its declining cost relative to other capital investments. IT also obviously affects the cost and quality of information and changes the economics of information. Information technology helps firms contract in size because it can reduce transaction costs - the costs incurred when a firm buys in the marketplace items it cannot make itself. According to transaction cost theory, firms and individuals seek to economise on transaction costs, much as they do on production costs.

Using markets is expensive because of costs such as locating and communicating with distant suppliers, monitoring contract compliance, buying insurance and obtaining information on products. Traditionally, firms have tried to reduce transaction costs through vertical integration, by getting bigger, hiring more employees, and buying their own suppliers and distributors, as both General Motors and Ford used to do. Information technology, especially the use of networks, can help firms lower the cost of market participation (transaction costs), making it worthwhile for firms to make contracts with external suppliers, instead of using internal sources. As a result, firms can shrink in size (numbers of employees) because it is far less expensive to outsource work to a competitive marketplace rather than hire employees.

For instance, by using computer links to external suppliers, the Chrysler Corporation can achieve economies by obtaining more than 70 percent of its parts from the outside. Information systems make it possible for companies such as Cisco Systems and Dell Inc. to outsource their production to contract manufacturers such as Flextronics instead of making their products themselves.

Because IT reduces both agency and transaction costs for firms, we should expect firm size to shrink over time as more capital is invested in IT. Businesses should have fewer managers, and we should expect to see revenue per employee to increase over time.

Organisational and Behavioural Impacts

Theories based in the sociology of complex organisations also provide some understanding about how and why firms change with the implementation of new IT applications.

IT Flattens Organisations

Large, bureaucratic organisations, which primarily developed before the computer age, are often inefficient, slow to change and less competitive than newly created organisations. Some of these large organisations have downsized, reducing the number of employees and the number of levels in their organisational hierarchies.

Behavioural researchers have theorised that information technology facilitates flattening of hierarchies by broadening the distribution of information to empower lower-level employees and increase management efficiency (see figure 3.5). IT pushes decision-making rights lower in the organisation because lower-level employees receive the information they need to make decisions without supervision. This empowerment is also possible because of higher educational levels among the workforce, which give employees the capabilities to make intelligent decisions. Because managers now receive so much more accurate timely information, they become much faster at making decisions, so fewer managers are required. Management costs decline as a percentage of revenues, and the hierarchy becomes much more efficient.

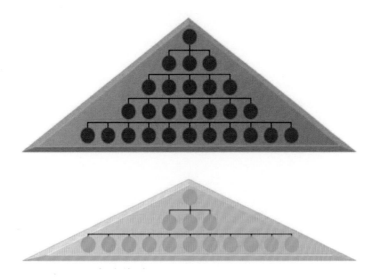

Figure 3.5 A traditional hierarchy of management with many levels (upper)
and a flattened management structure (lower).

These changes mean that the management span of control has also been broadened, enabling high-level managers to manage and control more workers, spread over greater distances. Many companies have eliminated thousands of middle managers as a result of these changes.

Post-industrial Organisations

Post-industrial theories based more on history and sociology than economics also support the notion that IT should flatten hierarchies. In post-industrial societies, authority increasingly relies on knowledge and competence, and not merely on formal positions. Hence, the shape of organisations flattens because professional workers tend to be self-managing and decision making should become more decentralised.

Information technology may encourage task force-networked organisations in which groups of professionals come together - face to face or electronically - for short periods of time to accomplish a specific task. Once the task is accomplished, the individuals join other task forces. The global consulting service Accenture is an example. It has no operational headquarters and no formal branches. Many of its 190,000 employees move from location to location to work on projects at client locations in 49 different countries.

Who makes sure that self-managed teams do not head off in the wrong direction? Who decides which person works on which team and for how long? How can managers evaluate the performance of someone who is constantly rotating from team to team? How do people know where their careers are headed? New approaches for evaluating, organising, and informing workers are required and not all companies can make virtual work effective.

Understanding Organisational Resistance to Change

Information systems inevitably become bound up in organisational politics because they influence access to a key resource—namely, information. Information systems can affect who does what to whom, when, where, and how in an organisation. Many new information systems require changes in personal, individual routines that can be painful for those involved and require retraining and additional effort that may or may not be compensated. Because information systems potentially change an organisation's structure, culture, business processes and strategy, there is often considerable resistance to them when they are introduced.

For a manager involved in future IT investments, the ability to work with people and organisations is just as important as technical awareness and knowledge.

PEST Analysis

Though structure and leadership play a large role in business success, external factors can also shape a company's potential. One method for systematically discovering and quantifying those factors is the PEST analysis. PEST is an acronym for political, economic, social, and technological factors that commonly affect business activities and performance. Created by Aguilar (1967), PEST can be used to determine an organisation's overall outlook.

Political

This factor looks at how government regulations and legal issues affect a company's ability to be profitable and successful. Issues that must be considered include tax guidelines, copyright and property law enforcement, political stability, trade regulations, social and environmental policy, employment laws and safety regulations. Companies should also consider their local and federal power structure and discuss how anticipated shifts in power could affect their business.

Economic

This factor examines the outside economic issues that can play a role in a company's success. Items to consider include economic growth, exchange, inflation and interest rates, economic stability, anticipated shifts in commodity and resource costs, unemployment policies, credit availability and unemployment policies.

Social

This factor analyses the demographic and cultural aspects of the company's market. These factors help businesses examine consumer needs and determine what pushes them to make purchases. Among the items that should be examined are demographics, population growth rates, age distribution, attitudes toward work, job market trends, religious and ethical beliefs, lifestyle changes, educational and environmental issues and health consciousness.

Technological

This factor takes into consideration technology issues that affect how an organisation delivers its product or service to the marketplace. Among the specific items that need to be considered are technological advancements, government spending on technological research, the life cycle of current technology and the role of the Internet. In addition, companies should consider how generational shifts, and their related technological expectations, are likely to affect those who will use their product and how it is delivered.

PEST example analysis: The Restaurant Industry

Political factors: Government regulations regarding employee hygiene, health and food regulations, food standards, etc. Government policies regarding the restaurant industry and managing eateries. These may include licenses, inspections by health and food departments etc.

Economic factors: Interest rates would affect the cost of capital, the rate of interest being directly proportionate to the cost of capital. Rate of inflation determines the rate of remuneration for employees and directly affects the price of the restaurant's products. Again, the proportion between the inflation rate and wages/prices is direct. Economic trends act as an indicator of the sustainability and profitability of a business in the chosen region and help you in deciding your marketing strategy.

Social factors: Eating habits of the people in a chosen business environment may, and certainly will, affect marketing decisions. Ratio of people preferring to eat out regularly.

Technological factors: A good technical infrastructure would lead to better production, procurement and distribution logistics, resulting in reduced wastage and lower costs. Effective technology may be a decisive factor for food technology innovation, better presentation, more effective business marketing etc.

Case Studies – Problem Solving in Business Organisations

Case Study: Primark - providing consumers with ethically sourced garments.

Synopsis: Primark's Code of Conduct is translated into 26 languages, all published on its website, to ensure clear communication on standards. The Code of Conduct sets out the company's policy and is part of its legal terms and conditions. See the full Code and additional detailed information on the eleven points of the code at:
www.primark.co.uk/Ethical/Values/Code_of_Conduct

The code states that within its supply chain:

- Employment is freely chosen
- Freedom of association and the right to collective bargaining are respected
- Working conditions are safe and hygienic
- Environmental requirements - Primark shares its commitment with suppliers
- Child labour shall not be used
- Living wages are paid
- Working hours are not excessive
- No discrimination is practised
- Regular employment is provided
- No harsh or inhumane treatment is allowed
- Legal requirements - Primark is committed to compliance of all countries' laws.

Primark works closely with the suppliers and factories that produce its goods. It provides training for suppliers, factories and its own buyers so that they understand ethical issues. For example, it offers guidance on issues such as child labour and home working in Asia, as well as immigration and right-to-work issues in the UK. The role of Primark buyers is important in helping to support ethical business practices. When selecting new suppliers and factories, Primark requires them to go through a selection process. This enables Primark to establish if working conditions are appropriate or if improvements are necessary before approval. For more information, refer to the full case study.

Questions for Discussion:

1. What are business ethics?
2. Give two examples of ways in which Primark is operating in an ethical way. Provide two additional examples of ethical practices or behaviours in a business not associated with retailing or clothing.
3. Why is it so important for businesses to operate in an ethical way? Explain your answer by referring to the fashion industry.
4. In what ways could ethical business practices incur costs to the business? Evaluate the extent to which the benefits to a business of operating in an ethical are likely to outweigh the costs.

Case Study: *Use of PEST analysis at Unison.*

Synopsis: UNISON is Britain and Europe's biggest public sector trade union, representing more than 1.3 million members working in public services. Job roles they represent in the public sector include, for example:

- librarians
- Human Resources, IT and finance workers
- teaching assistants and early years nursery staff
- secretaries
- cleaners, caretakers and school meals supervisors
- care workers, social workers and nurses

UNISON campaigns on a variety of issues relevant to its members. Currently, it is running the Migrant Workers Participation Project. This campaign focuses on the issues faced by migrant workers in the UK. Migrant workers are employees who have moved from overseas to the UK to find work. They form an important and growing part of the workforce in both the private sector and public sector. These workers are at particular risk of being exploited in the workplace. This may be due to lack of knowledge of their rights, their limited command of the English language and the fact that they are often reluctant to complain about their treatment by employers. They may also be exploited because of racist attitudes. UNISON believes that the best way of preventing exploitation is through trade union representation in the workplace. One of the objectives of the current UNISON campaign is to increase the number of migrant workers who are part of the union.

When making decisions, a business needs to take account of internal and external factors. Internal factors are ones that are within its control. Examples include how many staff the business employs, the number of machines it uses and how much money owners choose to invest in the business. External factors are those that are outside of its control. These may be direct or indirect influences. Direct influences include suppliers, customers and competitors. Indirect influences include legislation, the economy or technology.

External influences are summarised by the acronym PEST. This stands for Political, Economic, Social and Technological influences. For more information, refer to the full case study.

Questions for Discussion:

1. Explain the purpose and benefits of PEST analysis.
2. Outline the factors that could lead to exploitation of migrant workers.
3. Analyse factors which have led to recent increased immigration to the UK.
4. Evaluate the extent to which the UK economy benefits from migrant labour.

Exercises – Problem Solving in Business Organisations

1. {multiple choice – choose the most appropriate answer (a), (b), (c) or (d)}

A structure of organisation that can respond to rapidly changing environments, consisting of large groups of specialists organised into multidisciplinary teams is called:

   (a) Totalitarianism   b) Adhocracy   (c) Entrepreneurial   (d) Consultancy

2. {multiple choice – choose the most appropriate answer (a), (b), (c) or (d)}

Ethical behaviour of a business organisation is often referred to using the acronym:

   (a) EB   (b) CSR   (c) ETH   (d) MORAL

3. {multiple choice – choose the most appropriate answer (a), (b), (c) or (d)}

The patent for the *PageRank* algorithm, a method for ranking web pages in terms of popularity, is currently owned by:

   (a) Microsoft Corporation   (b) Alta Vista   (c) Google   (d) LinkedIn

4. {multiple choice – choose the most appropriate answer (a), (b), (c) or (d)}

In PEST analysis for business organisations, the "S" stands for:

   (a) Scientific   (b) Solving   (c) Spreadsheet   (d) Social

5. {multiple choice – choose the most appropriate answer (a), (b), (c) or (d)}

Which of the following activities has had the most a significant negative impact on Royal Mail revenues in the UK?

   (a) Emailing   (b) Phoning   (c) Texting   (d) Faxing

6.   <u>Information Systems</u>

Several types of information system can be used within an organisation. Research and summarise briefly the main features of each of the following:

     (i)   Transaction Processing System
     (ii)   Data Warehouse System
     (iii) Knowledge Based System
     (iv) Decision Support System

7.   Business Functions

Explain the following business functions:

   (i)   Purchasing Transaction
   (ii)   Marketing
   (iii)   Human Resource Management (Personnel)
   (iv)   Stock Control

8.   Unethical Business Practices

Unfortunately, there have been well-publicised unethical practices over the past decade. Thankfully most of the companies involved have since tried to repair their reputations.

Briefly summarise in one paragraph the circumstances surrounding the following events, with approximate dates given in parentheses.

   (i)   Adidas used animal skin (2011)
   (ii)   Apple used slave labour (2010)
   (iii)   Barrick Gold Corporation torched homes (2009)
   (iv)   BP spilled oil (2010)
   (v)   Toyota ignored safety (2009)

8.   Wordsearch

BUSINESS ORGANISATIONS & IS

```
X  X  D  E  T  K  G  E  R  R  U  E  N  E  R  P  E  R  T  N  E  N  N
H  S  N  U  B  O  B  J  E  N  V  I  R  O  N  M  E  N  T  Z  H  S  M
S  T  P  D  P  E  S  T  Y  K  R  D  N  C  E  D  C  U  J  W  Y  C  Z
J  R  J  M  W  S  E  L  D  A  T  A  S  T  M  Y  F  A  U  Q  I  I  S
V  T  S  E  S  S  E  C  O  R  P  F  U  W  E  O  S  I  P  W  R  T  I
Z  P  T  E  C  H  N  O  L  O  G  I  C  A  L  R  S  O  B  B  Y  I  W
D  N  U  N  N  Y  L  R  T  M  F  R  Q  K  U  A  N  L  C  W  V  L  L
N  V  Y  T  Z  S  A  Z  D  D  K  N  E  O  E  N  X  E  N  I  C  O  H
M  C  H  D  O  L  Y  S  E  E  Y  O  L  P  M  E  W  L  T  A  A  P  J
S  Q  Y  C  K  S  D  J  Q  P  N  M  A  S  L  X  E  N  K  R  N  L  V
Z  D  S  N  E  T  T  A  L  F  O  R  G  A  N  I  S  A  T  I  O  N  E
M  I  N  F  O  R  M  A  T  I  O  N  X  A  D  H  O  C  R  A  C  Y  S
X  W  K  J  U  B  Z  N  Q  P  M  S  S  S  Y  S  T  E  M  L  T  J  V
L  U  P  A  G  E  R  A  N  K  Z  Y  T  G  Q  W  J  P  Q  K  F  J  R
Z  X  L  H  X  I  V  P  O  H  G  I  P  G  C  M  N  A  O  N  A  K  K
E  F  M  G  W  P  E  C  O  N  O  M  I  C  K  Z  E  F  M  Y  T  Z  S
```

Find the following words in the puzzle.
Words are hidden ↑ ↓ → ← and ↘ .

ADHOCRACY	FLATTENS	POLITICS
DATA	INFORMATION	PROCESSES
ECONOMIC	INTERNET	SOCIAL
EMPLOYEES	ORGANISATION	SYSTEM
ENTREPRENEUR	PAGERANK	TECHNOLOGICAL
ENVIRONMENT	PEST	

4. SECONDARY DATA: GATHERING & REPRESENTING

Introduction to Secondary Data

Secondary data are data collected by someone other than the user. Common sources of secondary data for business management and social sciences include censuses, organisational records and data collected through qualitative methodologies or qualitative research. *Primary data*, by contrast, are collected by the investigator conducting the research. In this section, we will focus on secondary data.

Secondary data analysis saves time that would otherwise be spent collecting data and, particularly in the case of quantitative data, provides larger and higher-quality databases than would be feasible for any individual researcher to collect on his or her own. In addition, analysts of business and economic change consider secondary data essential, since it is impossible to conduct a new survey that can adequately capture past change or developments.

Secondary data can be obtained from different research strands, including:

- prior documentation, such as business reports and statistical databases
- internet searches, such as search engines and online databases
- library resources, such as public reports and specialist journals

A clear benefit of using secondary data is that much of the background work needed has already been carried out, for example: literature reviews, case studies might have been carried out, published texts and statistics could have been already used elsewhere, media promotion and personal contacts could also have been utilised. This wealth of background work means that secondary data generally can have a pre-established degree of validity and reliability which need not be re-examined by the researcher who is re-using such data. Furthermore, secondary data can also be helpful in the research design of subsequent primary research and can provide a baseline with which the collected primary data results can be compared. Therefore, it is always wise to begin any research activity with a review of the secondary data. If secondary research and data analysis is undertaken with care and diligence, it can provide a cost-effective way of gaining a broad understanding of research questions.

Secondary data analysis and review involves collecting and analysing a vast array of information. To help stay focused, a first step should be to develop a statement of purpose, i.e. a detailed definition of the purpose of the research and the research design. Having a clear understanding of why we are collecting the data and what kind of data we need to collect, analyse, and better understand, will help us to remain focused and prevent us becoming overwhelmed with the sheer volume of data. It is important to have a step-by-step plan that guides data collection and analysis.

For instance, in the case of secondary data reviews, it might simply be an outline of what we want the final report to look like, a list of the types of data that we need to collect or a preliminary list of data sources. The specific types of information and data needed to conduct a secondary analysis will depend, obviously, on the focus of the study.

Sources of Secondary Data

Two common situations when looking for good sources of secondary data are that we find very few relevant sources for the chosen study (in which case we may have chosen a study which is too narrow and or specialised and we need to widen its scope) or we find so many seemingly-relevant sources that we are overwhelmed by them and need to focus the study accordingly.

Types of Sources

Literature Review Articles: Literature review articles assemble and review original research dealing with a specific topic. Reviews are usually written by experts in the field and may be the first written overview of a topic area. Review articles discuss and list all the relevant publications from which the information is derived.

Official Statistics: Official statistics are statistics collected by governments and their various agencies, bureaux, and departments. These statistics can be useful to researchers because they are an easily obtainable and comprehensive source of information, usually covering long periods of time. However, because official statistics can be characterised by unreliability, data gaps, inaccuracies, mutual inconsistencies and lack of timely reporting, it is important to critically analyse official statistics for accuracy and validity. There are several reasons why these problems exist:

- The scale of official surveys generally requires large numbers of enumerators (interviewers) and, in order to reach those numbers enumerators contracted are often under-skilled
- The size of the survey area and research team usually prohibits adequate supervision of enumerators and the research process
- Resource limitations (human and technical) often prevent timely and accurate reporting of results

Reference Books: Reference books provide secondary source material. In many cases, specific facts or a summary of a topic is all that is included. Handbooks, manuals, encyclopaedias and dictionaries are considered as reference books.

Scholarly Journals: Scholarly journals generally contain reports of original research or experimentation written by experts in specific fields. Articles in scholarly journals usually undergo a peer review, where other experts in the same field review the content of the article for accuracy, originality and relevance. This level of review gives more confidence that the information is reliable.

Technical Reports: Technical reports are usually accounts of work done on research projects. They are written to provide research results to colleagues, research institutions, governments and other interested researchers. A report may emanate from completed research projects or on-going research projects.

Trade Journals: Trade journals contain articles that discuss practical information concerning various fields. These journals provide people in these fields with information pertaining to that field or trade.

Where to Find Sources

There are numerous sources of secondary data and information. The first step in collecting secondary data is to determine which institutions conduct research on the topic area. Large surveys and country-wide studies are expensive and time-consuming to conduct. Therefore, they are usually carried out by governments or large institutions with a research orientation. Thus, government documents and official statistics are good starting places for gathering secondary data.

For example, the UK Government's Statistical Service publishes broad reviews in a Monthly Digest of Statistics and an Annual Abstract of Statistics. Their *Guide to Official Statistics* lists the more specialised figures they publish. Other countries have similar publications, and the results are summarised by international bodies such as the United Nations, the European Union, the World Bank and the International Monetary Fund. Most of this data is available in official websites.

In addition to government information, a huge amount of data is published by individual companies and organisations, as well as information provided by services such as Reuters, CNN, BBC and the Financial Times or survey companies, such as Gallup, Nielsen and Mori. Some general and business-related sources are listed below:

General

1. **iSEEK Education**: iSeek is a targeted search engine, designed especially for students, teachers and administrators
2. **RefSeek**: With more than a billion documents, web pages, books, journals and newspapers, RefSeek offers authoritative resources in many subjects, without sponsored links and commercial results
3. **Virtual LRC**: The Virtual Learning Resources Center has created a custom Google search, featuring academic information websites. This search is created by teachers and library professionals around the world to share resources for academic projects
4. **BUBL LINK**: This Internet resource catalogue is a good resource in which we can search using our own keywords, or browse subject areas with Dewey subject menus
5. **OAIster**: We can search the OAIster database to find millions of digital resources from thousands of contributors, especially open access resources
6. **Internet Public Library**: We can find resources by subject through the Internet Public Library database

Business and Economics

7. **London Stock Exchange**: We can easily look up current and historical stock market information with charts and trends
8. **BPubs**: We can search the Business Publications Search Engine for access to business and trade publications
9. **Corporate Information**: For researching companies, we can use *Corporate Information* to find corporate financial records
10. **EconLit**: EconLit provides access more than a hundred years of economics literature from around the world, including journal articles, books, book reviews, articles and dissertations, as well as historic journal articles dating from 1886
11. **Inomics**: Economists use this site for finding economics resources, including jobs, courses, and conferences
12. **National Bureau of Economic Research**: On this site, we can learn about and find access to good resources in economic research.

Evaluating the Quality of Sources

One of the advantages of secondary data review and analysis is that individuals with limited research training or technical expertise can be trained to conduct this type of analysis. Key to the process, however, is the ability to judge the quality of the data or information that has been gathered. The following questions will help us to assess the quality of the data.

Is there a clear original purpose of the data collection?

Consider the purpose of the data or publication. Is it a government document or statistic, data collected for corporate and/or marketing purposes, or the output of a source whose business is to publish secondary data (e.g. research institutions)? Knowing the purpose of data collection will help us to evaluate the quality of the data and discern the potential level of bias.

What is the date of publication?

When was the source published? Is the source current or out-of-date? Topic areas of continuing or rapid development, such as the sciences, demand more current information.

Can we ascertain the credentials of the source?

What are the author's or source's credentials, background or experience in this area?

Does it include a methods section and are the methods sound?

Does the article have a section that discusses the methods used to conduct the study? If it does not, we can assume that it is a popular audience publication and we should look for additional supporting information or data. If the research methods are discussed, we should review them to ascertain the quality of the study.

Who is the intended audience?

Is the publication aimed at a specialised or a general audience? Is the source too elementary, aimed at the general public? What is the coverage of the report? Does the work update other sources, substantiate other reports that we have read or add new information to the topic area?

Is the document or report well-referenced?

When data and figures are given, are they followed by a footnote, endnote, which provides a full reference for the information at the end of the page or document or the name and date of the source (e.g. Burke 1997)? Without proper reference to the source of the information, it is impossible to judge the quality and validity of the information reported.

Do the numbers and results make sense?

Data reporting characteristics vary according to what the data is being collected for and the stage of reporting. For the purpose of secondary data analysis, the aggregated percentage figure, rather than the number of cases reported, should be used.

> **Checklist Questions for Evaluating Quality of Sources**
>
> - What are the source's credentials?
> - What methods were used?
> - Is the information current or out-of-date?
> - Is the intended audience researchers or the general public?
> - Is the source's coverage of the topic area too broad or too narrow?
> - Does the author provide references for the data and information reported?
> - Do the numbers and results make sense?

Data Disaggregation

The level of data aggregation or disaggregation simply refers to the extent to which the information or data is broken down.

Aggregated Data: Aggregate data are data that describe a group of observations, with the grouping made on a defined criterion. For example, geographic data are often grouped by spatial units such as region, state, census, etc. Aggregate data can also be defined by time interval, for example: the number of persons that migrated to European areas in the last five years. Over aggregating data can be used as a means of 'hiding' key issues and should be carefully checked.

Disaggregated Data: These are data on individuals or single entities, for example: age, gender, level of education, income, occupation etc. These data are generally more informative and useful than aggregate data.

What and Where to Why

Secondary data is sometimes referred to as outcome data. This is because secondary data generally describe the condition or status of phenomena or a group; however, these data alone do not tell us why the condition or status exists. This limitation can be overcome in two ways.

First, it can be overcome by using information from case studies and other research to fill in the gaps. For example, data on women's level of education can provide information relevant for understanding why those children whose mothers have low levels of education will likely exhibit higher malnutrition rates than children of mothers with higher levels of education. Thus consulting relevant literature can sometimes help us to illuminate causal relationships.

Second, analysis of additional key data and indicators can help us acquire more explanation as to why a problem exists. For example, if low farm income has been identified as a problem, data on land tenure, land size, types of crops, production value, cost of inputs, and so on, can be compared to help identify who has this problem and possible causes and solutions. Therefore, cross-analysing key indicators and using additional information sources help us understand or make reasonably sound inferences about unmeasured conditions or situations, thus allowing us to better understand not only *what* is happening and *where* it is happening but also *why* it is happening.

In summary, secondary data can be a valuable source of information for gaining knowledge and insight into a broad range of issues and phenomena. Review and analysis of secondary data can provide a cost-effective way of addressing issues, conducting cross-national business comparisons, understanding country-specific and local conditions, determining the direction and magnitude of changes and trends, and describing a current business situation. It complements, but does not replace, primary data collection, as we shall see in the next chapter, and should be the starting place for any research.

Simple Data Types

We can classify data in several ways. One way describes data as either quantitative (based on numbers) or qualitative (where there are no numbers). Quantitative data is often easier to collect, analyse and describe, so we should use it whenever possible. We can even transform data that is essentially qualitative into a quantitative form. For example, when people have different opinions about some issue, we cannot measure those opinions in precise units but we could ascertain if they 'strongly agree' with a particular statement, or 'agree', 'have no opinion', 'disagree' or 'strongly disagree'. Then we can map a notional scale 5, 4, 3, 2, 1 and work with these numbers to analyse our data.

Nominal data is the kind that we really cannot quantify with any meaningful units. The facts that a person is an accountant, or a country has a mixed economy, or a company has a particular name are examples of nominal data because there are no real measures for these. The usual analysis for nominal data is to define a number of distinct categories and say how many observations fall into each, which is why it is also called categorical or descriptive data. For instance, gender in a survey can normally take two values, 'male' or 'female'. A survey of the shirt colours of all Premier League clubs will give us nominal data with twenty categories. A key point about nominal data is that the order in which the categories are listed does not particularly matter.

Ordinal data is one step more quantitative than nominal data. Here we can rank the categories of observations into some meaningful order. For example, we can describe companies as 'large', 'medium' or 'small'. The order of these categories is important because we know that 'medium' comes between 'large' and 'small', but this is all we can say. Other examples of ordinal data are the strength of people's opinions on a scale of 1 to 5, and exam results as 'distinction', 'pass' or 'fail'. The key point is that the order of the categories is indeed important, which is why ordinal data is sometimes also described as *ordered* or *ranked*.

Cardinal data has at least one attribute that can be measured directly. For example, we can measure the time taken to finish a business project, count the number of mining companies in the UK or measure the profits of a retail company. These measures give a precise description, and are clearly the most relevant to quantitative methods. We can divide cardinal data into two types, namely 'discrete' or 'continuous'. Data is discrete if it takes countable values. The number of departments in a company and the age of employees are discrete data. Continuous data can take any value and are not restricted to integers. For instance, the times taken to serve customers are continuous data.

The following table classifies the various simple data types, associated distributions, permissible operations, etc. Regardless of the logical possible values, all of these data types are generally coded using real numbers, as we shall see later.

Data Type	Possible Data Values	Example Usage	Data Measurement
binary	0, 1 (arbitrary labels)	Binary outcome ('yes/no', 'true/false' ...)	nominal
categorical	1, 2, ..., N (arbitrary labels)	Categorical outcome (blood type, basic colour...)	nominal
ordinal	1, 2, 3,...N (arbitrary scale)	Relative score (significant for creating a ranking)	ordinal
binomial	0, 1, ..., N	Number of successes (e.g. 'yes' votes out of N possible)	cardinal (discrete)
count	0, 1, 2, 3, ...	Number of items in a given interval (telephone calls)	cardinal (discrete)
real-valued	real number	Varying continuously (temperature, size, distance ...)	cardinal (continuous)

Figure 4.1 Types of data: binary, categorical, ordinal, binomial, count, real-valued.

Representing Secondary Data

The most common ways of representing secondary data are tables, bar charts, histograms, pie charts, organisational charts, candlestick charts, line charts and scatter diagrams, the choice of which to use depends on the audience, personal preference and complexity of the information.

Tables

For instance, a table of shopping preferences for one hundred supermarket shoppers could be presented as a table containing one hundred rows:

Shopper ID	Preference
001	*Tesco*
002	*Sainsbury's*
003	*Tesco*
...	...
...	...
100	*Asda*

Figure 4.2   One hundred rows of categorical data values.

However, when completed this would be a very large table and most readers would expect us to present the data in a more concise and effective way, perhaps counting the information and using *grouped data* in a table. Remember, one main objective of representing data is to inform the reader in a simple, clear way and showing 'raw' data in hundreds of rows is neither concise nor effective.

The table in figure 4.3 shows a count of the preferences for each supermarket. It is easily seen that Tesco is the most preferred in the group of one hundred shoppers, Sainsbury's second and so on. Generally, grouped data can convey more useful information than the raw data.

Supermarket	Number of Preferences
Tesco	35
Sainsbury's	29
Asda	25
Others	11

Figure 4.3   A grouped data table.

When a table of secondary data has been obtained from a specific source, the details of the source must be properly referenced. There is no universally adopted referencing system for academic writing.

Most scholars and students employ one of the most popular systems currently in use in the UK and America, which include:

- American Psychological Association (APA)
- Chicago System
- Modern Humanities Research Association (MHRA)
- Modern Language Association of America (MLA)
- The Harvard System (sometimes called the 'Author Date System')

We will mainly use the *Harvard System* in this book.

For instance, consider the secondary data courtesy of 'The Guardian', April 2015, concerning supermarket share by sales and obtained through the Guardian website:

http://www.theguardian.com/business/2015/apr/08/aldi-overtakes-waitrose-to-become-uks-sixth-largest-supermarket-chain

The usual way to reference this article in the *Harvard system* is:

Butler, S. 2015. Aldi overtakes Waitrose to become UK's sixth-largest supermarket chain. [ONLINE] Available at:
http://www.theguardian.com/business/2015/apr/08/aldi-overtakes-waitrose-to-become-uks-sixth-largest-supermarket-chain. [Accessed 17 August 15].

Other references can be easily generated online at: http://www.harvardgenerator.com/references/

Supermarket Chain	Market Share (%)
Tesco	29.4
Asda	17.1
Sainsbury's	16.4
Morrisons	10.9
The Co-op	6.0
Aldi	5.3
Waitrose	5.1
Lidl	3.7
Others	6.1

Figure 4.4   A table of market share data based on secondary data taken from Butler (2015).

Picking out key information from data is important to assist the reader's understanding. In this case, the headline used by the Guardian was 'German discounter increases market share to 5.3%, compared with the John Lewis-owned chain's 5.1%, as sales in 12 weeks to 29 March jumps by almost 17%'. We can also present the information in a **Bar Chart**, as a visualisation of the data (see figure 4.5).

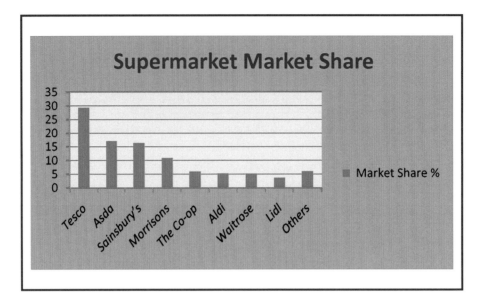

Figure 4.5   A bar chart of market share data based on secondary data taken from Butler (2015).

The bar chart shows rectangular bars with lengths proportional to the values that they represent. The bars are plotted vertically in this case but can be plotted horizontally, according to preference.

Three advantages of using bar charts rather than tables are:

- ease of interpretation for the reader
- ease of identifying the maxima/minima in the data
- ease of representing more than one data set in the same chart

For instance, with regard to the latter, if data sets were available for both male and female shoppers, we could show the information in a single chart (see figure 4.6), using different colours for each set.

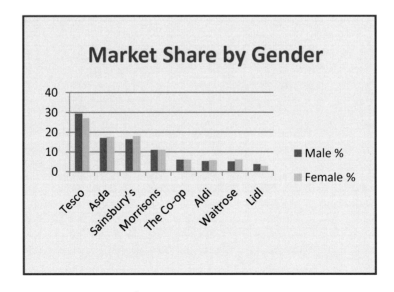

Figure 4.6   A bar chart of market share data for male and female supermarket shoppers.

Example

Using the data courtesy of http://www.statista.com/statistics, create a simple data table and bar chart with a properly-referenced caption.

Solution

CURRENT ACCOUNT MARKET SHARE OF UK BANKS IN 2014									
BANK	**Lloyds**	**Barclays**	**RBS**	**HSBC**	**Santander**	**Nationwide**	**TSB**	**Co-op**	**Others**
%share	27	18	18	12	10	6	4	2	2

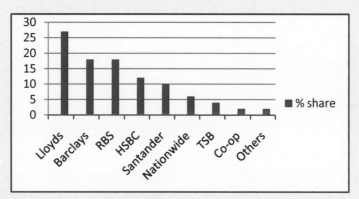

Figure 4.7 A data table and bar chart showing bank market share of UK banks in 2014, based on data taken from *Statista* (2014).

Histograms are generally used for continuous data, where there are no gaps between rectangles and the areas of the rectangles are meaningful, while a bar chart is generally a plot of categorical variables and gaps appear between the rectangles from which only the length is meaningful. Sometimes this is overlooked, which may lead to a bar chart being confused with a histogram.

A histogram often represents frequencies, shown as adjacent rectangles drawn over equal intervals, with each area equal to the frequency of the observations in the interval. For example, William (2014) prepared salary data for thousands of job advertisements in the UK citing specific keywords and figure 4.8 shows a histogram of results for the keyword 'Java'. Notice that the reference in the caption does not say 'based on data taken from ...' because the histogram shown is the actual figure shown in the source and not our own diagram based on the source's data.

If we were to pick out key information from the figure 4.8, we might say that very few Java-related jobs were advertised below £20K or over £100K and in Chapter 6 we will see that summary statistics can be also be calculated and quoted usefully.

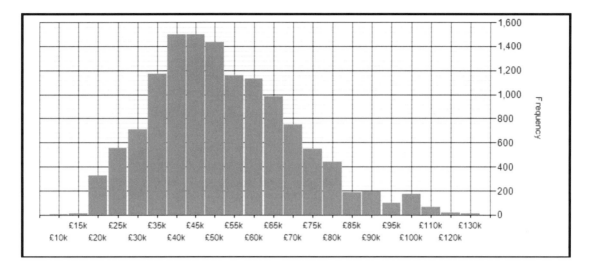

Figure 4.8   This histogram is taken from https://www.biostars.org/p/109225 and provides salary data for IT jobs citing "Java" over the last three months of 2014.

Practice Exercise

Prepare a similar histogram and caption for IT jobs citing 'Data Modelling' taken from the same William (2014) source.

Pie Charts generally show similar information to bar charts in the form of percentage values as a slice of a pie. Representing differently coloured slices of the pie can be a very effective visualization of relative size or proportion in the data. However, there needs to be a balance of the number of slices (or sectors). Too few (two or three) will look too simplistic and too many (more than a dozen or so) will look too complicated. Remember, the main idea here is to put across data in a straightforward, clear, visual way and not to confuse the reader.

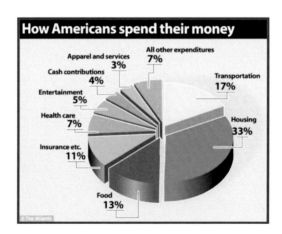

Figure 4.9 This pie chart is taken from a newspaper article Buchdahl (2013).

Consider secondary data taken from *The Daily Mail* link:

http://www.dailymail.co.uk/news/article-2423730/U-S-spending-poorest-families-spent-60-income-clothing-food-housing-year.html

relating to the typical ways that Americans spent their income in 2012, according to the *U.S. Bureau of Labor Statistics*. This is shown in figure 4.9. Percentages have been added to the nine coloured labelled sectors, giving a good visualisation of proportions in household spending. Adding percentage values is usually optional, depending on how simple we wish to make the chart.

Example

Represent the top five bank data shown in figure 4.7 in the form of a pie chart in which the colours are themed to those of each bank logo.

Solution

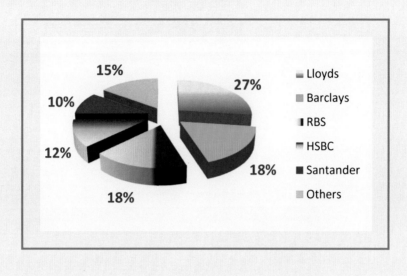

Practice Exercise

Find a reliable source of secondary data on the world's richest football clubs and represent the top eight in a pie chart with sectors labelled according to value in $US and sectors coloured according to shirt colour.

Organisational Charts are a specific example of *SmartArt* graphics in business software, such as Excel. They are an effective way of presenting the hierarchical nature of organisations, including reporting lines and appraisal structure.

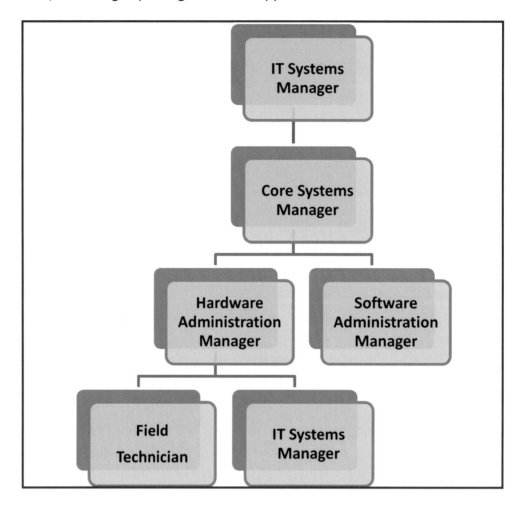

Figure 4.10   An Organisational chart taken from *Library Technology and Media Services (2014)*, http://www.roehampton.ac.uk/.

Other SmartArt Graphics categories include:

- list
- process
- cycle
- relationship
- matrix
- pyramid

Practice Exercises

Using the SmartArt Graphics section in Excel, prepare organisational charts similar to figure 4.10 for:

(i)   *Roehampton Business School*
(ii)   *Chelsea Football Club*

Line Charts

A line chart or line graph is a type of chart which displays information as a series of data points called markers connected by straight line segments. It is a basic type of chart common in many business fields, including revenues, sales and stock prices. A line chart is often used to visualise a trend in data over intervals of time (time series). Thus the line is often drawn chronologically. In these cases they are also known as run charts.

Figure 4.11 shows a line chart courtesy of *Business Insider* of Apple Corporation's revenues over seventeen quarters.

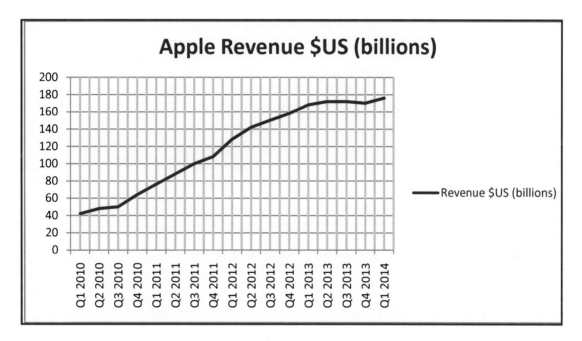

Figure 4.11 A line chart showing *Apple Trailing Twelve Month Revenue* based on data
taken from http://www.businessinsider.com/apple-q2-earnings-2014-4?IR=T.
Note that 'billion' here represents a European definition of 10^{12}, one million
millions, whereas the US definition of a billion is 10^9, one thousand million.

Figure 4.12 shows unemployment fluctuations in the UK.

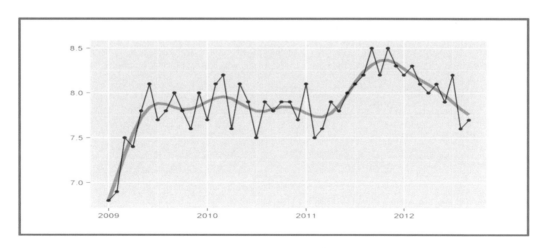

Figure 4.12 A line chart showing UK unemployment rates from 2009 until late 2012
as a red fluctuating line (data courtesy of www.seasonladjustment.com).
The purple smooth line can be generated using the 'smoothing' option,
available in most business software packages.

Gantt Charts

A Gantt chart is a type of bar chart, adapted by Adamiecki in 1896, and independently by Gantt in the 1910s, that illustrates a project schedule and planner. Gantt charts illustrate the start and finish dates of the main tasks of a project. Each task is represented by a linear or rectangular shape in which the length is proportional to the task's duration. Modern Gantt charts also show the dependency (i.e. precedence network) relationships between tasks and differently-coloured lines or rectangles to indicate tasks completed so far or different types of task.

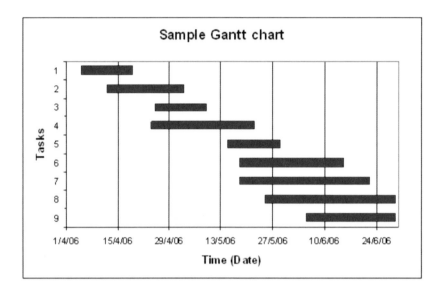

Figure 4.13   A sample Gantt chart for a project starting early April and finishing late June, comprising nine tasks, courtesy http://www.examplesof.com/business/gantt_charts.html.

Of course, business research includes many areas of business activity. For instance, university students are often required to complete a business dissertation or project on a topic (see figure 4.14).

	Summer	Sept	Oct	Nov	Dec	Jan	Feb	Mar	Apr	May	Jun
Background reading	├─────┼─────┤										
Proposal/initial meetings		├───┤									
Literature review		├───────────┤									
Research methods planning			├─────┤								
Data collection					├───┤						
Check on progress / Data analysis						├┤ ├──┤					
Submit some draft work		├─────┤		├──┤							
Discuss conclusions						├──┤	├──┤				
Further drafts						├──┤					
Final meeting								├──┤			
Final draft									├──┤		

Figure 4.14 A sample Gantt chart for completing
a year-long university project.

Scenario

Suppose that a certain university student is planning a fourteen-week Business Research Project starting on Saturday 09/01/16 with a deadline of 15/04/16. She has decided to make a time-management plan of the key tasks involved. These tasks are shown in the table below. To avoid the stress of deadlines and to give a 'contingency' week, she has (sensibly) planned to finish a week early on 08/04/16. As in most projects, some tasks must be carried out before others and these are shown as predecessors in the table. Complete the finish dates and represent her time-management plan in a simple Gantt chart.

No.	Task	Duration	Start date	Finish date	Predecessors
1	Learn Excel & SPSS basics	3 weeks	Sat 09/01/16		
2	Carry out a comprehensive literature review	4 weeks	Sat 16/01/16		
3	Identify reliable secondary data sources /references	4 weeks	Sat 23/01/16		
4	Investigate potential methodologies & strategies	4 weeks	Sat 06/02/16		
5	Design questionnaire and assimilate primary data	5 weeks	Sat 06/02/16		
6	Start writing up the project report (longest task)	9 weeks	Sat 06/02/16		
7	Identify potential tests and significant results	3 weeks	Sat 20/02/16		3
8	Carry out tests (hypotheses, correlations ...)	2 weeks	Sat 05/03/16		4
9	Summarise findings, check for errors	1 week	Sat 26/03/16		8
10	Draw conclusions & make recommendations	2 weeks	Sat 26/03/16		8

Solution

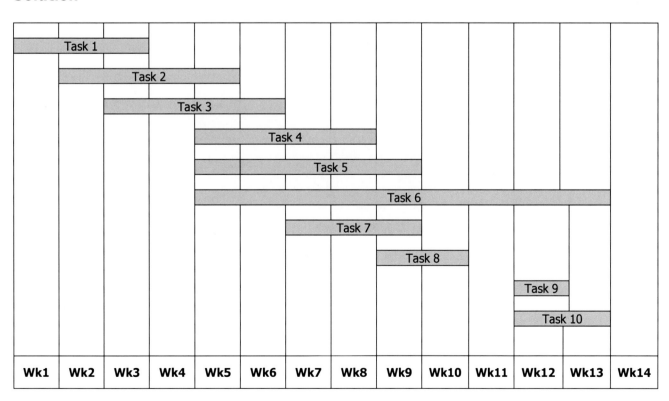

Scatter diagrams

A *scatter diagram* or *scatterplot* is a basic type of mathematical diagram using Cartesian coordinates to display data values for typically two variables. The data is displayed as a collection of points, each having the value of one variable (**x**) determining the position on the horizontal axis and the value of the other variable (**y**) determining the position on the vertical axis. Examples are shown in figures 4.15 and 4.16. We shall see later how to investigate possible associations between variables **x** and **y**.

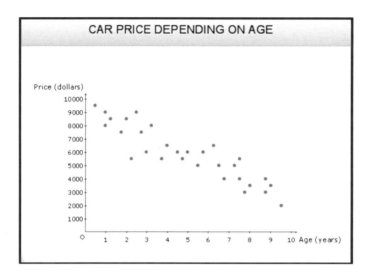

Figure 4.15   A scatter diagram showing car price versus age, courtesy of http://conceptdraw.com.

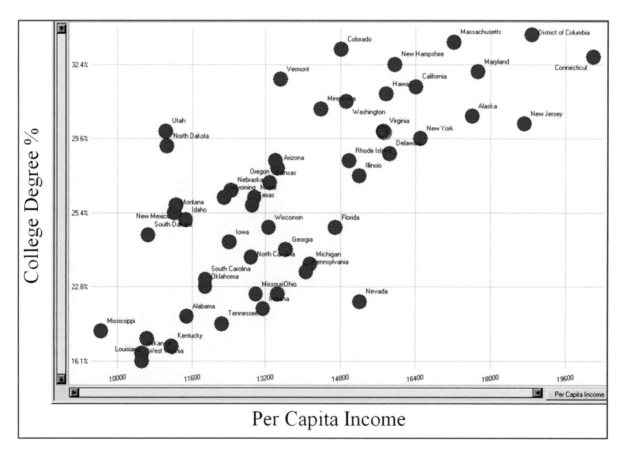

Figure 4.16   A scatter diagram showing per capita income versus college degree
courtesy http://www.aviz.fr.

Candlestick Charts

A candlestick chart is a style of financial chart used to describe price movements of an equity or currency. Each "candlestick" typically shows one day; so for example a one month chart may show the 20 trading days as 20 'candlesticks'. Each bar represents all four important pieces of information for that day: the open, the close, the high and the low, with green representing a positive gain on the day and red a negative loss.

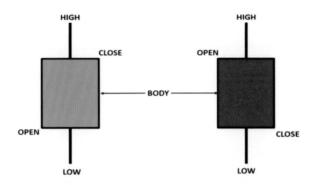

Figure 4.17   Components of a candlestick chart.

Candlestick charts are thought to have been developed in the 18th century by Homma, a Japanese rice trader of financial instruments. They were introduced to the Western world by Nison in his book on *Japanese Candlestick Charting Techniques*. In order to create a candlestick chart, we must have a data set that contains open, high, low and close values for each time period. The hollow or filled portion of the candlestick is called 'the body' (also referred to as 'the real body'). The long thin lines above and below the body represent the high-low range and are called 'shadows' (also referred to as 'wicks' and 'tails'). The high is marked by the top of the upper shadow and the low by the bottom of the lower shadow. If the stock closes higher than its opening price, a green candlestick is drawn with the bottom of the body representing opening price and the top of the body representing closing price. If the stock closes lower than its opening price, a red candlestick is drawn with the top of the body representing opening price and the bottom of the body representing closing price.

Figure 4.18   A candlestick chart of Forex movements in November 2009, courtesy of http://forexwatchers.org/tag/basic-guide-to-candlestick-chart/.

Mixed Charts

We have seen several basic forms of charts used in business reports and presentations. Of course, we need to keep the charts simple but effective. Too many unstructured details can confuse the reader. However, sometimes we can use one diagram to show two or more charts, provided the information is still readily understandable.

Mixed Pie Charts

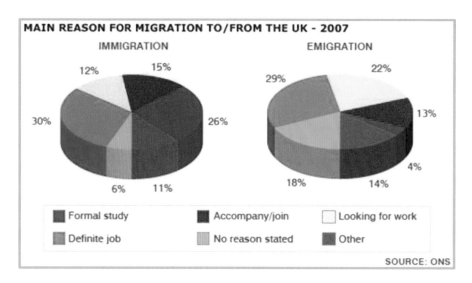

Figure 4.19 UK immigration and emigration in 2007, courtesy of
http://www.ieltsbuddy.com/ielts-pie-chart.html

Candlestick and Bar Chart

Consider the diagram in figure 4.20. The candlestick chart is shown in the normal way over specific time periods. Analysts would also often like to know the volume of stock traded, just in case volatile movements were due to unusually low volumes. The diagram additionally shows volume traded in feint grey in the form of a bar chart.

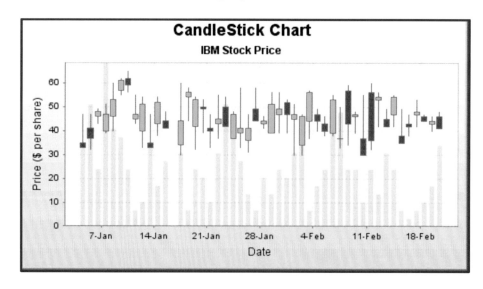

Figure 4.20   A mixed chart of IBM stock price movements, containing both a candlestick and bar chart, courtesy of http://www.java2s.com/Code/Java/Chart/JFreeChartCandlestickDemo.htm.

Mixed Gantt Charts

Consider the diagram in figure 4.21. The Gantt chart shows an interim state of a project, in which some tasks have already been completed and some are still outstanding.

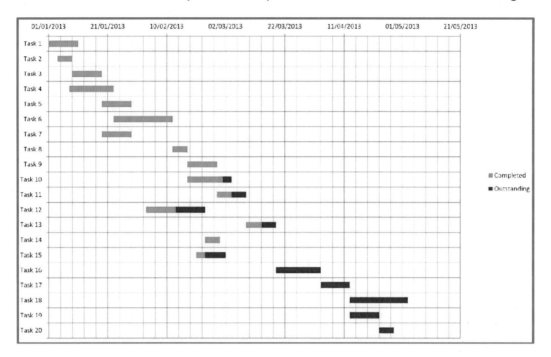

Figure 4.21   A mixed Gantt Chart with task bars shown in green (completed tasks) and red (outstanding) - ref: http://leahrn.org/gantt-chart-excel-template.html

Mixed Line Charts

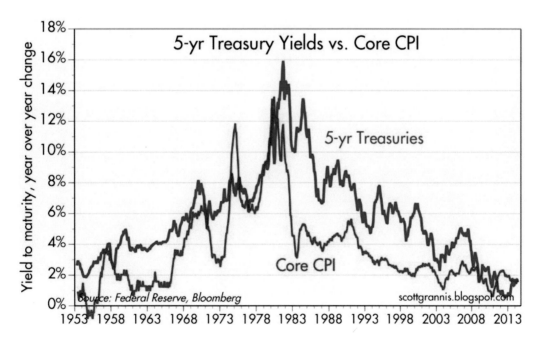

Figure 4.22   A mixed line chart showing two superimposed line diagrams for comparison
http://scottgrannis.blogspot.co.uk/2014/06/10-valuation-charts.html

Line Chart and Bar Chart

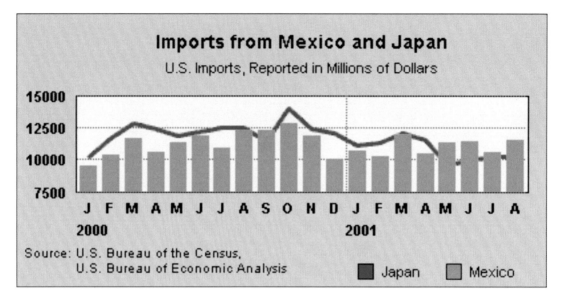

Figure 4.23   A chart showing import data in the form of a line chart (Japan) and bar chart (Mexico).
http://docs.oracle.com/html/A96127_01/jcb_advanced.htm

Mixed Histograms

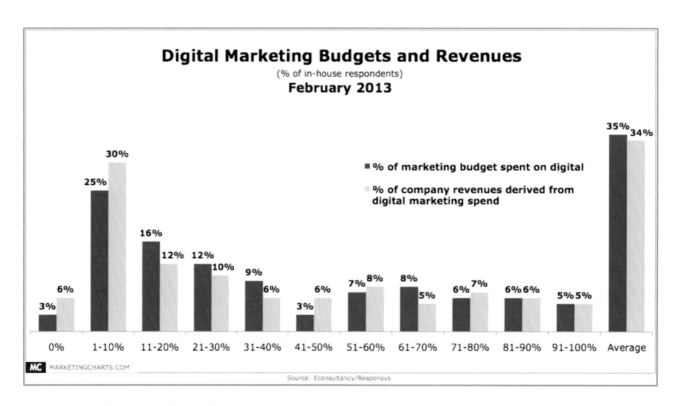

Figure 4.24   A digital marketing chart combining two histograms for budgets and revenues, courtesy www.marketingcharts.com.

Mixed Line Chart and Histogram

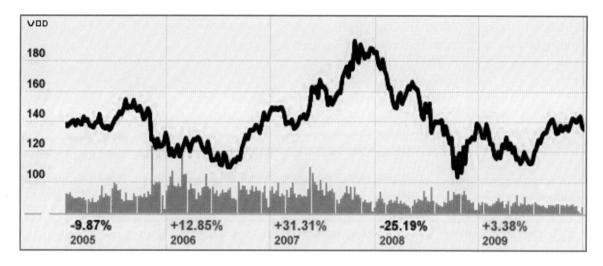

Figure 4.25   A chart showing the share price fluctuations of *Vodafone* from 2005 to 2009, inclusively. Ticker symbol **VOD**.

Day–to–day fluctuations of share prices can be very interesting, although analysts will often look at quarterly or annual average prices to gain an understanding of trends over short and long terms. From the above figure, we can compile an approximate average estimate of the Vodafone share price for the years 2005 to 2009, inclusively. This information is shown in rows one and two of the following matrix.

YEAR	2005	2006	2007	2008	2009
S.P.	140	120	160	140	130
Absolute inc from previous year	N/A	−20	+40	−20	−10
% increase from previous year	N/A	−14.4	+33.3	−12.5	−7.1

Figure 4.26   A table containing values obtained from figure 4.25.

Data in rows three and four in figure 4.26 show relative increases from the previous year, in the forms of absolute or percentage values. Other useful techniques involve statistical measures of *moving averages*, also called *rolling averages*, which are ways to analyse share prices over a given period. One popular such measure, for example, the *10–day simple moving average of closing price* (SMA) is simply the mean of the previous 10 days' closing prices. Consider the share data given below which is based on actual VOD data from January 4th, 2010.

143	142	142	139	138	138	138	138	137	135

The 10–day SMA $= \dfrac{143+142+142+139+138+138+138+138+137+135}{10} = 139.$

SWOT Analysis

SWOT is an acronym for strengths, weaknesses, opportunities and threats. It is a structured planning method that evaluates some of the key data and information relating to those four elements of a project or business venture.

A SWOT analysis can be carried out for a business, product, place, industry or person. It involves specifying the objective of the business venture or project and identifying the internal and external factors that are favourable and unfavourable to achieve that objective.

- Strengths are characteristics of the business that give it an advantage over others
- Weaknesses are characteristics that place the business at a relative disadvantage
- Opportunities are elements that the business could exploit to its advantage
- Threats are elements in the environment that could cause trouble for the business

Identification of strengths, weaknesses, opportunities, and threats is important because they can inform later steps in planning to achieve the objective. First, decision makers should consider whether the objective is attainable, given the strengths, weaknesses, opportunities, and threats. If the objective is not attainable, they must select a different objective and repeat the process.

Users of a SWOT analysis must ask and answer questions that generate meaningful information for each category (strengths, weaknesses, opportunities, and threats) to make the analysis useful and find their competitive advantage.

Internal and external factors

Internal factors usually include the strengths and weaknesses internal to the business whereas external factors include the opportunities and threats presented by the environment external to the business. The analysis may view the internal factors as strengths or as weaknesses depending upon their effect on the organization's objectives. What may represent strengths with respect to one objective may be weaknesses (distractions, competition) for another objective. The factors may include all of the 4Ps of business (price, product, promotion, and place) as well as personnel, finance, manufacturing capabilities and so on.

The external factors may include macroeconomic matters, technological change, legislation, and socio-cultural changes, as well as changes in the marketplace or in competitive position. The results are often presented in the form of a matrix.

SWOT Matrix

SWOT analysis is just one method of categorisation and has its own weaknesses. For example, it may tend to persuade its users to compile lists rather than to think about actual important factors in achieving objectives. It also presents the resulting lists uncritically and without clear prioritisation so that, for example, weak opportunities may appear to balance strong threats. However, it is prudent not to eliminate any candidate SWOT entry too quickly.

The importance of individual SWOTs will be revealed by the value of the strategies they generate. A SWOT item that produces valuable strategies is important. A SWOT item that generates no strategies is not important. Consider the following SWOT matrix example analysing the market position of a small management consultancy with specialism in Human Resource Management (HRM).

Strengths	Weaknesses	Opportunities	Threats
Reputation in marketplace	Shortage of consultants at operating level rather than partner level	Established position with a well defined market niche	Large consultancies operating at a minor level
Expertise at partner level in HRM consultancy	Unable to deal with multi-disciplinary assignments because of lack of ability	Identified market for consultancy in areas other than HRM	Other small consultancies looking to invade the marketplace

Figure 4.26   A SWOT matrix for a consultancy in HRM.

The usefulness of SWOT analysis is not limited to profit-seeking organizations. SWOT analysis may be used in any decision-making situation when a desired end-state (objective) is defined. Examples include: non-profit organizations, governmental units, and individuals. SWOT analysis may also be used in pre-crisis planning and preventive crisis management. SWOT analysis may also be used in creating a recommendation during a viability study/survey.

The SWOT analysis has been utilized in community work as a tool to identify positive and negative factors within organizations, communities, and the broader society that promote or inhibit successful implementation of social services and social change efforts. It is used as a preliminary resource, assessing strengths, weaknesses, opportunities, and threats in a community served by a non-profit or community organization. This organizing tool is best used in collaboration with community workers and/or community members before developing goals and objectives for a program design or implementing an organizing strategy. The SWOT analysis is a part of the planning for social change process and will not provide a strategic plan if used by itself.

Example: A simple SWOT Analysis for a local Community Centre.

Strengths and Weaknesses: These are the internal factors within an organization.

- Human resources - staff, volunteers, board members, target population
- Physical resources - your location, building, equipment
- Financial - grants, funding agencies, other sources of income
- Activities and processes - programs you run, systems you employ
- Past experiences - building blocks for success, your reputation in the community

Opportunities and Threats: These are external factors stemming from community or societal forces.

- Future trends in your field or the culture
- The economy - local, national, or international
- Funding sources - foundations, donors, legislatures
- Demographics - changes in the age, race, gender, culture of those you serve or in your area
- The physical environment (Is your building in a growing area? Is the bus service regular?)
- Legislation (Do new council requirements make your job harder...or easier?)
- Local, national or international events

Case Studies – Secondary Data: Gathering & Representing

Case Study: *IKEA - SWOT analysis and sustainable business planning*

IKEA is an internationally known home furnishing retailer. It has grown rapidly since it was founded in 1943. Today it is the world's largest furniture retailer, recognised for its Scandinavian style. The majority of IKEA's furniture is flat-pack, ready to be assembled by the consumer. This allows a reduction in costs and packaging. IKEA carries a range of 9,500 products, including home furniture and accessories. This wide range is available in all IKEA stores and customers can order much of the range online through IKEA's website. There are 18 stores in the UK to date, the first of which opened in Warrington in 1987. In July 2009 IKEA opened a store in Dublin too - its first in Ireland.

IKEA stores include restaurants and cafés serving typical Swedish food. They also have small food shops selling Swedish groceries, everything from the famous meatballs to jam. Stores are located worldwide. In August 2008 the IKEA group had 253 stores in 24 countries, with a further 32 stores owned and run by franchisees. It welcomed a total of 565 million visitors to the stores during the year and a further 450 million visits were made to the IKEA website. IKEA sales reached 21.2 billion Euros in 2008 showing an increase of 7%. The biggest sales countries are Germany, USA, France, UK and Sweden.

In 2008 IKEA opened 21 new stores in 11 countries and expects to open around 20 more in 2009 as part of its strategy for growth. Low prices are one of the cornerstones of the IKEA concept and help to make customers want to buy from IKEA. This low price strategy is coupled with a wide range of well designed, functional products. IKEA's products cater for every lifestyle and life stage of its customers, who come from all age groups and types of households. This is vital in times when the retail sector is depressed, as it increases IKEA's potential market.

For more information, refer to the full case study.

Questions for Discussion:

1. Describe what is meant by a SWOT analysis.
2. Explain the difference between internal and external factors.
3. Analyse ways in which IKEA has managed to minimise threats to its business.
4. Discuss the contribution of SWOT analysis to IKEA's business growth.
5. Crossword (see over the page).

IKEA

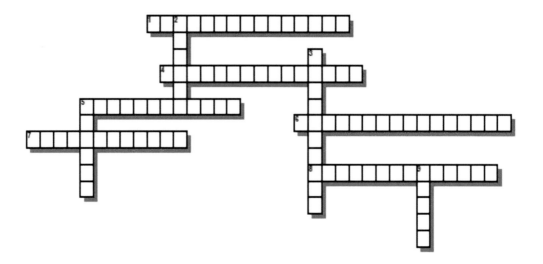

Across

1 - Those features that prevent businesses entering a particular market

4 - A measure of the amount of carbon dioxide produced by individuals, businesses or countries as a result of their activities

5 - IKEA recently used this tool as part of its strategic planning process

6 - Reductions in average costs that stem from operating on a large scale

7 - A term that generally refers to the inter-play between supply and demand that determines both the price of a product and the volume sold

8 - Practices which do not adversely affect the future use of resource

Down

2 - In which sector of industry is IKEA?

3 - Person licensed to trade using a particular well known name in return for a fee or share of revenues made

5 - IKEA started in this particular country

9 - A name, symbol or design used to identify a specific product and to differentiate it from its competitors

Possible Answers:

barriers to entry, brand, carbon footprint, economies of scale, franchisee, market forces, retail, sustainability, sweden, swot analysis

Case Study: *Kellogg's - Building a brand in order to sustain its life cycle.*

Kellogg's All-Bran has a long and distinguished history. Like many other famous products, however, it is important from time to time to re-energise its life cycle. While All-Bran continues to be a powerful brand, a number of other high fibre brands made by Kellogg have not had the promotional support or sales of the All-Bran brand. Kellogg has therefore sought to support these other fibre products by associating them with the master-brand All-Bran. Kellogg has looked to raise consumer interest by creating a family of fibre-based cereal brands focused around the All-Bran banner in order to create a power-brand structure. These bran products have now been marketed as a family. This has added extra strength to each separate product.

The decision to create the power-brand was a strategic change, made at a high level. It involved managers at Kellogg planning for the long term future. It also needed heavy resource commitments e.g. to finance and market the initiative.

The product life cycle is the period over which it appeals to customers. The cycle can be illustrated in a series of stages showing how consumer interest, and hence sales, has altered over time. For example, a company like Kellogg is continually developing new product lines, which it then market tests. For many of these products, test marketing will indicate that the product might be popular for a short while and then interest would quickly fizzle out.

For more information, refer to the full case study.

Questions for Discussion:

1. Give a concise summary of the SWOT analysis given in the case study for Kellogg's All Bran. Include TWO strengths, weaknesses, opportunities and threats, respectively, as a concise list with bullet points.
2. Several **Sales vs. Time** diagrams are given in the case study. Place an image of any ONE diagram into a Word document and properly reference the source.
3. Summarise the TWO main approaches to market research used by Kellogg's (one paragraph).
4. Research high fibre brands similar to Kellogg's All Bran to find a table of data for high fibre cereals. Your table should show the quantity of sodium (mg) and the quantity of sugar per serving size for at least TEN different high fibre cereals.
5. Represent SIX breakfast cereals with highest **sodium content** in the form of a histogram.
6. Represent SEVEN breakfast cereals with highest **sugar content** in the form of a pie chart.

[Kellogg's Questions continued]

7. In 2014, *Markets and Markets* explained in a business report how Breakfast Cereals (BFCs) are a healthier alternative to the traditional breakfast items such as white bread, high-calorie spreads, or meat-based dishes. The report provided a study on the global breakfast cereal ingredients market categorizing these ingredient based on their types, applications, and geography.

Cereal Ingredient Market Share Analysis, 2012–2019 ($Million)

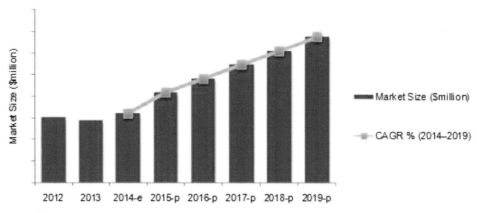

<u>Figure courtesy:</u> http://www.marketsandmarkets.com/Market-Reports/cereal-ingredients-market-150230788.html

With reference to the chart in the figure above, taken from the report,

   (i) Explain the term CAGR
   (ii) What types of cereal are included in the report

8. In 2016, *The Food & Agriculture Organisation of the United Nations* produced a mixed chart relating to forecast data of world cereal production, utilization and stocks.

Summarise the data in one concise paragraph written in simple terms (you can mention that there are expectations of a lower world wheat production).

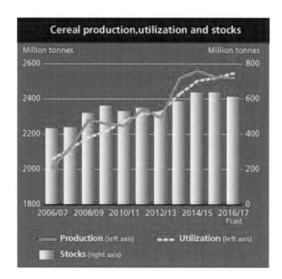

<u>Figure courtesy:</u> http://www.fao.org/worldfoodsituation/csdb/en/

Exercises– Secondary Data: Gathering & Representing

1. {multiple choice – choose the most appropriate answer (a), (b), (c) or (d)}

A business researcher has found good reliable secondary data about customer preference in car buying and hopes to look for differences between female and male customer preferences but mistakenly collects and represents data as a single (female and male combined) customer group. This is called:

    (a) Under-aggregation (b) Dis-aggregation (c) Aggregation   (d) Over-aggregation

2. {multiple choice – choose the most appropriate answer (a), (b), (c) or (d)}

A company has found good reliable secondary data about two types of customers, those who pay invoices on time and those who do not. This type of data is called:

    (a) Nominal   (b) Categorical   (c) Ordinal   (d) Binomial

3. {multiple choice – choose the most appropriate answer (a), (b), (c) or (d)}

Based on "How Americans Spend Their Money" (pie chart, figure 4.9), the fraction NOT spent on housing in 2013 was approximately:

    (a) $1/3$ (b) $1/2$ (c) $2/3$ (d) $3/4$

4. {multiple choice – choose the most appropriate answer (a), (b), (c) or (d)}

If you were searching for good, reliable secondary data in a trade and business publication, which of these websites would you most likely use?

    (a) www.lse.co.uk   (b) www.bpubs.com (c) www.aeaweb.org (d) www.inomics.com

5. {multiple choice – choose the most appropriate answer (a), (b), (c) or (d)}

Based on Apple revenue shown in the histogram of figure 4.11, revenue for the entire year 2013 was approximately:

    (a) $575 billion   (b) $625 billion   (c) $675 billion   (d) $725 billion

6. <u>Data for ten new London universities</u> ranked in alphabetical order are shown in the figure below. Overall scores are based upon entry standards, student satisfaction, research quality and graduate prospects.

CUG Rank		University Name	Entry Standards		Overall Score	
2016	**2015**					
124	122	East London	273	▌	406	▌
107	99	Greenwich	309	▌▌	505	▌
104	107	Kingston	297	▌▌	511	▌
126	123	London Metropolitan	220	▌	327	▌
119	120	London South Bank	244	▌	429	▌
89	94	Middlesex	271	▌	565	▌▌
66	93	Roehampton	284	▌	625	▌▌▌
109	-	St Mary's, Twickenham	287	▌	486	▌
108	110	West London	257	▌	492	▌
100	96	Westminster	309	▌▌	525	▌▌

Figure based on data courtesy of http://www.thecompleteuniversityguide.co.uk/league-tables
(Note that St Mary's has no 2015 ranking because it only became a university in January, 2014)

Carry out the following steps leading finally to an ordered table and mixed histogram. Note that *The Complete University Guide* claims to be 'independent and trusted'.

(i)   Which consultants compiled the guide and how independent would you consider them to be?
(ii) Place the table into a suitable business software package
(iii) Sort the table according to overall score (highest first, lowest last)
(iv) Present the data in (ii) in the form of a mixed histogram with improving universities shown in green and the others shown in red.

7. <u>Unemployment Data.</u> According to U.S. Bureau of Statistics secondary data, long-term, medium term and short-term unemployment since the 2008 recession, varied as shown in the figure below.

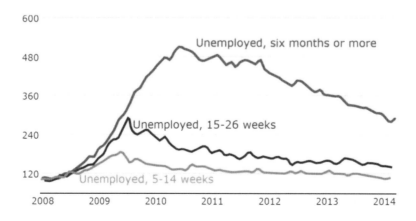

Figure Q7 Unemployment data, courtesy of the *U.S. Bureau of Labor Statistics* (2014).

Carry out the following steps leading finally to a mixed line graph showing both US and EU total unemployment in one comparative graph.

  (i)   From the data in the above chart, aggregated total US employment showing results in the form of a simple table.
  (ii) Search for similar reliable data for EU total unemployment in the same time period 2008-2014.
  (iii) Create a simple EU-unemployment table similar to the one you made in (i).
  (iv) Place tables made in (i) and (iii) together into a suitable business software package.
  (v)   Show both US and EU total unemployment data in one comparative mixed line chart.

8.   Planning.   Suppose that you are a university student taking in the twelve-week Autumn Term a Business Research module plus other modules, all of which have different assessment deadlines and types, e.g. on-line test, essay, reports, etc. In a similar manner to the project planning scenario covered earlier in this chapter, create a planning table and Gantt chart for each module on the key tasks involved, making sure that advertised deadlines will be met in good time. Include specific dates, duration and appropriate predecessor information.

9.   Stock Market.

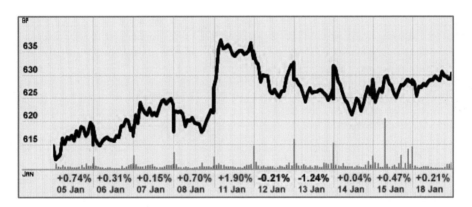

The above figure shows fluctuations in the share price of British Petroleum (ticker: **BP**) for ten consecutive days in January 2010 when the stock market was open.

Complete a table similar to the one shown below which contains (approximate) daily average and absolute/percentage increase information for the five-day period 11[th]Jan - 15[th]Jan.

DAY	11 Jan	12 Jan	13 Jan	14 Jan	15 Jan
Daily S.P. average	635				
Absolute inc from previous day					
% increase from previous day					

10. <u>Research</u> daily stock market data for any major UK banking stock of your choice for which the UK government owns a large stake, following the bailouts of 2008/9. Represent your raw data in the form of a mixed chart (see figure 4.25) combining closing price as a line chart and volume traded as a histogram.

11. <u>Wordsearch</u>

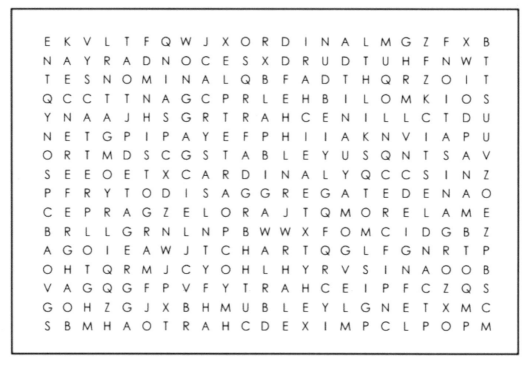

Find the following words in the puzzle.
Words are hidden ↑ ↓ → ← and ↘ .

AGGREGATED   HISTOGRAM   PIECHART
CANDLESTICK   LINECHART   REFERENCE
CARDINAL   MIXEDCHART   SCATTERPLOT
CHART   NOMINAL   SECONDARY
DISAGGREGATED   ORDINAL   TABLE
GANTT   ORGANISATION

5. INFORMATION SYSTEMS FOR COMPETITIVE ADVANTAGE

In almost every business in every sector, we find that some do better than most others. There is almost always a 'stand-out' business. In pure online retail, Amazon is a recognised leader. In off-line retail, Walmart, the world's largest retailer, is a leader. In online music, Apple's iTunes is considered a leader with more than seventy percent of the downloaded music market. In the related industry of digital music players, the iPod is the leader and in Web search, Google is presently the front runner.

Businesses that excel more than others are said to have a *competitive advantage* over others. They either have access to special resources that others do not or they are able to use commonly-available resources more efficiently, usually because of superior knowledge or information assets. In any case, they do better in terms of revenue growth, profitability or productivity growth (efficiency), all of which ultimately translates into higher stock market valuations than their competitors.

But why do some firms do better than others and how do they achieve competitive advantage? How can we analyse a business and identify its strategic advantages? How can we develop a strategic advantage for our own business? And how do information systems contribute to strategic advantages? One way to answer to those questions involves Michael Porter's competitive forces model.

Porter's Competitive Forces Model

Arguably, the most widely used model for understanding competitive advantage is Porter's competitive forces model (see figure 5.1).

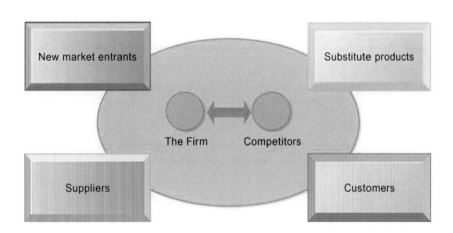

+

Figure 5.1 Organisational structure types.

This model provides a general view of a business, its competitors and its business environment. Porter's model is essentially about the business' general environment. In this model, <u>five</u> competitive forces shape the fate of the business. These are *traditional competitors, new market entrants, substitute products, customers* and *suppliers*.

Traditional Competitors

All businesses share market space with other competitors who are continuously devising new, more efficient ways to produce by introducing new products and services, and attempting to attract customers by developing their brands and imposing switching costs.

New Market Entrants

In a free economy with mobile labour and financial resources, new companies are regularly entering the marketplace. In some industries, there are very low barriers to entry, whereas in others, entry is very difficult. For instance, it is fairly easy to start a pizza business or just about any small retail business, but it is much more expensive and difficult to enter the computer chip business, which has very high capital costs and requires significant expertise and knowledge that is hard to build up. New companies have several possible advantages. They are not locked into old plants and equipment, they often hire younger workers who are less expensive and perhaps more innovative, they are not encumbered by old worn-out brand names and they are "more hungry" (more highly motivated) than traditional occupants of an industry. These advantages can also be their weakness. They depend on outside financing for new plants and equipment, which can be expensive. They also have a less-experienced workforce and little brand recognition.

Substitute Products and Services

In just about every industry, there are substitutes that customers might use if prices become too high. New technologies create new substitutes all the time. For example, oil has substitutes - ethanol can substitute for gasoline in cars and vegetable oil for diesel fuel in trucks. Wind, solar, coal, and hydro power are all used for industrial electricity generation. Similarly, the Internet telephone service can be substituted for traditional telephone services and fibre-optic telephone lines to the home can be substituted for cable TV lines. The more substitute products and services we have in a business, the less we can control pricing and the lower the profit margins.

Customers

A profitable company depends in large measure on its ability to attract and retain customers (while denying them to competitors), and charge high prices. The power of customers grows if they can easily switch to a competitor's products and services, or if they can force a business and its competitors to compete on price alone in a transparent marketplace where there is little product differentiation, and all prices are known instantly (such as on the Internet). For instance, in the used college textbook market on the Internet, students (customers) can find multiple suppliers of just about any current college textbook. In this case, online customers have extraordinary power over used-book firms.

Suppliers

The market power of suppliers can have a significant impact on a business' profits, especially when the business cannot raise prices as fast as can suppliers. The more different suppliers a business has, the greater control it can exercise over suppliers in terms of price, quality, and delivery schedules. For instance, manufacturers of laptop computers almost always have multiple competing suppliers of key components, such as keyboards, hard drives, and display screens.

Strategies for Dealing with Competitive Forces

What is a business to do when it is faced with all these competitive forces? And how can it use information systems to counteract some of these forces? How do we prevent substitutes and inhibit new market entrants? There are four generic strategies, each of which is often enabled using information technology and systems. They are strategies of low-cost leadership, product differentiation, focus on market niche and strengthening links between customers and suppliers.

Low-Cost Leadership

We can use information systems to achieve the lowest operational costs and the lowest prices. A classic example is Walmart. By keeping prices low and shelves well stocked using a legendary inventory replenishment system, Walmart became the leading retail business in the United States. Walmart's continuous replenishment system sends orders for new merchandise directly to suppliers as soon as consumers pay for their purchases at the cash register. Point-of-sale terminals record the bar code of each item passing the checkout counter and send a purchase transaction directly to a central computer at Walmart headquarters. The computer collects the orders from all Walmart stores and transmits them to suppliers. Suppliers can also access Walmart's sales and inventory data using Web technology. Because the system replenishes inventory with lightning speed, Walmart does not need to spend much money on maintaining large inventories of goods in its own warehouses. The system also enables Walmart to adjust purchases of store items to meet customer demands. Competitors, such as Sears, have been spending approximately 25% of sales on overhead. But by using systems to keep operating costs low, Walmart pays only 17% of sales revenue for overhead. (Operating costs average 20% of sales in the retail industry.) Walmart's continuous replenishment system is also an example of an efficient customer response system. An efficient customer response system directly links consumer behaviour to distribution and production and supply chains. Walmart's continuous replenishment system provides an efficient customer response.

Product Differentiation

We can use information systems to enable new products and services or to greatly change the customer convenience in using your existing products and services. For instance, Google continuously introduces new and unique search services on its Web site, such as Google Maps. By purchasing PayPal, an electronic payment system, in 2003, eBay made it much easier for customers to pay sellers and expanded use of its auction marketplace.

Apple created the iPod, a unique portable digital music player, plus a unique online Web music service where songs can be purchased for just a small cost. Apple has continued to innovate with its multimedia iPhone, iPad tablet computer, and iPod video player. Manufacturers and retailers are using information systems to create products and services that are customised and personalised to fit the precise specifications of individual customers. For example, Nike sells customised trainers through its NIKEiD program on its Web site. Customers are able to select the type of shoe, colours, material, outsoles, and even a logo of up to 8 characters. Nike transmits the orders via computers to specially-equipped plants in China and Korea. The trainers cost only a small amount extra and take about three weeks to reach the customer. This ability to offer individually tailored products or services using the same production resources as mass production is called *mass customisation*.

Focus on Market Niche

We can use information systems to enable a specific market focus and to serve a narrow target market better than competitors. Information systems support this strategy by producing and analysing data for finely-tuned sales and marketing techniques. Information systems enable companies to analyse customer buying patterns, tastes, and preferences closely so that they efficiently pitch advertising and marketing campaigns to smaller and smaller target markets.

The data come from a range of sources, including credit card transactions, demographic data, purchase data from checkout counter scanners at supermarkets and retail stores and data collected when people access and interact with Web sites. Sophisticated software tools find patterns in these large pools of data and infer rules from them to guide decision making.

Analysis of such data drives one-to-one marketing that creates personal messages based on individualised preferences. For example, Hilton Hotels' OnQ system analyses detailed data collected on active guests in all of its properties to determine the preferences of each guest and each guest's profitability. Hilton uses this information to give its most profitable customers additional privileges, such as late check-outs. Contemporary customer relationship management (CRM) systems feature analytical capabilities for this type of intensive data analysis.

Business	Competitive Advantage
Amazon: One-click shopping	Amazon holds a patent on one-click shopping that it licenses to other online retailers
Online music: Apple iPod	The iPod integrated handheld player backed up with an online and iTunes library of over ten million songs
Golf club Club customisation:	Ping Customers can select from more than one million different golf club options and a build-to-order system
Online person-to-person payment: PayPal.com	PayPal enables the transfer of money between individual accounts and between bank accounts

Figure 5.2 A table of some IT-enabled products providing competitive advantage.

Strengthening Customer and Supplier Links

We can use information systems to tighten links with suppliers and to develop 'intimacy' with customers. Chrysler Corporation uses information systems to facilitate direct access by suppliers to production schedules and even permits suppliers to decide how and when to ship supplies to Chrysler factories. This allows suppliers more lead time in producing goods. On the customer side, Amazon.com keeps track of user preferences for book purchases and can recommend titles purchased by others to its customers. Strong links to customers and suppliers increase switching costs (the cost of switching from one product to a competing product) and loyalty to the business.

The Internet's Impact on Competitive Advantage

Since the inception of the Internet, traditional competitive forces are still at work but competitive rivalry has arguably become much more intense (Porter, 2001). Internet technology is based on universal standards that any company can use, making it easy for rivals to compete on price alone and for new competitors to enter the market. Because a vast array of information is available to everyone, the Internet raises the bargaining power of customers, who can quickly find the lowest-cost provider on the Web. Profits have been dampened.

Competitive Force of the Internet

The Internet reduces barriers to entry, such as the need for a sales force, access to channels, and physical assets. It provides a technology for driving business processes that makes other things easier to do. It also widens the geographic market, increasing the number of competitors and reducing differences among existing competitors.

On the other hand, the Internet has nearly destroyed some industries and has severely threatened more. For instance, the printed encyclopaedia industry and the travel agency industry have been nearly decimated by the availability of substitutes over the Internet. Likewise, the Internet has had a significant impact on the retail, music, book, retail brokerage, software, telecommunications and newspaper industries. However, the Internet has also created entirely new markets, formed the basis for thousands of new products, services, and business models and provided new opportunities for building brands with very large and loyal customer bases. Amazon, eBay, iTunes, YouTube, Facebook, Travelocity, and Google are such examples. In this sense, the Internet is constantly transforming entire businesses, forcing them to change how they do business.

The Business Value Chain Model

Although the Porter model is very helpful for identifying competitive forces and suggesting generic strategies, it is not very specific about what exactly to do and it does not provide a methodology to follow for achieving competitive advantages. If your goal is to achieve operational excellence, where do you start? Here's where the business value chain model is helpful.

The value chain model highlights specific activities in the business where competitive strategies can best be applied and where information systems are most likely to have a strategic impact. This model identifies specific critical leverage points where a firm can use information technology most effectively to enhance its competitive position. The value chain model views the firm as a series or chain of basic activities that add a margin of value to a firm's products or services. These activities can be categorised as either primary activities or support activities. Primary activities are most directly related to the production and distribution of the firm's products and services, which create value for the customer.

Primary activities include inbound logistics, operations, outbound logistics, sales/marketing and service:

- Inbound logistics includes receiving and storing materials for distribution to production
- Operations transform inputs into finished products
- Outbound logistics entails storing and distributing finished products
- Sales/marketing includes promoting and selling the business' products
- Service activity includes maintenance and repair of goods and services that coordinate the flow of resources into the business and customer relationship management

Using the business value chain model will also cause you to consider benchmarking your business processes against your competitors or others in related industries, and identifying industry best practice. Benchmarking involves comparing the efficiency and effectiveness of your business processes against strict standards and then measuring performance against those standards. Industry best practices are usually identified by consulting companies, research organisations, government agencies, and industry associations as the most successful solutions or problem-solving methods for consistently and effectively achieving a business objective. Once you have analysed the various stages in the value chain at your business, you can come up with candidate applications of information systems. Then, once you have a list of candidate applications, you can decide which to develop first. By making improvements in your own business value chain that your competitors might miss, you can achieve competitive advantage by attaining operational excellence, lowering costs, improving profit margins, and forging a closer relationship with customers and suppliers.

Extending the Value Chain: The Value Web

A business' value chain is linked to the value chains of its suppliers, distributors and customers. After all, the performance of most businesses depends not only on what goes on inside but also on how well it coordinates with direct and indirect suppliers, delivery firms (logistics partners, such as couriers) and, of course, customers. How can information systems be used to achieve strategic advantage at the industry level? By working with other businesses, industry participants can use information technology to develop industry-wide standards for exchanging information or business transactions electronically, which forces all market participants to subscribe to similar standards. Such efforts increase efficiency, making product substitution less likely and perhaps raising entry costs. Also, industry members can build industry-wide, IT-supported consortia, symposia, and communications networks to coordinate activities concerning government agencies, foreign competition and competing industries.

Looking at the industry value chain encourages us to think about how to use information systems to link up more efficiently with your suppliers, strategic partners and customers. Strategic advantage derives from an ability to relate our value chain to the value chains of other partners in the process. For instance, Amazon.com wants to build systems that:

- make it easy for suppliers to display goods and open stores on the Amazon site
- make it easy for customers to pay for goods
- develop systems that coordinate the shipment of goods to customers
- develop shipment tracking systems for customers

Internet technology has made it possible to create highly synchronised industry value chains called 'value Webs'. A value Web is a collection of independent businesses that use information technology to coordinate their value chains to produce a product or service for a market collectively. It is more customer driven and operates in a less linear fashion than the traditional value chain.

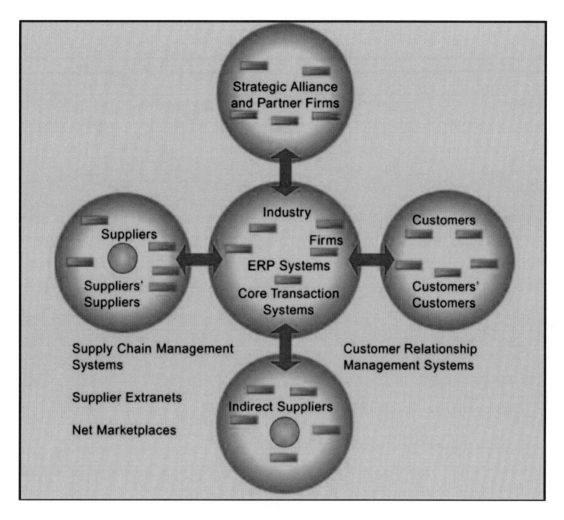

Figure 5.3 The Value Web.

Figure 3.3 shows that the value Web synchronises the business processes of customers, suppliers and trading partners among different companies. These value Webs are flexible and adaptive to changes in supply and demand. Relationships can be bundled or unbundled in response to changing market conditions. Firms will accelerate time to market and to customers by optimising their value Web relationships to make quick decisions on who can deliver the required products or services at the right price and location.

Synergies, Core Competencies and Network-based Strategies

A large corporation is typically a collection of businesses. Often, the firm is organised financially as a collection of strategic business units and the returns to the firm are directly tied to the performance of all the strategic business units. Information systems can improve the overall performance of these business units by promoting synergies and core competencies.

Synergies

The idea of synergies is that when the output of some units can be used as inputs to other units, or two organisations pool markets and expertise, these relationships lower costs and generate profits. Recent bank and financial firm mergers, such as the merger of JP Morgan Chase and Bank of New York in 2006, as well as Bank of America and Countrywide Financial Corporation, occurred precisely for this purpose.

One use of information technology in these synergy situations is to tie together the operations of disparate business units so that they can act as a whole. For example, acquiring Countrywide Financial enabled Bank of America to extend its mortgage lending business and to tap into a large pool of new customers who might be interested in its credit card, consumer banking, and other financial products. Information systems would help the merged companies consolidate operations, lower retailing costs, and increase cross-marketing of financial products.

Enhancing Core Competencies

Yet another way to use information systems for competitive advantage is to think about ways that systems can enhance core competencies. The argument is that the performance of all business units will increase insofar as these business units develop, or create, a central core of competencies. A core competency is an activity for which a firm is a world-class leader. Core competencies may involve being the world's best miniature parts designer, the best package delivery service, or the best thin-film manufacturer. In general, a core competency relies on knowledge that is gained over many years. This practical knowledge is typically supplemented with a long-term research effort and committed employees.

Any information system that encourages the sharing of knowledge across business units enhances competency. Such systems might encourage or enhance existing competencies and help employees become aware of new external knowledge; such systems might also help with business leverage in related markets.

Network-Based Strategies

The availability of Internet and networking technology have inspired strategies that take advantage of firms' abilities to create networks or network with each other. Network-based strategies include the use of network economics, a virtual company model and business ecosystems.

Network Economics

Business models based on a network may help firms strategically by taking advantage of network economics. In traditional economics, such as the economics of factories and agriculture, production experiences diminishing returns. The more any given resource is applied to production, the lower the marginal gain in output, until a point is reached where the additional inputs produce no additional gain. This is the law of diminishing returns, and it is the foundation for most of modern economics.

In some situations, the law of diminishing returns does not apply. For instance, in a network, the marginal costs of adding another participant are about zero, whereas the marginal gain is much larger. The larger the number of subscribers in a telephone system (or the Internet), the greater the value to all participants because each user can interact with more people. It is not much more expensive to operate a television station with 1,000 subscribers than with 10 million subscribers. The value of a community of people grows with size, whereas the cost of adding new members is inconsequential. From this network economics perspective, information technology can be strategically useful.

Internet sites can be used by businesses to build communities of users and like-minded customers who want to share their experiences. This builds customer loyalty and enjoyment, while building unique ties to customers.

eBay, the giant online auction site, and iVillage, an online community for women, are examples. Both businesses are based on networks of millions of users, and both companies have used the Web and Internet communication tools to build communities. The more people offering products on eBay, the more valuable the eBay site is to everyone because more products are listed, and more competition among suppliers lowers prices.

Network economics also provides strategic benefits to commercial software vendors. The value of their software and complementary software products increases as more people use them, and there is a larger installed base to justify continued use of the product and vendor support.

Virtual Company Model

Another network-based strategy uses the model of a 'virtual company' to create a competitive business. A virtual company, also known as a 'virtual organisation', uses networks to link people, assets, and ideas, enabling it to ally with other companies to create and distribute products and services, without being limited by traditional organisational boundaries or physical locations. One company can use the capabilities of another company without being physically tied to that company.

The virtual company model is useful when a company finds it cheaper to acquire products, services, or capabilities from an external vendor or when it needs to move quickly to exploit new market opportunities and lacks the time and resources to respond on its own. Fashion companies, such as Ann Taylor, Levi Strauss and Reebok, enlist Hong Kong-based Li & Fung to manage production and shipment of their garments. Li & Fung handles product development, raw material sourcing, production planning, quality assurance and shipping. Li & Fung does not own any fabric, factories, or machines, outsourcing all of its work to a network of more than 7,500 suppliers in 37 countries all over the world. Customers place orders to Li & Fung over its private extranet. Li & Fung then sends instructions to appropriate raw material suppliers and factories where the clothing is produced. The Li & Fung extranet tracks the entire production process for each order. Working as a virtual company keeps Li & Fung flexible and adaptable so that it can design and produce the products ordered by its clients quickly to keep pace with rapidly changing fashion trends.

Business Ecosystems: Keystone and Niche Firms

The Internet and the emergence of digital firms call for some modification of the industry competitive forces model. The traditional Porter model assumes:

- a relatively static industry environment
- relatively clear-cut industry boundaries
- a relatively stable set of suppliers, substitutes, and customers, with the focus on industry players in a market environment

Instead of participating in a single industry, some of today's businesses are much more aware that they should participate in industry sets, i.e. collections that provide related services and products. 'Business ecosystem' is another term for these loosely coupled but interdependent networks of suppliers, distributors, outsourcing firms, transportation service firms, and technology manufacturers. The concept of a business ecosystem builds on the idea of the value Web mentioned earlier, the main difference being that co-operation takes place across many *industries* rather than many businesses.

For instance, both Microsoft and Walmart provide platforms composed of information systems, technologies and services that thousands of other firms in different industries use to enhance their own capabilities. Microsoft has estimated that more than 40,000 firms use its Windows platform to deliver their own products, support Microsoft products and extend the value of Microsoft's own firm. Walmart's order entry and inventory management system is a platform used by thousands of suppliers to obtain real-time access to customer demand, track shipments and control inventories.

Business ecosystems can be characterised as having one or a few keystone firms that dominate the ecosystem and create the platforms used by other niche firms. Keystone firms in the Microsoft ecosystem include Microsoft and technology producers such as Intel and IBM. Niche businesses include thousands of software application developers, service businesses, networking businesses and consulting firms that both support and rely on the Microsoft products.

Information technology plays a powerful role in establishing business ecosystems. Obviously, many firms use information systems to develop into keystone firms by building IT-based platforms that other firms can use. In the digital era, we can expect greater emphasis on the use of IT to build industry ecosystems because the costs of participating in such ecosystems are continuously falling and the benefits to all will increase rapidly as the platform grows. Individual businesses need to consider how their information systems will enable them to become profitable niche players in larger ecosystems created by keystone firms. For instance, in making decisions about which products to build or which services to offer, a business should consider the existing business ecosystems related to these products and how it might use IT to enable participation in these larger ecosystems.

An example of a rapidly expanding ecosystem is the mobile Internet platform. In this ecosystem, there are several industries, including device makers (Apple iPhone, Samsung Galaxy), wireless telecommunication firms (BT, EE), independent software applications providers (generally small businesses selling games and applications) and Internet service providers (who participate as providers of Internet service to the mobile platform).

Each of these industries has its own history, interests and driving forces. But these elements come together in a sometimes co-operative, and sometimes competitive, new industry we refer to as the mobile digital platform ecosystem. More than any other, Apple has managed to combine these industries into a unified system. It is Apple's mission to sell physical devices (iPhones) that are nearly as powerful as today's personal computers.

These devices work only with a high-speed broadband network, supplied by the wireless phone carriers. In order to attract a large customer base, the iPhone had to be more than just a mobile phone. Apple differentiated this product by making it a "smart phone," one capable of running thousands of different, useful applications. Apple could not realistically develop all these applications itself. Instead it relies on generally small, independent software developers to provide the applications.

Using Systems for Competitive Advantage: Management Issues

Strategic information systems often change the organisation as well as its products, services and operating procedures, driving the organisation into new behavioural patterns. Successfully using information systems to achieve a competitive advantage is challenging and requires precise coordination of technology, organisations and management.

Sustaining Competitive Advantage

The competitive advantages that strategic systems create do not necessarily last long enough to ensure long-term profitability. This is because competitors can react and copy strategic systems. Hence, competitive advantage is not always sustainable. Markets, customer expectations and technology change. Globalisation has made these changes even more rapid and unpredictable. The Internet can make competitive advantage disappear very quickly because virtually all companies can use this technology. Classic strategic systems, such as American Airlines' SABRE computerised reservation system, Citibank's ATM system, and FedEx's package tracking system, all benefitted by being the first in their industries. Then rival systems emerged. Amazon.com was an e-commerce leader but now faces competition from eBay, Yahoo and Google. Information systems alone cannot provide an enduring business advantage. Systems originally intended to be strategic frequently become tools for survival, required by every firm to stay in business or they may inhibit organisations from making the strategic changes essential for future success.

Aligning IT with Business Objectives

The research on IT and business performance has found that the more successfully a business can align information technology with its business goals, the more profitable it will be. Furthermore, only about a quarter of businesses achieve alignment of IT with the business. About half of a business firm's profits can be explained by alignment of IT with business. Many businesses get it wrong. Information technology takes on a life of its own and does not serve management and shareholder interests very well. Instead of business people taking an active role in shaping IT to the enterprise, they ignore it, claiming not to understand IT or tolerating failure in the IT area as just a nuisance to work around. Such businesses pay a hefty price in poor performance. Successful businesses and managers understand what IT can do and how it works, taking an active role in shaping its use and measuring its impact on revenues and profits.

Management Checklist: Performing a Strategic Systems Analysis

To align IT with the business and use information systems effectively for competitive advantage, managers need to perform a strategic systems analysis. To identify the types of systems that provide a strategic advantage to their firms, managers should ask the questions shown in figure 5.4.

1.   What is the structure of the industry in which the business is located?
<ul><li>What are some of the competitive forces at work in the industry?</li><li>Are there new entrants to the industry?</li><li>What is the relative power of suppliers, customers, and substitute products and services over prices?</li><li>Is the basis of competition quality, price, or brand?</li><li>What are the direction and nature of change within the industry?</li><li>From where are momentum and change coming?</li><li>How is the industry currently using information technology?</li><li>Is the organisation behind or ahead of the industry in its application of information systems?</li></ul>
2.   What are the business and industry value chains for this particular business?
<ul><li>How is the company creating value for the customer - through lower prices snd transaction costs or higher quality?</li><li>Are there any places in the value chain where the business could create more value for the customer and additional profit for the company?</li><li>Does the business understand and manage its business processes using the best practice available?</li><li>Is it taking maximum advantage of supply chain management, customer relationship management and enterprise systems?</li><li>Does the business leverage its core competencies?</li><li>Is the industry supply chain and customer base changing in ways that benefit or harm the business?</li><li>Can the business benefit from strategic partnerships and value Webs?</li><li>Where in the value chain will information systems provide the greatest value?</li></ul>
3.   Have we aligned IT with our business strategy and goals?
<ul><li>Have we correctly articulated our business strategy and goals?</li><li>Is IT improving the right business processes and activities to promote this strategy?</li><li>Are we using the right metrics to measure progress towards those goals?</li></ul>

Figure 5.4 Table showing questions for performing strategic systems analysis.

Managing Strategic Transitions

Adopting the kinds of strategic systems described here generally requires changes in business goals, relationships with customers and suppliers and business processes. These socio-technical changes, affecting both social and technical elements of the organisation, can be considered strategic transitions, i.e. a movement between levels of socio-technical systems.

Such changes often entail blurring of organisational boundaries, both external and internal. Suppliers and customers become intimately linked and may even share each other's responsibilities. Managers need to devise new business processes for coordinating their business activities with those of customers, suppliers and other organisations. The organisational change requirements surrounding new information systems are so important that they merit careful attention.

The Internet has transformed the music industry. Sales of CDs in retail music stores have been steadily declining while sales of songs downloaded through the Internet to iPods and other portable music players are skyrocketing. Moreover, the music industry is still contending with millions of people illegally downloading songs for free. Will the television industry experience a similar fate? Widespread use of high-speed Internet access, powerful PCs with high-resolution display screens, iPhones, iPads, other mobile handhelds and leading edge file-sharing services have made downloading of video content from movies and television shows faster and easier than ever. Free and often illegal downloads of some TV shows are abundant. However, the Internet is also providing new ways for television studios to distribute and sell their content and they are trying to take advantage of that opportunity.

YouTube, which started up in February 2005, quickly became the most popular video-sharing website in the world. Even though YouTube's original mission was to provide an outlet for amateur filmmakers, clips of copyrighted Hollywood movies and television shows soon proliferated on the YouTube website. It is difficult to gauge how much proprietary content from TV shows winds up on YouTube without the studios' permission. Viacom claimed in a 2008 lawsuit that over 150,000 unauthorised clips of its copyrighted television programmes had appeared on YouTube. YouTube tries to discourage its users from posting illegal clips by limiting the length of videos to 10 minutes each and by removing videos when requested by their copyright owner. YouTube has also implemented Video ID filtering and digital fingerprinting technology that allows copyright owners to compare the digital fingerprints of their videos with material on YouTube and then flag infringing material. Using this technology, it is able to filter many unauthorised videos before they appear on the YouTube website.

If infringing videos do make it online, they can be tracked using Video ID. The television industry is also striking back by embracing the Internet as another delivery system for its content. Television broadcast networks such as NBC Universal, Fox, and CNN have put television shows on their own websites.

Case Studies – Information Systems for Competitive Advantage

Case Study: *Sheffield Forgemasters - creating competitive advantage through R&D.*

The origins of Sheffield Forgemasters can be traced back to 1805. In that year, Edward Vickers, a traditional miller, made the largest steel ingot of its time. He manufactured (cast) steel bells, which were exported around the world. Over 200 years later, Sheffield Forgemasters International Ltd (SFIL) is the largest independently owned forgemaster and one of the oldest steel businesses in the world. It is one of the biggest private sector employers in South Yorkshire.

With its headquarters in Sheffield, SFIL is the parent company of seven subsidiary companies. These provide steel forgings, castings and engineering solutions to customers around the world. The business operates in many sectors, including defence, nuclear, offshore oil and gas, power generation, marine and construction. Despite a steady decline in steel manufacture in the UK over the past few decades, SFIL has continued to grow. It is now a world leader in heavy steel castings and steel forgings. Like any business, SFIL can be affected by various factors in the external environment in which it operates. These factors are often grouped under six headings: political, economic, social, technological, environmental and legal (PESTEL). Companies need to understand these factors to make sure they develop strategies to remain competitive. They need to find ways to manage and influence the external environment effectively. This case study shows how SFIL uses research and development (R&D) to sustain its competitive advantage.

For more information, refer to the full case study.

Questions for Discussion:

1. Explain the terms innovation, research and development.
2. Describe how modelling is useful in research.
3. Analyse how SFIL's strategy for research and development has created a competitive advantage.
4. Evaluate the effectiveness of SFIL's focus on developing new materials and processes within the steel industry.

Case Study: ACCA Professional - interpreting and understanding accounts.

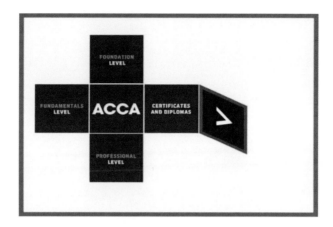

How much is the business worth? Are sales growing or declining? What about cash flow? These and many other vital questions are regularly tackled by qualified accountants of the Association of Chartered Certified Accountants (ACCA). Some of the answers are found fairly easily; others are much more difficult to uncover and need the skills and expertise of a qualified accountant.

ACCA is the largest professional body for accountants and its qualified accountants work in over 170 countries. For ACCA qualified accountants, no two days are ever the same. Each business is unique and business performance is constantly changing. Accountants use both financial and non-financial data to investigate business performance to aid strategic decision making and help make educated forecasts for the future. In addition to their technical skills, ACCA qualified accountants use their knowledge and professional experience every day, so they have to be complete finance professionals.

Finance is at the heart of every business so there is a constant demand for qualified accountants in all sectors. Accountancy is a highly skilled, multi-disciplinary profession. ACCA qualified accountants are well equipped to cope. Established over a hundred years ago, ACCA offers qualifications that are recognised all over the world. Its global network supports over 432,000 students and 154,000 members in accounting, finance and management. Many top employers actively look for applicants with ACCA qualifications.

There are many routes to becoming an ACCA qualified accountant. ACCA's foundation level suite of awards is ideal for non graduates with no prior accountancy experience. The ACCA Qualification is what you need to be a fully qualified accountant, and graduates may gain exemptions from some exams if they have studied a relevant degree. For more information, refer to the full case study.

Questions for Discussion:

1. Describe the role of an accountant.
2. Explain why ethical standards are so important for accountants.
3. Analyse how an Income Statement enables a judgement of a firm's profitability? How could a Balance Sheet further assist that judgement?
4. Evaluate the extent to which an accountant can help managers and directors to formulate a business strategy.
5. Create your own spreadsheet to simulate the income statement and balance sheet in this case study.

Exercises – Information Systems for Competitive Advantage

1. {multiple choice – choose the most appropriate answer (a), (b), (c) or (d)}

A specific market focus which enables a business to serve a narrow target market better than its competitors is called:

   (a) Market variety   (b) Market niche   (c) Market value   (d) Market share

2. {multiple choice – choose the most appropriate answer (a), (b), (c) or (d)}

Using information systems to achieve the lowest operational costs and the lowest prices has enabled several successful businesses in the UK. They have been able to keep prices low and shelves well stocked using an efficient inventory replenishment system. Which of the following businesses would fall in that category?

   (a) Boots   (b) H. Samuel   (c) W.H. Smith   (d) Poundland

3. {multiple choice – choose the most appropriate answer (a), (b), (c) or (d)}

Which of the following industries has been most negatively affected by e-commerce and the Internet?

   (a) Car Dealers   (b) Travel Agents   (c) Supermarkets   (d) Banks

4. {multiple choice – choose the most appropriate answer (a), (b), (c) or (d)}

What is the name given to the well-known model of competitive forces?

   (a) Peter   (b) Porter   (c) Pater   (d) Pellegrini

5. {multiple choice – choose the most appropriate answer (a), (b), (c) or (d)}

The ability to offer individually tailored products or services using the same production resources as mass production is called mass ....?

   (a) Customisation   (b) Custom   (c) Customer   (d) Conte

6. <u>Strategic Transitions</u>

Summarise briefly (one paragraph) the main business strategic transitions of *Youtube* since its start-up in 2005.

7. <u>Resource-based view on strategy.</u>

A 'resource-based view' on strategy suggests that a sustainable competitive advantage enables firm managers to answer "yes" to the following questions:

   (i)   Is your resource valuable?
   (ii)   Is it rare?
   (iii) Is it inimitable?
   (iv)   Is it non-substitutable?
   (v)   Is it operationalisable?

Briefly explain the issues involved in each question.

8. <u>Sustained competitive advantage</u>

Give an example of any ONE well-known company with sustained competitive advantage

   (i)   Strong research and innovation
   (ii)   Brand popularity
   (iii) Corporate reputation
   (iv)   Strategic assets
   (v)   Access to working capital
   (vi)   Barriers to entry
   (vii) Superior product or customer support

9. Wordsearch

```
   IS FOR COMPETITIVE ADVANTAGE
```

```
Z U S E H C I N R H P R O D U C T D F E O F B
V A L U E M O G V N E G I N D K S X I L T S H
D T M P B U B X W O L C Q H X D R N W S E G M
T K S T R A T E G I E S R A B L E Q B Y E T B
L J F T Z D N C S T A Z M X C K I M I N H W H
E U W R W Q Q W J A B N Q F U B L O S E S K Q
A M J A L E R D O I Y N J C S L P D X R E S N
D H Z N P G W C O T A Z C H T Q P E V G C E R
E N J S R R S R S N D O O B O O U L R I N C L
R T J I O E L E N E T Z C C M H S L X E A I E
S L C T D N I T Y R N J C F E S C I H S L V L
H R D I U E F R T E M O A E R B Z N B Q A R D
I R O O C J S O V F P V H U S Z S G F G B E O
P B A N T L O P H F L I N T E R N E T V B S P
G C R S S W A G N I T N U O C C A T T Y Q R U
H C U Q V W O E H D P P I V U D S Z V L P C C
```

Find the following words in the puzzle.
Words are hidden ↑ ↓ → ← and ↘ .

ACCOUNTING	MODELLING	STRATEGIES
BALANCESHEET	NICHE	SUPPLIERS
CUSTOMERS	PORTER	SYNERGIES
DIFFERENTIATION	PRODUCT	TRANSITIONS
INTERNET	PRODUCTS	VALUE
LEADERSHIP	SERVICES	

6. BUSINESS PROBLEM SOLVING SKILLS

In day-to-day business operations, problem solving is frequent and essential. Indeed some senior managers claim that most of their time is spent solving and resolving problems with customers, employees and product development. In many cases, the problems necessitate the need for reliable data and clear information in order for a manager to arrive at appropriate, effective solutions.

Frequently-occurring Business Problems

In relation to customers, frequent problems surround questions such as

- Why don't they buy our products?
- Why don't they use our services?
- Are they satisfied with us and how do we know?
- Are they receiving our goods on time?
- What do they think of the quality of our services and goods?

In relation to employees, important questions include:

- Are they happy and productive in our organisation?
- Do we offer them a rewarding working environment?
- Do we operate an effective staff training scheme?
- Are we promoting our highest achievers?
- Do our employees "believe in" our strategies and goals?

In relation to product development, frequent questions include:

- Do we invest appropriately in product development?
- Do we understand the life-cycle of our products?
- Are we sufficiently innovative to bring good products to market?
- Do we understand the market for our products?
- What is a realistic product stream that will lead to commercial success?

Once we have formulated the questions, we need information to guide us to realistic answers. For instance, obtaining *measures* for key variables is particularly important. Even if we find a disappointing measure for, say, employee satisfaction today, we can work on the reasons why we have such a disappointing measure and seek to improve it next time. Similarly, if customers are telling us that their estimate of "receiving goods on time" is only five out of ten, we can work to get to the bottom of why this is happening and strive to improve the situation.

Of course, in the real world of business, we neither achieve perfect answers to every question nor perfect solutions to every problem. However, what we can do is apply general problem-solving skills to business situations, improve our performance over time and, with an element of good fortune, create a thriving, successful business.

General Business Problem Solving Skills

There are general problem-solving skills that separate a very good manager from an ordinary one. With so many problems that we are all faced with in our work and life, it seems as if there is never enough time to solve each one without dealing with some adversity along the way. Problems can keep mounting so fast that we often find ourselves taking short-cuts to temporarily alleviate tension points and move onto the next problem, without really solving the current one. In the process, we might fail to solve the core of several problems facing us. In turn, we inevitably get caught in the trap of a never-ending cycle of problems that makes it difficult to find any real resolutions.

Problem solving is the essence of what managers do. As leaders, the goal is to minimize the occurrence of problems, which means we must be courageous enough to tackle them head-on before circumstances force our hand. We must be resilient in our quest to create and sustain momentum for the organization and people we serve. But the reality of the workplace finds us dealing with people (including colleagues and competitors) that complicate matters with negative behaviour such as corporate politicking, self-promoting or power-playing. Communication barriers, lack of budgets and resources, and many other random acts or circumstances also make it harder for people associated with problems to be productive.

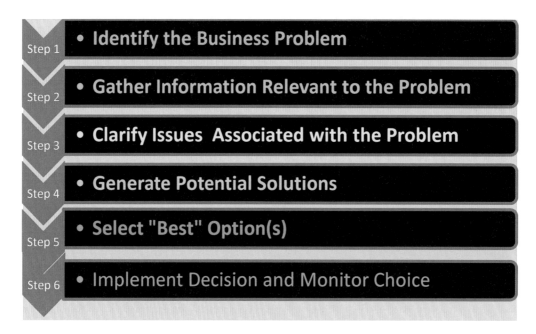

Step 1 • Identify the Business Problem

Step 2 • Gather Information Relevant to the Problem

Step 3 • Clarify Issues Associated with the Problem

Step 4 • Generate Potential Solutions

Step 5 • Select "Best" Option(s)

Step 6 • Implement Decision and Monitor Choice

Figure 6.1 Six steps in business problem solving.

Figure 5.1 shows some basic steps to follow in the course of solving problems. Missing out any of the steps can be calamitous. For instance, we need to identify the <u>correct</u> business problem. If customers are not buying our premier product, going back to its product development and redesigning it might be solving the wrong problem if in fact it is not being properly marketed to the right target customers by our marketing department, when indeed the product is fine as it is!

Similarly, selecting a present best solution and implementing it without following up with careful monitoring, could lead to blissful ignorance that the best solution has changed over time. Remember, virtually everything we do in business is time-dependent. A great product or best solution today is unlikely to be a great product or best solution next year (or even next month).

It can be argued that "All life is problem solving". Some managers contended that the best leaders are the best problem solvers. They have the patience to step back and see the problem at-hand through broadened observation and circular vision. They see around, beneath and beyond the problem itself. They see well-beyond the obvious. The most effective leaders approach problems through a lens of opportunity. Leaders who lack this wisdom approach problems with linear vision, only seeing the problem that lies directly in front of them and blocking the possibilities that lie within the problem. As such, they never see the totality of what the problem represents; that it can actually serve as an enabler to improve existing best practices, protocols and standard operating procedures for growing and competing in the marketplace. They never realize that, in the end, all problems are the same – just packaged differently. A leader must never view a problem as a distraction, but rather as a strategic enabler for continuous improvement and opportunities previously unseen. Therefore, there are four important features in general problem solving:

- maintaining transparent communication
- breaking down barriers
- encouraging open-minded people
- working to a clear strategy

Maintaining Transparent Communication

Problem solving requires transparent communication where everyone's concerns and points of view are freely expressed. Too many times, it is to almost impossible to get to the root of the matter in a timely manner when people do not speak up. Yes, communication is a fundamental necessity. That is why when those involved in the problem would rather not express themselves, fearing they may threaten their job and/or expose their own or someone else's wrong-doing, the problem-solving process becomes a treasure hunt. Effective communication towards problem solving happens because of a leader's ability to facilitate an open dialogue between people who trust her/his intentions and feel that they are in a safe environment to share why they believe the problem happened as well as specific solutions.

Once all voices have been heard and all points of view accounted for, the leader (with the rest of the team) can collectively map out a path toward a viable and sustainable solution. As fundamental as communication may sound, we shouldn't ever assume that people are comfortable sharing what they really think. This is where a leader must trust intuition enough to challenge the team until accountability can be fairly enforced and a solution can be reached. Some managers might argue that it is best to control communication lines between groups of colleagues when, in fact, this is simply a smoke screen to divert from their own poor management.

Breaking Down Barriers

If we do have good, transparent communication within our business, we can try to break down barriers and enable a boundary-less organisation whose culture is focused on the improvement of a healthier whole.   Unnecessary barriers encourage hidden agendas rather than welcome efficient, cross-functional collaboration and problem solving.

Organisational barriers are one root cause of most workplace problems and are why many of them never get resolved. This is why today's new workplace must embrace an entrepreneurial spirit where employees can freely navigate and cross-collaborate to connect the *problem-solving dots*, where everyone can be a passionate explorer who knows their own workplace dot and its intersections.   When colleagues know this information, they have a much greater sense of their sphere of influence. This is almost impossible to gauge when they operate in isolation, which potentially keeps them from having any significant influence at all. In a workplace where significant barriers exist, problem solving is more difficult because we are likely to be dealing with self-promoters, rather than team players fostered by a cross-functional environment.

Encouraging Open-minded Colleagues

Breaking down barriers requires people to be open minded. Ultimately, problem solving is about people working together to make the organisation and the people it serves better. Therefore, if we are stuck working with people that are closed minded, effective problem solving can become a long and winding road of misery.

There are some people in the workplace that enjoy creating unnecessary chaos so that their inefficiencies are never exposed. These make it difficult for problems to get solved because they slow the process down while trying to look more important. Discovering the *lifters* and *high-flyers* within the organisation enables us to see examples of the benefits of being open minded and how this eventually leads to more innovation and initiative.

Open-minded colleagues see beyond the obvious details before them and view risk as their best friend. They tackle problems head-on and get on with the business of driving growth and innovation. Closed-minded employees often turn things around to make it more about them and less about what is required to convert a problem into a new opportunity. With this explanation in mind, we should carefully observe the actions of others the next time we are presented with a real problem.

Working to a Clear Strategy

Without a clear strategy, change is merely substitution, not evolution. A solid strategy must be implemented in order to solve any problem. Many leaders attempt to dissect a problem rather than identify the strategy for change that lies within the problem itself.

Effective leaders that are comfortable with problem solving always seem to know how to gather the right people, resources, budget and knowledge from past experiences. They inspire people to lift their game by making the problem-solving process highly collaborative.

For them, it is an opportunity to bring people closer together. Effective leaders also connect the dots and map out a realistic plan of action in advance. They have a strategy that serves as the foundation for how the problem will be approached and managed. They anticipate the unexpected and utilize the strengths of their colleagues to assure the strategy leads to a sustainable solution.

It is unwise to shoot from the hip when problem solving. We should avoid guessing and take enough time to step back and assess the situation and the opportunities that each problem represents. We should make the problem-solving process more efficient by recognising that each problem has its own nuances that may require a distinct strategy towards a viable resolution.

We know that we have great leadership in our organisation when problem solving becomes a seamless process that enables the people and the organisation to grow and get better. If problem solving creates chaos, we may have a serious leadership deficiency. Some managers might argue that it is best to keep one's cards close to one's chest but this approach is usually self defeating.

Problem solving is the greatest enabler for growth and opportunity. This is why they say failure serves as the greatest lesson in business and in life. A good leader shows maturity, acts courageously and requires accountability.

Applying each of these lessons can help us to become an expert problem solver. Each experience teaches us new things.

Decision-making Skills

For more complex decisions, several options can be assessed against differing significant criteria, or against a single set of important factors. In any case, factors and options can be weighted and scored appropriately. The 'pros and cons method' can be used especially for two-option problem-solving and decision-making issues where implications need to be understood and a decision has to be made in a measured objective sense.

A weighted list is especially useful in business decisions, especially those which involve lots of different strategic considerations (as in SWOT and PEST and Porter's Five Forces concepts). In such situations, we can assess different options according to a single set of criteria (the most important considerations) or we can allocate weighted (scored) criteria differently to each option (see figure 6.2).

Should I replace my old, faulty car with a nearly-new, warranted one?			
Pros	**Score/10**	**Cons**	**Score/10**
Better comfort	3	Cost means sacrifices	7
Better reliability	7	Decisions upset me	4
Better for family use	3	Disposal of old car	2
Lower servicing costs	4	Hassle and Change	2
Lower fuel costs	3	Higher insurance	3
Load off my mind	7	Idiots "key" new cars	6
Needs no MOT	8		
Total Pros	35	Total Cons	24
Average Pros	**5**	**Average Cons**	**4**

Figure 6.2   A 'pros and cons method' table for a two-option car problem.

The two options in this problem are whether or not to buy a nearly new car, given that the old car is falling to pieces and will probably fail its MOT (roadworthiness test) next time. At first sight, it might seem that all of the issues can be easily formulated in one's head but in practice, noting down the issues in this way can help us to reason about the problem. Perhaps we have missed an issue or given an inaccurate weighting but after several iterations, we can usually arrive at a sensible list of pros and cons with appropriate weight. In this case, the *Average Pros* score (5/10) significantly exceeds the *Average Cons* score (4/10), so it might be a good idea to replace the old car.

The methodology is easily adapted for more complex decisions, such as in business strategy and consideration of more complex factors (notably found within other tools such as in SWOT, PEST and Porter's Five Forces).

Should I invest in UK buy-to-let market or not?			
Pros	**Score/10**	**Cons**	**Score/10**
House prices rising	5	Rent-receiving problems	7
Rental market increasing	7	Increase in stamp duty	7
Capital appreciation long term	8	Capital gains tax	8
UK houses "safe bet"	5	Tight profit margins	4
Very low bank savings rates	5	Risk of large repairs	4
		High agents fees	6
Total Pros	30	Total Cons	36
Average Pros	**6**	**Average Cons**	**6**

Figure 6.3   Pros and cons method table for a two-option investment problem.

The two options in this problem are whether or not to invest in the UK Buy-to-let market rather than, say, invest in savings or the stock market. In this case, the Average Pros Score (6/10) is comparable with the Average Cons Score (6/10), so it might be good wait until the situation becomes clearer, one way or the other.

Decision-making criteria depend on our own personal situations and preferences. Criteria and weighting will change according to time, situation, etc. Mood and intuition can also affect how we assess things, which is additional justification for the need of a measurable and robust method.

In bigger strategic business decision-making, it is often beneficial to seek input from others as to factors and weighting scores. In such situations, a template offers a way for people to contribute in a managed structured way. For more complex situations and more variables, especially which entail many more rows and columns, it is sensible to use a spreadsheet.

Negotiation Skills

Negotiation is a method by which people arrive at mutual agreement or settle differences. It is a process by which compromise or agreement is reached, hopefully while avoiding argument and dispute.

In any disagreement, individuals understandably aim to achieve the best possible outcome for their position or perhaps the business organisation they represent. However, the principles of fairness, seeking mutual benefit and maintaining a relationship are often the keys to a successful outcome. Specific forms of negotiation are used in many situations, including international affairs, the legal system, government, industrial disputes or domestic relationships. However, general negotiation skills can be learned and applied in a wide range of activities. Negotiation skills can be of great benefit in resolving any differences that arise between individuals and others. Every parent will testify that raising children is more about negotiation than it is about parental "control".

It is inevitable that, from time-to-time, conflict and disagreement will arise as the differing needs, wants, aims and beliefs of people are brought together. Without negotiation, such conflicts may lead to argument and resentment resulting in one or all of the parties feeling dissatisfied. The point of negotiation is to try to reach agreements without causing future barriers to communications.

Stages of Negotiation (Disputes)

In order to achieve a desirable outcome, it may be useful to follow a structured approach to negotiation. For example, in a work situation a meeting may need to be arranged in which all parties involved can come together. The process of negotiation to resolve a dispute can often include the following stages of preparation, discussion, clarification of goals, negotiation towards a win-win outcome, agreement and implementation of a course of action.

Preparation

Before any negotiation takes place, a decision needs to be taken as to when and where a meeting will take place to discuss the problem and who will attend. Setting a limited timescale can also be helpful to prevent the disagreement continuing. This stage involves ensuring all the pertinent facts of the situation are known in order to clarify our own position. This would include knowing the 'rules' of our business organisation. Most businesses will have policies to which we can refer in preparation for the negotiation.

Undertaking preparation before discussing the disagreement will help to avoid further conflict and unnecessarily wasting time during the meeting.

Discussion

During this stage, individuals or members of each side put forward the case as they see it, i.e. their understanding of the situation. Key skills during this stage include questioning, listening and clarifying. Sometimes it is helpful to take notes during the discussion stage to record all points put forward in case there is need for further clarification. It is extremely important to listen, as when disagreement takes place it is easy to make the mistake of saying too much and listening too little. Each side should have an equal opportunity to present their case.

Clarification of Goals

From the discussion, the goals, interests and viewpoints of both sides of the disagreement need to be clarified. It is helpful to list these factors in order of priority. Through this clarification it is often possible to identify or establish some common ground. Clarification is an essential part of the negotiation process; without it, misunderstandings are likely to occur which may cause problems and barriers to reaching a beneficial outcome.

Negotiation Towards a Win-Win Outcome

This stage focuses on what is termed a 'win-win' outcome where both sides feel they have gained something positive through the process of negotiation and both sides feel their point of view has been taken into consideration. A win-win outcome is usually the best result. Although this may not always be possible, through negotiation, it should be the ultimate goal. Suggestions of alternative strategies and compromises need to be considered at this point. Compromises are often positive alternatives which can usually achieve greater benefit for all concerned, compared to holding to the original positions.

Agreement

Agreement can be achieved once understanding of both sides' viewpoints and interests has been considered. It is essential for everybody involved to keep an open mind in order to achieve an acceptable solution. Any agreement needs to be made perfectly clear so that both sides know what has been decided.

Implementing a Course of Action

From the agreement, a course of action has to be implemented to carry through the decision. If the process of negotiation breaks down and agreement cannot be reached, then re-scheduling a further meeting is called for. This avoids all parties becoming embroiled in heated discussion or argument, which not only wastes time but can also damage future relationships. At the subsequent meeting, the stages of negotiation should be repeated. Any new ideas or interests should be taken into account and the situation looked at afresh. At this stage it may also be helpful to look at other alternative solutions and/or bring in another person to mediate.

Stages of Negotiation (Business & Customers)

There are often times when there is a need to negotiate more informally. At such times, when a difference of opinion arises, it might not be possible or appropriate to go through the stages in a formal manner. Nevertheless, remembering the key points in the stages of formal negotiation may be very helpful in a variety of informal situations.

In any negotiation with a business or customer, the following three elements are important and likely to affect the ultimate outcome of the negotiation:

- Attitudes
- Knowledge
- Interpersonal Skills

Attitudes

All negotiation is strongly influenced by underlying attitudes to the process itself. For example, attitudes to the issues and personalities involved in the particular case or attitudes linked to personal needs for recognition. We should always be aware that negotiation is not an arena for the realisation of individual achievements. There can be resentment of the need to negotiate by those in authority. Certain features of negotiation may influence a person's behaviour, for example some people may become defensive.

Knowledge

The more knowledge we possess of the issues in question, the greater our participation in the process of negotiation. In other words, good preparation is essential. It is important to do one's homework and gather as much information about the issues as possible.

Furthermore, the way issues are negotiated must be understood as negotiating will require different methods in different situations.

Interpersonal Skills

Good interpersonal skills are essential for effective negotiations, both in formal situations and in less formal or one-to-one negotiations.

These skills include effective verbal communication, listening, politeness, assertiveness and ability to deal with difficult situations.

It is particularly important to remember in negotiating business contracts, especially if we hope to secure repeat business, that the second party needs to feel that they are winning. As with a valued customer, trying to achieve a total win will simply leave the second party feeling taken advantage of or aggrieved. This means they are not likely to want to do business with us again and even worse, generate bad word-of-mouth reports about us.

Core Skills for Problem Solving in Senior Management

Providing Effective Leadership

Leadership is predominantly about setting direction and creating the right organisational conditions for heading in that direction. This is as true for the team leader as it is for the chief executive, although the scope and scale of the task varies significantly. Truly effective leaders have a clear vision of the future and the capability to communicate that vision to others, so that they are inspired to share it and work collaboratively to achieve it. It means ensuring that the right working conditions and physical resources are available but, more importantly, creating the culture, relationships and motivation to inspire people to make the most effective use of them. The best leaders face problems head on and have the confidence to propose sometimes innovative or difficult solutions. They also have the humility to accept that they do not have all the answers and will encourage others to make decisions by delegating authority. All managers need to be effective leaders. While a command and control culture will ensure that employees comply with organisational procedures and the terms of their employment contract, it does not create the enthusiasm, innovation and engagement that modern organisations need to compete effectively in a global marketplace. By developing their leadership capability, managers can achieve outstanding results from ordinary people and businesses, getting the best out of their employees. Above all, effective leaders need to inspire trust in their capability to take the organisation in the right direction.

Strategy and Planning

Sustainable performance requires good leadership and management capability at all levels of the organisation. Managers need to develop the skills to manage immediate operational needs whilst simultaneously planning for the future. Senior managers must be able to see the big picture, developing long term strategies that maximise opportunities to add value and support sustainable economic growth. They must have a clear understanding of the organisation's direction and the ability to continuously seek out ways to improve and build a leaner, more flexible and responsive business.

People Management

Core skills for people managers include reviewing and guiding performance, offering constructive feedback and praise, and identifying current and future skills needs. Good managers lead from the front, communicating with clarity, conviction and enthusiasm and mapping out for their employees a clear direction for the business. Managers should also create a learning culture within their team, taking responsibility for people's career development and promotion, as well coaching team members and supporting informal, on-the-job learning. It is claimed that nearly half of employees say their line manager rarely or never coaches them. Furthermore, a third of employees report that their line manager rarely or never discusses their training and development needs. If organisations want to ensure that their investment in training and development has maximum impact, they must make sure that they develop managers' ability to support, accelerate and direct learning in the workplace. Line management behaviour will also decide to a large extent which employees are given the opportunity to use their skills and are motivated to put in discretionary effort.

Budgeting & Financial Planning

Planning and control of financial resources lies at the heart of good management, from the most junior front line manager to the chief executive. Budgeting and financial planning ensure that the organisation is capable of achieving its goals. The monitoring and control of financial flows, and the people and physical resources that generate those financial flows, should be a primary responsibility if those goals are to be achieved. Whilst most senior managers are aware of the significance of financial management, too often managers in more junior positions do not have the knowledge or skills to appreciate fully its significance, nor are they given the responsibility for planning and control that would enable them to gain these insights.

Risk Management

If UK businesses are to lead the way from recession to economic growth, they need to be innovative and entrepreneurial, both of which mean being willing and able to assess risks and seize opportunities. From the front-line manager, ensuring a safe and healthy workplace that minimises its environmental impact, to the senior management team, identifying and taking advantage of new product and market opportunities, risk permeates business. The challenge for managers at all levels is to be able to assess the level of risk and the potential benefits that will accrue from taking them. This is what risk management is all about. Not avoiding risk but ensuring that the scale of risk facing the organisation is understood and acceptable.

Fostering innovation and creativity

Managers have a key role to play in fostering innovation, by adopting business strategies which focus on innovative products and services, and by leading the adoption of new technologies and work processes which improve productivity. There is now significant evidence to support the view that effective use of knowledge and technologies depends on the quality of management, with studies showing that firms adopting continuous innovation strategies are managed by more highly-educated and better informed managers. With employers facing a number of skills shortages, employers also need to be better at harnessing talent from across the UK's increasingly diverse workforce. Managers are responsible for ensuring fairness and equality in the workplace from the point of recruitment onwards. Drawing on diverse experiences and abilities can strengthen performance and may help businesses serve diverse customers, domestically or in global markets. **FACUP** is a useful mnemonic way of remembering the key elements to consider with any product's design: *Function, Appearance/Aesthetics, Cost, Unleashes, Profits*.

Partnership Working

An increasingly important role for managers is to foster the development of collaborative or partnership working with other organisations. Developing mutually beneficial 'win-win' relationships requires a range of skills, including personal skills, negotiating skills, the ability to build alliances, and the strategic abilities needed to define an organisation's purpose and anticipate changes in its operating environment. Reflecting the 'political' nature of building such relationships, these skills are sometimes referred to as political awareness, or political astuteness.

Case Studies – Business Problem Solving Skills

Case Study: *Enterprise Rent-a-car – Locating to enhance the customer experience*

One of the most important decisions a business has to make is where to locate. The location of the business can have a significant effect on how it performs. Businesses will aim to operate from locations that provide the maximum competitive advantage. These decisions need to be reviewed regularly. By selecting the best location, a business could get more customers, improve its efficiency and generate greater profits. For example, choosing an out-of-town shopping park instead of a high street may allow a retail business to have greater shop space, better overheads and attract more customers because parking is easier.   Multi-national businesses need to make many decisions about the location of their operations.

At an international level, they might need to choose which countries or territories to operate within to maximise opportunities. Within each country, they would need to locate the head office. At a more local level, they may need to choose whether to locate within or around major cities. Enterprise Rent-A-Car is an internationally recognised brand, operating within the United States, Canada, the UK, Ireland and Germany. It is the UK's largest car rental company. As the company has developed, it has sought to retain the personal feel of a smaller business. The company encourages its branch managers to take responsibility for local operations. This approach helps to create a dynamic service, driven by the individual branches. This means that each branch is free to focus on the needs of its local customers, while delivering Enterprise's values and high standards of customer service.

For more information, refer to the full case study.

Questions for Discussion:

1   Using an example of a service that you know, describe what is meant by customer service.
2.   Explain why Enterprise Rent-A-Car tries to locate branches close to its customers.
3.   Analyse factors that influence Enterprise's decisions about locating a new branch.
4.   Assess how organisations might evaluate any investment that they may make.

Case Study: *Portakabin – Product development, innovation and the product life-cycle.*

Profitable and innovative commercial businesses are ones which provide customers with exactly what they need and want. Portakabin is an example of such a business. Portakabin has been the UK's market leading modular building innovator for more than 50 years, operating in 6 countries and employing more than 1,300 people. The marketing of Portakabin is central to its past, present and future success. Portakabin is a business to business (B2B) organisation. Its customers are other businesses. This makes its approach to marketing different to more consumer-focused organisations.

Portakabin operates both in the secondary and tertiary sector, manufacturing and hiring a range of modular buildings. These vary from one-off portable buildings for doctor's surgeries to vast modular schools, hospitals and office complexes. Its buildings are made off-site, transported and constructed on site. Portakabin began supplying the first portable PK16 building in 1961. At the time this was a unique product and the business has built its success by continued innovation. One of its major extension strategies involved hiring out its buildings locally as an interim arrangement for businesses. It currently has more than 90 Visitor and Hire Centres.

Recently Portakabin launched its latest product, the Yorkon Building System (YBS). This new product is at the cutting edge of modular building technology. Its design is the culmination of extensive planning involving market research, research and development. Yorkon is a brand that belongs to the Portakabin Group, dating back to 1980. Any large, permanent building that needs to be designed and then built is sold under the Yorkon brand. The case study focuses on the processes involved in creating the Yorkon Building System and the role of marketing in launching the new product.

For more information, refer to the full case study.

Questions for Discussion:

1. Describe four main factors to take into account when designing a new product.
2. Explain two benefits of new product development to a business in a competitive market.
3. Analyse the role of promotion in extending a product's life cycle.
4. Evaluate the extent to which constant innovation guarantees business success.

Exercises – Business Problem Solving Skills

1. {multiple choice – choose the most appropriate answer (a), (b), (c) or (d)}

Which of the following questions is the most likely odd one out in relation to frequent problems relating to our customers?

      (a)   Why don't they buy our products?
      (b)   What is the colour theme of their website?
      (c)   Are they receiving our goods on time?
      (d)   What do they think of the quality of our services and goods?

2. {multiple choice – choose the most appropriate answer (a), (b), (c) or (d)}

Which of the following questions is the most likely odd one out in relation to frequent problems relating to our employees?

      (a)   Are they happy and productive in our organisation?
      (b)   Do we offer them a rewarding working environment?
      (c)   Do we operate effective marketing campaigns?
      (d)   Are we promoting our highest achievers?

3. {multiple choice – choose the most appropriate answer (a), (b), (c) or (d)}

Which of the following questions is the most likely odd one out in relation to frequent problems relating to our product development?

      (a)   Do we invest appropriately in product development?
      (b)   Do we understand the life-cycle of our products?
      (c)   Are we located in a purpose-built building?
      (d)   What is a realistic product stream that will lead to commercial success?

4. {multiple choice – choose the most appropriate answer (a), (b), (c) or (d)}

Research the following books on "negotiations" and identify which you would recommend to a friend:

      (a)   *Getting to yes* by Roger Fisher and William Ury
      (b)   *How to Win Friends and Influence People* by Dale Carnegie
      (c)   *Negotiation Genius* by Deepak Malhotra
      (d)   *Influence: the Psychology of Persuasion* by Robert B. Cialdini.

5. {multiple choice – choose the most appropriate answer (a), (b), (c) or (d)}

To whom is the following quote attributable: "We cannot negotiate with people who say what's mine is mine and what's yours is negotiable."?

  (a) John F Kennedy   (b) Bill Gates   (c) Taylor Swift   (d) Richard Branson

6. <u>Negotiation.</u> Discuss FOUR advantages and FOUR disadvantages of a 'win-lose' approach to negotiation.

7. <u>Decision Making.</u> Complete a decision-making table similar to the one below where the two-option problem is:

    Should I continue for a Masters Degree (MBA) after graduating?

    (Note: Try to find at least four pros and four cons)

Should I continue for a Masters Degree (MBA) after graduating?			
Pros	**Score/10**	**Cons**	**Score/10**
Total Pros		Total Cons	
Average Pros		**Average Cons**	

8. <u>Negotiation.</u> During a negotiation meeting, a supplier offers a price and payment terms that are on offer 'today only' and the buyer can 'take or leave' this deal. The buyer explains that more discussion is required because the price is above the buyer's budget and the payment terms are shorter than the buying organisation's standard terms. The supplier listens selectively and then repeats his ultimatum. The buyer does not want an impasse to end the meeting. Using the scenario outlined above, suggest THREE different types of question that the buyer can use and explain why these questions might be effective.

9. <u>Decision Making.</u> Complete a decision-making table similar to the one below where the two-option problem is:

Should I invest in the UK stock market at the moment or not?

(Note: Try to find at least four pros and four cons)

Should I invest in the UK stock market at the moment or not?			
Pros	**Score/10**	**Cons**	**Score/10**
Total Pros		**Total Cons**	
Average Pros		**Average Cons**	

10. <u>Negotiation.</u> Explain some of the factors a buying business organisation might consider when establishing its bargaining position in relation to a supplier.

11.   Wordsearch

Problem Solving

```
G F K V K I G X P A Z T T V S F R X E U P G Y
A T T I T U D E S G H O Y C T R I U S E B Y N
V W O L T I N O V R S E P H R P S M B T X Z F
S I T N X W W Z N E N R R C A E K S Y H R P V
W N W R S N N T E E O S O J T P A Z T V Y Y U
I W D P A J C Z G M I Z B K E Z Y T G J I Y Y
E I M L S N R E O E S N L N G O R A I O D W F
G N G A O K S M T N I R E S I Z T X L V L V T
D Y Y N L G Z P I T C K M I E F A C U P I V K
E H J N U F L W A S E E S Z S P T Z W P Q T Y
L P Q I T K B M T R D P I H S R E D A E L D Y
W K T N I Q G P I R E W T F O X Q F P Q T U H
O K S G O I I T O C T N A F T V S Z B C S Z K
N L F S N P J G N U J M T W W S T B U B H P R
K D C L S I Z L S Z Q S N O I T A V O N N I J
D R P D W O R Y B A R R I E R S D P B O Y L G
```

Find the following words in the puzzle.
Words are hidden ↑ ↓ → ← and ↘ .

AGREEMENTS   INNOVATION   RISK
ATTITUDES   KNOWLEDGE   SOLUTIONS
BARRIERS   LEADERSHIP   STRATEGIES
CREATIVITY   NEGOTIATIONS   TRANSPARENT
DECISIONS   PLANNING   WINWIN
FACUP   PROBLEMS

7. PRIMARY DATA: CUSTOMERS

Introduction to Primary Data

Primary data is collected first hand for specific focused purposes whereas secondary data has been collected second hand, usually for general purposes.

The first step in collecting primary data is to pre-define as clearly as possible the purposes of the information emanating from the data and how it will be used. The second step is to decide which data is needed to achieve these purposes. If we already have good secondary data, we could perhaps compare and contrast it with our new primary data. Then the third and fourth steps are to determine primary sources and actually set about collecting data. At first sight, it seems easy to collect data. Unfortunately, a significant proportion of the primary data that we realistically find is either not directly relevant or unlikely to help in answering salient questions. If we want data that is relevant for our needs and is reliable, we have to plan the collection carefully.

In summary, four important issues in primary data collection are:

- Deciding the amount of data needed
- Determining the types of data needed
- Determining its sources
- Organising the best means of collection.

Amount of Primary Data

Good managers would like to have enough data to enable wise decision making, but not so much data that they are swamped by irrelevant detail. The balance can be difficult. There is often a large amount of data that could be collected and we need to figure out which might be useful. However, all data collection and analysis costs money, so we must resist the temptation to go overboard and simply collect everything.

There is always pressure on a manager's time, so they prefer faster methods, arguing that when data collection takes too long, the results sometimes become obsolete and irrelevant even before they are fully prepared. Unfortunately, when managers do not allow enough time for proper data collection, they encourage shortcuts and assume that any data, even if slightly inaccurate, is better than no data at all. Sometimes this is true. If a company does not have time for a full market survey, it can still get useful information from a limited study.

Often, though, incorrect data can be worse than no data at all. A limited or flawed market survey might give us misleading results that encourage a company to start a hopeless venture. Inaccurate data can lead to bad decisions, so the clear message is that managers need both <u>accurate</u> data and careful data <u>planning</u>.

Types of Primary Data

Primary data has the advantages of fitting our needs quite precisely, being more up to date and hopefully being more reliable. Secondary data, on the other hand, might be much cheaper, faster and easier to collect and certainly, if there is reliable secondary data available which fits the bill, we should use it. There is no point in spending time and effort in duplicating data that has already been prepared. Unfortunately, it is also the case that secondary data is often not reliable enough for a particular purpose, is in the wrong form or is simply out of date. Therefore, we have to balance the benefits of collecting primary data with the cost and effort of collecting it.

For major investment decisions, it is essential to collect primary data. If Chelsea football club is deciding on the feasibility of a new football stadium, secondary data on other new football stadia would really only provide historical or budgetary information and so collecting primary data on engineering costs, local reactions, transportation effects, etc. would be essential. In practice, the best option is often a combination of primary and secondary data, perhaps with secondary data giving the overall picture and primary data adding the finer detail. For example, a UK logistics business might get a broad view of industrial prospects from secondary data collected by the government and the European Union, further details could then come from secondary data collected by the *Chartered Institute for Transport and Logistics*. Then the company could collect specific primary data from its customers.

We have already discussed different types of data in figure 4.1 and we always try to identify the type of data needed for our purposes. Problems can occur if we don't do this. For example, a project student hoping to answer questions such as "Do older women spend more on fashion than older men in the UK?" should not forget to record the <u>gender</u> of respondents in her primary data.

Sources of Primary Data

When we collect primary data, we identify the relevant *population*. Here we are using 'population' in the statistical sense of all people or entities that share some common characteristic. For instance, if the Human Resources (HR) department of a small and medium enterprise (SME) company wishes to analyse employee preferences and feedback, it might be practicable to contact all fifty or so members of this population (i.e. employees).

However, some populations are not as simple as they seem to identify or to contact. The population for a survey of student opinion is clearly the student but does this mean only full-time students or does it include part-time, day-release, short-course and distance-learning students? What about students who are doing a period of work experience school students and those studying but not enrolled in courses? Once we have established the more detailed situation, we might actually have several thousand members of the population making it impracticable to include everyone in our data. When we compile a complete idea of members of a population, we have a 'sampling frame'. Some common sources of sampling frames include electoral registers and lists of credit account holders. Collecting data from all entries in the sampling frame or the whole population is called a 'census'. Collecting data from only a representative sample of entries in the sampling frame is called 'sampling'. A common challenge with primary data is choosing an appropriate sample.

A 'random' sample has the essential feature that every member of the population has exactly the same chance of being chosen to supply data. If we randomly choose one member of a customer database for a company, it means that each member of the database population has exactly the same chance of being chosen. However, this does not mean that a random sample is haphazard. It does mean that our multiple random samples have avoided deliberate bias.

Suppose that the auditors for a particular company receive 10,000 invoices covering the last financial year. The auditors do not have time to examine each and every invoice, so they take a random sample of a particular size, say 100 by forming the sampling frame, labelling the invoices from 0000 to 9999 then they can generate a set of one hundred four-digit random numbers, e.g. 2315, 4569, ... and select invoices labelled 2315, 4569, etc. Various business software packages contain so-called RAND-related functions as standard to help with the process.

Practice Exercises

Create a simple spreadsheet to illustrate the use of:

(i) The RAND functions contained in the 'Mathematical and trigonometry functions' section of Appendix B,
(ii) The RANDBETWEEN function.

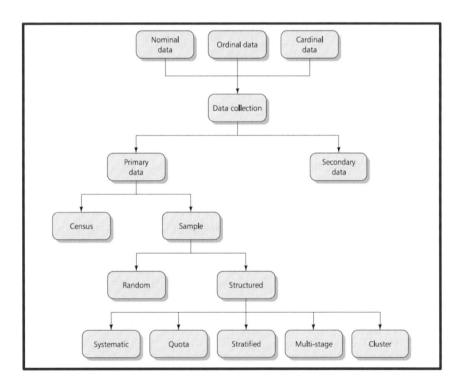

Figure 7.1 An organisational chart showing types and sources of primary data.

If a sample does fairly reflect the population, we might consider it reasonable to make inferences about the population from it. If a sample does not fairly reflect the population it is said to be *biased*. Avoiding bias is an important part of sampling because even a well-organised random sample can be affected by atypical results.

For example, a project student hoping to answer questions such as "Does age affect the healthy-eating choices of customers in McDonalds?" but then randomly samples distributes questionnaires at eight o'clock in the morning (when the restaurant was full of teenagers breakfasting before school) should beware. The completed questionnaires were never going to answer his main question because of bias towards the younger age group.

Structured sampling provides an alternative to random sampling in the form of systematic, quota, stratified, multi-stage and cluster sampling.

Systematic samples are one way of organizing our sampling to collect data at regular intervals. For example, we might interview every fifth person in an airport lounge or test every tenth unit from a production line. Clearly this is not a random sample because every member of the population does not have the same chance of being chosen. Unfortunately, a systematic sample can also introduce bias, e.g. if every tenth unit in the production line is made from the same machine, the sample is clearly biased towards that machine.

Stratified samples are appropriate when there are distinct groups (strata) in the population; it is a good idea to make sure that members from each stratum are fairly represented in a sample. For a stratified sample we divide the population into strata and then take a random sample from each, with the number chosen from each stratum ensuring that the overall sample contains a balanced mix. For example, 40% of people working in a company might be women. To get a stratified sample of views, we could divide the population of employees into two strata (women and men) and randomly select 40% of our sample from women and 60% from men.

Quota samples extend the idea of stratified sampling by adding a more rigid structure. They look at the characteristics of the population and then specify the characteristics needed in the sample to match this more precisely. Suppose we want to see how people will vote in an election. For a quota sample, we could choose a sample that contains exactly the same proportions of people with different characteristics as the population of people eligible to vote. If the population consists of 4% of men who are over 60, retired from manual work and living alone, then the sample is chosen to also have this proportion. Quota sampling often uses interviewers who are given a number of the actual people, so there is still a significant random element. However, the sample is clearly not random because interviewers who have filled one quota do not interview any more people in it and those people have no chance of being chosen.

Multi-stage samples: Suppose that we want a sample of people who subscribe to a particular magazine. If we take a random sample, we will probably find that they are spread over a wide geographical area, and it is inconvenient and expensive to travel to interview them. A cheaper option is to use multi-stage sampling which makes sure that a sample is confined to a smaller geographical area. The usual approach is to divide the country into a number of geographical regions, such as television or local radio regions. Then select some of these regions at random and divide them into smaller subdivisions, perhaps parliamentary constituencies or local government areas. Then select some of these subdivisions at random and again divide them into smaller areas, perhaps towns or parliamentary wards. We continue in this way until we have small enough areas and then identify a sample of individuals from within these areas.

Example

How could we set about choosing a multi-stage sample of approximately one thousand people in Greater London?

Solution

One approach is to select the thirty-two boroughs in Greater London then randomly select eight streets in each borough, then randomly select four individuals living in each street. This would give us $32 \times 8 \times 4 = 1024$ individuals. Of course, there are other suitable ways.

Cluster sampling chooses the members in a sample not individually, but in the form of clusters. This is useful when a population naturally falls into distinct groups and then we randomly select a number of groups and collect information from some or all of the members. For example, we might divide the population of a town into households, then select households at random and collect information from everyone within the chosen households. One disadvantage of using a cluster sample, for instance, is if the cluster group chosen has a biased opinion, then the entire population is inferred to have the same opinion. This may not be the actual case. However, it is still often used in marketing research as a reasonable cost-effective approach.

Organising Data Collection

After identifying an appropriate sample, the next stage is to collect the data. There are two main ways of doing this. Firstly, we can use direct observations to see what is happening. Secondly, we can ask people questions.

Observations

Direct observation of situations can be a very effective means of data collection. Then an observer watches some activity and records what happens, typically counting a number of events, taking some measurements or seeing how something works. Observing queues at supermarket checkouts or recording consumer behaviour in department stores can be highly informative. But the 'observers' do not have to be human because so much data these days is collected automatically; simple tasks like digitally recording online shopping transactions or CCTV monitoring of traffic conditions are carried out millions of times daily.

Generally speaking, observing is more reliable than asking people for data, although we must be careful because human observers get tired and distracted, while automatic observers sometimes break down and technological devices develop programming faults.

Asking Questions

When we cannot collect data by observation, we usually have to ask people to supply it. Unstructured open-ended questionnaires are typically not pre-planned and allow respondents to express views with a very wide range of possible replies. Unstructured close-ended questionnaires are typically not pre-planned but allow respondents to express views but with a relatively limited range of possible replies.

Structured open-ended questionnaires usually contain a list of pre-planned questions to which respondents can reply in their own judgment e.g. 'Which of these banks would you rate best for customer service?' Structured closed-ended questionnaires usually require responses limited to the stated alternatives and the respondents cannot express their own judgment. So questions on gender, age (years), spending (£) and frequency will often be answered with a specific value or range of values.

STRUCTURED, CLOSE-ENDED	STRUCTURED, OPEN-ENDED
e.g. Are you male or female? What is your age? How much did you spend in Debenhams today?	e.g. Which institutions caused the crash of 2008? Which of these banks would rate best for service?
UNSTRUCTURED, CLOSE-ENDED	UNSTRUCTURED, OPEN-ENDED
e.g. What was the colour of the car in this accident? When did you hear about the proposed merger?	e.g. Who caused this car accident? Why do you think this merger is a good idea?

Figure 7.2   General types of questionnaires.

In qualitative analysis, the questions we ask might be answered subjectively, e.g. "How strongly do you hold your view on this subject?" By contrast, in quantitative analysis, the questions we ask tend to be more objective and structured, e.g. "How many times do you access internet banking each week?"

Obviously both approaches can lead to very good data. As with all data collection, there may be inherent errors of estimation and recall but hopefully the respondent will try to answer as honestly and precisely as possible. There are ways to deal statistically with deliberate errors or bias. There are several means of eliciting data by asking a series of questions in a variety of ways. These include

- Interviewing experts
- Online surveying
- Panel surveying
- Personal interviewing
- Postal surveying
- Questionnaire distribution
- Social media surveying
- Telephone interviewing
- Text surveying

Interviewing experts

Eliciting knowledge from an expert can lead to very interesting data but this is more likely to be qualitative than quantitative. It can certainly be difficult for the expert to put into words precisely how they do things so well. For instance, a stock market investor might use intuition to make the right investment decision without realising themselves precisely all of the factors involved in the decision making. Nevertheless, carefully carrying out interviews with successful entrepreneurs or leading business figures can be expected to lead to data collection of high value.

Online surveys

Using a computer or mobile phone to connect to company websites and access web-based content provides a good platform to carry out surveys, polls and questionnaires. However, visitors are in these places to find information and answering more than two or three questions may well slow them down. So, conciseness is critical in most cases.

Panel surveys

These assemble a representative panel of respondents who are monitored to see how their opinions change over time. For example, we could monitor the business views of a panel on, say, 'The future of the UK Economy' asking questions about interest rates and areas of economic growth. Panel surveys are expensive and difficult to administer, so they use relatively small samples.

Personal interviews

These normally involve an interviewer directly asking questions to respondents, and they can be a reliable way of getting detailed data. They have a high response rate (only about ten percent of people refuse to answer on principle) but this depends on circumstances and few people will agree to a long, complicated or inconvenient interview. In principle, collecting data by personal interviews is relatively easy because it only needs someone to ask questions and record the answers. The reality is more complicated and depends on skilled interviewers. For instance, we must be careful not to direct respondents to a particular answer by our expression, tone of voice or comments. We should not explain the questions or offer any help because this would introduce bias.

Postal surveys

These normally involve sending questionnaires through the post, and asking people to complete them and return the answers. They are cheap, easy to organise and suitable for very large samples. But there are drawbacks such as the difficulty of getting a questionnaire to the right people. A major problem with postal surveys is the low response rate, which is usually lower than 20% and sometimes close to zero. This might be improved by making the questionnaire short and easy to complete, sending it to a named person, enclosing a covering letter to explain the purpose of the survey, including a pre-paid return envelope, promising anonymity of replies, using a follow-up letter or telephone call if replies are slow and promising a summary of results. Many surveys try to increase the response rate by offering some reward (typically a small gift, discount on a future purchase or entry to a prize draw) but we will see shortly that this often introduces bias because respondents now feel more kindly towards the questionnaire.

Questionnaire distribution

Designing and distributing hard copies of a questionnaire is arguably one of the most efficient means of primary data collection. Of course, a badly-designed questionnaire or poor distribution will create a significant negative effect. Nevertheless, the proportion of respondents can be very high, particular in areas of relaxation or social groups, such as coffee bars, libraries and fast-food restaurants. Visitors are expecting to stay perhaps only a few minutes and they just might be inclined to complete a well-designed concise questionnaire during that time.

Social media surveys

Of course, the way that users behave in social networking such as <u>Facebook</u> can be variable. Nevertheless, an anticipated high number of responses can generally provide good data. Professional networks such as <u>Linkedin</u> are likely to experience less irresponsible behaviour and data relating to professional issues.

Telephone interviews

These can be used for the 95% of people who own a telephone, and it is relatively cheap and easy, involves no travel and sometimes gets a good response rate. On the other hand, it has the disadvantage of bias because it uses only people who will accept anonymous calls. Other weaknesses are that observers cannot see the respondents and phone calls annoy people who object to the intrusion. The usual procedure for telephone interviews has a computer selecting a phone number at random from a directory listing. Then an interviewer asks the questions presented on a computer screen and types in the answers. This allows the computer to analyse answers interactively, choose an appropriate set of questions and prevents errors during the transfer of data.

Text surveys

These normally involve sending short questions via text and provided the answer is straightforward, e.g. "How would you rate the customer service at our store today?" Many of us will respond to a quick question provided that the answer likely to be straightforward, e.g. "On a scale 1 to 5, 1 being the best ..." particular if the receiver can send free texts. However, further questioning can be annoying. This type of data collection is best for a single easy-to-understand easy-to-answer question.

Others methods of data collection include email surveys and focus groups, the latter being particularly useful for qualitative analysis.

Bias in Primary Data

The following list of bias in primary data collection is divided into interviewer bias and respondent bias. In research methodology, we should consider ways of conducting the research so as to reduce bias.

Interviewer-induced bias

- Desire to help the respondent: The interviewer may become too sympathetic to the problems and conditions of the respondent, and this can affect the conduct of, and results obtained from, the interview. Objectivity must be retained at all times.

- Failure to follow instructions in administering the questions: It is often tempting for the interviewer to change the wording of a question or introduce inflection in questions. This can affect the respondent's understanding and can bias the replies.

- Reactions to responses: When respondents give answers, the interviewer must be careful not to 'react.' A note of 'surprise' or 'disbelief may easily bias the respondent's subsequent answers. Interviewers must respond with a uniform polite interest only.

Respondent-induced bias

- Courtesy bias: In interview situations, there might be a tendency for respondents to give answers that they think the interviewer wants to hear rather than what they really feel. The respondents may not wish to be impolite or to offend the interviewer, and may therefore endeavour to give 'polite' answers.

- Exaggeration and dishonesty: There can be a tendency on the part of some respondents to exaggerate claims about their conditions and problems if they think it will further their cause and lead to improvement in their well being. The interviewer must be alert to, and note any, inconsistencies arising. Age can sometimes be minimised and income maximised.

- Faulty memory: Some respondents may answer a question incorrectly simply because they have a poor memory. The key to avoiding this problem is to steer clear of questions requiring feats of memory. For example, questions such as, "Can you tell me how many cars you sold three years ago?" should be avoided.

- Failure to answer questions correctly: If rapport is not developed sufficiently, the respondent may be unwilling to respond or fail to give sufficient attention or consideration to the questions asked and, if the respondent does not understand a question properly, she/he may give inappropriate answers. For instance, an overly-long questionnaire can result in the questions towards the end being rushed.

- Influence of groups at interview: During interviews the presence of other individuals is almost inevitable. Such a situation can have important implications for the type of data obtained. The respondent may be tempted to answer in a way that gives him or her credibility in the eyes of the others, rather than giving a truthful reply.

- Misunderstanding purpose of interview: Some respondents may perceive the purpose of the survey to be a long-winded form of 'selling', particularly if the interviewer is asking them what they think about a new product. To avoid such problems, it is important to carefully explain the objectives of the survey, the identity of the interviewer and the sponsor, and what is required of the respondent, prior to the interview.

Customer Satisfaction Surveys – University Students

Universities across the world now realise that students are customers. With the advent of student fees and increasing competition, the satisfaction of university and college students needs to be measured, analysed and shared.

For instance, the University of Roehampton works in partnership with its students to enhance learning and teaching. The centre often works directly within departments or across the university in dialogue with students. Student views are then taken back to programme teams to help improve the student experience.

Programme representatives are also play a key role in the student voice. Every programme has a Programme Representative from each year who liaises with academic staff and students on academic matters, and the student experiences of the programme. Every year the University holds a conference which brings all Programme Reps together to share ideas and clarify key messages for the University. Typical issues for students have been speedy feedback on assessed work and links with employers. Significant changes have been made in response.

Student Surveys

National surveys take place every year in UK higher education. For undergraduates, the National Student Survey (NSS) is published for prospective applicants to read and make decisions on their own choices. These surveys measure satisfaction in a number of areas including teaching, facilities, support, research and careers.

Module Evaluations

Before the end of every module, most university students are invited to give anonymous feedback on teaching, student support, resources and assessment. In this way, their university can find out how students are experiencing the teaching and assessment and thus make changes where they are required.

See Case Study: *Module Evaluations at the University of Roehampton*

Questionnaire Design

When respondents complete a questionnaire, their answers are usually done so in isolation in the sense that they probably do not know the overall characteristics of the population from which they are drawn. Their role is simply to answer relatively straightforward questions and it is the data analyser's job to make sense of (or inferences about) the resulting data.

Of course, all businesses depend on a variety of *stakeholders* and it is important to survey them all. Some stakeholders are internal to the business, such as a company's employees. Other stakeholders are external to the business, such as suppliers, customers, trade unions, civil society groups, shareholders and the communities in which the business operates.

This questionnaire is designed to support research as part of an undergraduate dissertation at the University of Roehampton on "relationships between air travel, age and gender" Your answers will be completely anonymous and the data provided will not be used for any purposes other than research.

Your views are greatly appreciated.

Thank you!

START

1. Are you?

   ☑   ☐

   Female   Male

2. What is your age group?

   ☐   ☑   ☐   ☐   ☐   ☐   ☐
   <16   16–25   26–35   36–45   46–55   56–65   >65

3. Using a scale 1-5, '1' being highest and '5' lowest, how would you rate in-flight service on your flight today?

   ☐   ☑   ☐   ☐   ☐
   1   2   3   4   5

4. Approximately, how many times per year you travel on an airline?

   ☐   ☑   ☐   ☐   ☐   ☐   ☐
   1-3   4–6   7–9   10–12   13–15   16–18   >18

FINISH

Figure 7.3   Part of sample 'airline' questionnaires (already completed).

In the example of figure 7.3, the questions have been phrased clearly and in this case, the respondent has answered all four questions. In fact, most of the twenty respondents answered all four sections, probably because the design was attractive, straightforward and concise. We have already seen that data can be classified as nominal, ordinal and cardinal. In the case of figure 6.3, question 1 will give us nominal (binary) data; question 3 ordinal and questions 2 and 4 cardinal (discrete).This is an example of a mixed questionnaire, in which one question is qualitative and three questions are quantitative. We need to note a few areas of good practice when designing questionnaires. In figure 7.3, Question 2 uses mainly equal-interval grouped data; any questionnaires completed by respondents under 16 will be disregarded, unless we specifically obtain individual parental consent (not likely). Question 3 makes it very clear that '1' is the highest rating, avoiding any misunderstanding about the rating scale. Question 4 does not offer a possible answer of zero, since the respondents have already been on the flight so must have travelled at least once. Other tips are shown in figure 7.4.

Tips for Questionnaire Design

- Indicate clearly the *Start*
- Use a logical sequence for questions
- Make a questionnaire as short as reasonably possible
- Check for ambiguity by testing with others before distribution
- Use equal intervals for cardinal data
- Avoid asking two or more questions in one question
- Make sure the possible answers are complete
- Indicate clearly the *End*

Figure 7.4   Tips for questionnaire design.

Initially, it might seem surprising that our preferred way of presenting raw data table should take the form of numbers only (see figure 6.5). Nevertheless, it is the way that quantitative analysts work. As we shall see later, a main reason for this lies in the fact that we can deal statistically with all data types in the form of numbers, even those that are categories or labels.

ID	GENDER	AGE_GP	INFLT_RT	TRVL_FREQ
01	2	2	2	2
02	1	4	1	5
03	2	3	2	5
04	1	5	2	11
05	2	6	2	11
06	1	6	4	11
07	1	6	4	14
08	1	3	1	5
09	2	4	2	5
10	2	3	3	6
11	2	5	1	9
12	1	6	4	14
13	1	3	1	14
14	1	4	1	10
15	2	3	4	5
16	1	5	2	10
17	2	6	5	7
18	1	3	2	11
19	1	2	1	14
20	2	3	1	5
DATA KEY				
ID	01 ... 99: ANONYMISING IDENTIFIER			
GENDER	2=FEMALE;1=MALE; (0=MISSING DATA)			
AGE_GP	1...7 FOR AGE GROUPS (1=youngest, etc);(0=MISSING DATA)			
INFLT_RT	In-flight service rating: 1 ... 5 (1= HIGHEST;5= LOWEST); (0=MISSING DATA)			
TRVL_FREQ	Frequency of travel each year (midpoint values 2,5,8,11 ...).; (0=MISSING DATA)			

Figure 7.5   Results from twenty distributed "airline" questionnaires.

It is important to include a data key to show what the number means for each variable GENDER, AGE_GP, INFLT_RT and TRVL_FREQ, thereby avoiding confusion.

The ID is also vital in the sense that we have promised anonymity and using numbers rather than names or any other personalised information supports our promise. Large business organisations failing to properly anonymise their data can be subject to heavy penalties. In figure 7.5, there are no missing data values but if there were, we would be able to use different ways of identifying and analysing such data, as described later.

It should be noted that customers are just one of the stakeholders with which a business might be concerned. Others include suppliers, governments, shareholders, unions and employees. Issues relating to the latter are covered in the next chapter.

Customer Satisfaction Surveys – Business Customers

Figure 7.6 shows a typical business customer questionnaire. Of course, questions can vary in terms of phrasing and focus but the questions here relate to common issues that generally interest all businesses.

1. When was the last time you purchased a product or service from us? (please tick one)

☐ Within the last month
☐ Between 1 month and 3 months
☐ Between 3 and 6 months
☐ Between 6 months and 1 year
☐ More than 1 year
☐ Never

2. How long have you used our products/services? (please tick one)

☐ Fewer than 6 months
☐ Between 6 months and 1 year
☐ Between 1 and 3 years
☐ Between 3 and 5 years
☐ More than 5 years
☐ Never

3. Please rate us on the following: (please tick one: Excellent = 4, Good = 3, Fair = 2, Poor = 1)

	4	3	2	1
Customer service/support				
Quality of products/service				
Sales staff				
Price/value				

4. How would you rate your overall satisfaction with us? (please tick one)

☐ Very satisfied
☐ Satisfied
☐ Neutral
☐ Dissatisfied
☐ Very dissatisfied

5. How likely are you to continue doing business with us? (please tick one)

☐ Very likely
☐ Likely
☐ Neutral
☐ Unlikely
☐ Very unlikely

6. How likely are you to recommend our products/services to others? (please tick one)

☐ Very likely
☐ Likely
☐ Neutral
☐ Unlikely
☐ Very unlikely

7. Please suggest how we can improve our products/services to better serve you.

Figure 7.6   A typical questionnaire used to ascertain business custome opinion.

However, the questions might have been ordered, in overall terms they need to cover money, time and satisfaction ratings. The overall features should be simplicity and clarity with ease of completion in an appropriate time. If customers do not have enough time to complete it, they probably will not do so, particularly if a question becomes too hard to fathom.

In the case of figure 7.6, the questionnaire is to be completed by hand using tick boxes but it is very simple to convert it to an online version where the input involves clicking a button in a form.

Various online resources (e.g. www.surveymonkey.co.uk) provide easy ways to create surveys, including customer satisfaction surveys.

The important issue to remember with all of the different ways to collect customer satisfaction is that the data created should be useful, reliable and correct. We have already discussed ways to avoid bias and businesses which collect and analyse customer data effectively can expect to track satisfaction over time, thereby leading to successful strategies and processes.

Case Studies – Primary Data: Customers

Case Study: *University of Roehampton & Surrey – Module Evaluation Surveys*

Each semester, students in the Business School at the University of Roehampton are invited to complete an anonymous in-class paper-based questionnaire. The University uses the results to decide on actions relating to resources management, staff performance, curriculum enhancements and improvements to the virtual learning environment (Moodle).

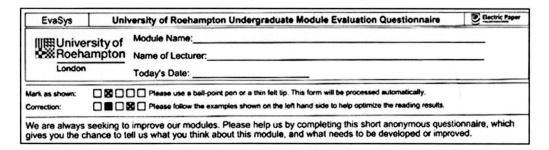

A similar system is used at the University of Surrey where the evaluations are conducted online (http://www.surrey.ac.uk/dhe/Online_MEQ/). The University replaced paper-based module evaluation with an online Module Evaluation Questionnaire (MEQ) survey system in the 2013/4 academic year in order to provide a more comprehensive and reliable measurement of students' learning experience. In terms of psychometric validity of the new 25-item questionnaire design (consisting of five key module scales: teacher support, learning experience & pedagogy, module design, student interaction, assessment & feedback; and a scale for each lecturer involved), a robust reliability was found across Faculties and disciplines. The extended online MEQ provides a better understanding of students' learning experience, quality of assessment & feedback and student-teacher interaction. All questions generally follow a five-point *Likert Scale*: Strongly Agree (SA), Agree (A), Undecided (U), Disagree (D), Strongly Disagree (SD) with numerical assignment scores 5, 4, 3, 2, 1, respectively.

For more information, refer to the full case study.

Questions for Discussion:

1. Explain three advantages and three disadvantages of paper-based questionnaires, as compared with online questionnaires.
2. Suppose that in one module, sixty completed questionnaires showed ten SA, ten A, ten U, ten D and the rest SD. What was the <u>average</u> score in this case?
3. What other forms of survey do universities use to gauge student satisfaction?
4. Students are just <u>one</u> of the stakeholders in a university. Suggest three others.

Case Study: *Primark: Engaging with Stakeholders*

The textile manufacture and clothing distribution industry has seen dramatic changes in recent years. Consumers' expectations are higher today than ever before, they expect fashionable clothing at affordable prices. As a result many clothing retailers, including Primark, source clothes from countries like China, Bangladesh, India and Vietnam where materials and labour costs are lower. Primark works with a variety of manufacturers from around the world to provide consumers with what they want. Primark has stores across the UK, Ireland, Spain, Portugal, Germany, Holland and Belgium and employs over 70,000 people across the globe. Primark is a subsidiary company of Associated British Foods (ABF). As part of ABF, the company shares important values. These values provide an ethical dimension to Primark's activities. Being ethical means doing the right thing. For example, ethical companies provide fair working conditions for their employees, and build fair relationships with suppliers. For Primark, acting ethically means:

- taking care of its people
- being a good neighbour
- respecting human rights
- engaging with its stakeholders.

For more information, refer to the full case study.

Questions for Discussion:

1. Make a list of ten stakeholders that have an interest in the products that Primark source from India. In each case, briefly explain their stake in the process. Produce a diagram showing the position where you would place each of the stakeholders in relation to the two dimensions of power and interest.
2. This case study features several initiatives that Primark is supporting to help workers and communities in developing countries. Which of these do you think should be most effective? Can you suggest some other helpful initiatives?
3. Primark has developed some collaborative educational programmes. Do you think that it is a good idea to engage with young people in this way? In what other ways could Primark engage with young people?
4. How important do you think it is for Primark to be a member of the ETI? Discuss the ways you think Primark's stakeholders will be benefit from Primark's work with the ETI.

Exercises – Primary Data: Customers

1. {multiple choice – choose the most appropriate answer (a), (b), (c) or (d)}

A researcher analysing a small used car business knows that the number of employees in the three fundamental departments (salesroom, marketing and accounts) are split more or less evenly (one third of employees in each). Unfortunately, the first sample chosen to gauge overall employee preferences, while obtained randomly, surprisingly contained no-one from accounts. On balance, what is her best sampling option now?

(a) Cluster   (b) Stratified   (c) Give up   (d) Random (again)

2. {multiple choice – choose the most appropriate answer (a), (b), (c) or (d)}

A researcher decides to use multi-stage sampling technique for his research methodology. This involves randomly selecting seven streets from each and every borough of Greater Manchester then randomly choosing three residents in each street. Approximately, how many people will he have in the whole sample?

(a) 20   (b) 200   (c) 2000   (d) 20000

3. {multiple choice – choose the most appropriate answer (a), (b), (c) or (d)}

Of 100 randomly selected people in the area of Roehampton in London, twenty had the last name 'Smith' and twenty had the first name 'John'. Which of the following sentences is descriptive but not inferential?

(a) 20% of the people of Greater London have 'Smith' as the last name
(b) 20% of these people of Roehampton have 'Smith' as the last name
(c) 20% of the people of London have 'John' as the first name
(d) 20% of the people in the UK have 'John' as the first name.

4. {multiple choice – choose the most appropriate answer (a), (b), (c) or (d)}

In her answer to a question in a questionnaire, a respondent lied about her age, claiming to be ten years younger than she actually was. Which compound term best describes the bias created by the claim?

(a) Accidental, interviewer-induced
(b) Interviewer-induced, deliberate
(c) Deliberate, respondent-induced
(d) Respondent-induced, accidental.

5. {multiple choice – choose the most appropriate answer (a), (b), (c) or (d)}

Generally, which of the following would you expect to lead to a higher response rate?

(a) Postal surveying, personalised letter
(b) Text surveying, targeted audience
(c) Email surveying, targeted audience
(d) Questionnaire distribution and collection.

6. <u>Over-complication.</u> One form of bias in general questionnaires involves the use of more complicated words than necessary. This has the effect of alienating those respondents who simply do not know what the words mean. Accordingly, they might miss the question out even though they might have had useful information to offer.

Complete the table below of uncommon and less common words (in alphabetical order), noting that we should use the most common word in general questionnaires.

Uncommon	Common
Consider	Think
Effectuate	
Elucidate	
Employ	
Initiate	
Major	Important/Main
Perform	
Quantify	Measure
Require	
Reside	
State	Say
Sufficient	
Terminate	
Ultimate	Last
Utilize	
Assist	

7. <u>Airline Data files.</u>   Input the data from Figure 6.5 into three separate Excel spreadsheet files, as follows:

   (i)   Name your data file for all of the data 'airline.xls'
   (ii) Name your data file for only male-related data 'airline_male.xls'
   (iii) Name your data file for only female-related data 'airline_female.xls'.

(Note: Save your files for use later).

Without performing any statistical calculations, would you estimate that for this sample that the airline travel frequency for men was higher than for women?

8. <u>Bad design</u>. The questionnaire below is based on a real questionnaire that the researcher claimed to have checked and pre-tested. He felt ready and willing to distribute it randomly outside the Santander Bank, Aldgate East, London. In fact, he went ahead with his plan hoping to analyse 'business banking' and the research project ended in tears.

Identify problems with:

(i) His distribution methodology (you should find at least two problems here)
(ii) The questions in his questionnaire (you should find at least ten problems here)

This questionnaire is designed to support research on "business banking". Your answers will be completely anonymous and the data provided will be used for any purpose.

Cheers!

NAME: [_____]   AGE: [____]

1. Are you?

[ ]   [ ]   [ ]
Female   Male   Other

2. What is your UK bank?

[ ]   [ ]   [ ]   [ ]   [ ]
HSBC   Santander Lloyds   RBS   Halifax

3. Using a scale 1-3, how would you rate customer service at your bank?

[ ]   [ ]   [ ]
3   2   1

4. Aproximately, how much do you pay over the counter (£) each year?

[ ]   [ ]   [ ]   [ ]   [ ]
0-50   51-500   501-1000   1001-10000 >10001

---

9. <u>Wordsearch</u>

Primary Data: Customers

Find the following words in the puzzle.
Words are hidden ↑ ↓ → ← and ↘ .

BIAS	MULTISTAGE	STRATIFIED
CLUSTER	OBSERVATIONS	STRUCTURED
COLLECTION	QUESTIONNAIRES	STUDENTS
EXAGGERATION	PANEL PERSONAL	SURVEYING
INFLUENCE	QUOTA	SYSTEMATIC
INTERVIEWING	SAMPLING	

8. PRIMARY DATA: EMPLOYEES

We have already discussed the enormous volumes of secondary data available to businesses covering customers, employees and other stakeholders. In the case of employee data, even small to medium businesses hold very large volumes of primary data. Part of the reason for this is that each country's regulations require data to be stored, processed and secured in specific ways. In Human Resource Management (HRM), extensive resources are needed to handle all of the employee data and information and, in turn, research departments use data modelling to make estimates and projects.

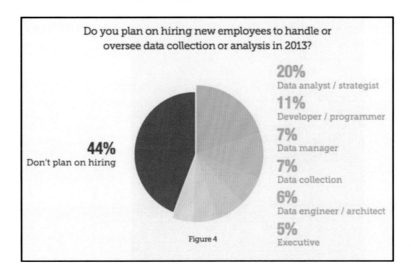

Figure 8.1   A sample graphic illustrating typical employee hiring to handle data in a business.

It is often the case that businesses underestimate the resources needed to handle their data. Figure 8.1 shows a typical distribution of hiring specifically relating to data collection and data analysis.   While it is to be expected that technological enhancements and lowering cost of computer processing and storage will all serve to reduce costs, regulations such as The Data Protection Act and The International Standards Organisation place responsibilities on any organisation to process personal information that it holds in a 'fair and proper way'. Indeed, failure to do so can ultimately lead to civil or criminal offences being committed. Fines by regulatory authorities can be very high.

In this chapter, we consider employee primary data in five sections:

- Recruitment & Selection
- Employment Records
- Monitoring at Work
- Employee Health
- Data Analytics

Recruitment & Selection

The recruitment and selection process necessarily involves an employer in collecting and using information about workers. Much of this information is personal in nature and can affect a worker's privacy. The various regulations do not prevent an employer from carrying out an effective recruitment exercise but help to strike a balance between the employer's needs and the applicant's right to respect for his or her private life.

Recruitment and selection covers all aspects of the recruitment and selection process from the advertising of vacancies through to the deletion of information on unsuccessful applicants.

Verification and vetting

Figure 8.2   The UK Disclosure and Barring Service (DBS) is a *verification* service.

The terms verification and vetting are both used in recruitment to cover the process of checking that details supplied by applicants (e.g. qualifications) are accurate and complete. Verification, therefore, is limited to checking of information that is sought in the application or supplied later in the recruitment process. As used here, the term also includes the taking up of references provided by the applicant. Where a UK employer is justified in asking an applicant about any criminal convictions, Disclosure and Barring Service (DBS), previously called the Criminal Records Bureau (CRB), provides a verification service covering certain, high risk areas of employment. Vetting covers the employer actively making its own enquiries from third parties about an applicant's background and circumstances. It goes beyond the verification of details addressed above. As such it is particularly intrusive and should be confined to areas of special risk. It is for example used for some government workers who have regular access to highly classified information. In some sectors vetting may be a necessary and accepted practice. Limited vetting may be a legal requirement for some jobs, for example, child care jobs under the Protection of Children Act. Presently, the Department of Health has developed a Protection of Vulnerable Adults list which employers intending to recruit certain types of care workers are required to consult. Such vetting usually takes place through the DBS Service.

Advertising

Advertising covers any method used to notify potential applicants of job vacancies, using such media as notices, newspapers, radio, television and the internet. Advertisements normally inform individuals responding to job advertisements of the name of the organisation to which they will be providing their information and how it will be used, unless this is self-evident.

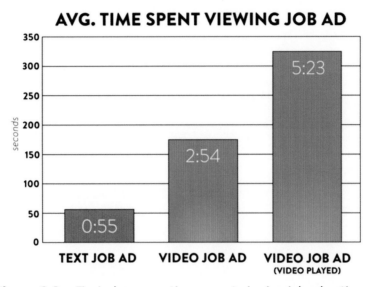

Figure 8.3   Typical average times spent viewing job advertisements.

For businesses advertising vacancies, there are key points and possible actions to note:

- Ensure that the business name in all recruitment advertisements
- Ensure the business is named on its website before collecting personal information
- Describe the purposes for which personal information may be used

Businesses with advertising experience should usually know the best forms of advertising. For example, online job advertising might yield results similar to the bar chart shown in figure 8.3. If prospective applicants spend a few minutes viewing the details in an advertisement containing a video, whereas only a minute or so viewing advertisement containing text only, this could have an impact on the prospective applicant pool.

Applications

Sometimes curriculum vitae (CVs) might be sent as informally enquiries, as well as more formal responses to job advertisements. These are nevertheless considered to be applications. On any application form, it is important to indicate clearly to whom the information is being provided and how it will be used, if this is not self-evident.

For businesses receiving applications, there are key points and possible actions to note:

- Inform the applicant as soon as possible of any uses for the information received
- Ensure the business is named on its website before collecting personal information
- Ensure the name of the business is stated on the application form
- Request information about an applicant's criminal convictions only if it can be justified in terms of the role offered
- Remove questions that are not relevant to unsuccessful applicants (e.g. bank details)
- Provide a secure method for sending applications
- Ensure that once electronic applications are received, they are saved in a directory or drive which has access limited only to those involved in the recruitment process
- Ensure that postal applications are given directly to the person processing the applications and that these are stored in a locked cabinet area

Short-listing

A business should be consistent in the way personal information is used in the process of short-listing candidates for a particular position.

For businesses short-listing, there are key points and possible actions to note:

- Ensure applicants provide signed consent, if this is required to secure the release of documents to you from another organisation or person
- Check shortlist methods with sources of good practice such as the Equality and Human Rights Commission
- Remember that if we mislead another person or organisation into giving personal information about an applicant, we may be committing a criminal offence
- Inform applicants if an automated short-listing system will be used as the sole basis of making a decision
- Ensure that tests based on the interpretation of scientific evidence, such as psychological tests, are only used and interpreted by those who have received appropriate training

Interviewing

Figure 8.4   A typical panel interview situation.

There are several types of job interview available to an employer:

1. **Traditional one-on-one job interview**. The traditional one-on-one interview is where you are interviewed by one representative of the company, most likely the manager of the position you are applying for. Because you will be working with this person directly if you get the job, he/she will want to get a feel for who you are and if your skills match those of the job requirements. You may be asked questions about the experience on your resume and what you can offer to the company or position. Many times the interviewer will ask you questions such as "Why would you be good for this job?" or "Tell me about yourself." The one-on-one interview is by far one of the most common types of job interviews.

2. **Panel interview**. In a panel interview, you will be interviewed by a panel of interviewers. The panel may consist of different representatives of the company such as human resources, management, and employees. The reason why some companies conduct panel interviews is to save time or to get the collective opinion of panel regarding the candidate. Each member of the panel may be responsible for asking you questions that represent relevancy from their position.

3. **Behavioural interview**. In a behavioural interview, the interviewer will ask you questions based on common situations of the job you are applying for. The logic behind the behavioural interview is that your future performance will be based on a past performance of a similar situation. You should expect questions that inquire about what you did when you were in a certain situation and how did you dealt with it. In a behavioural interview, the interviewer wants to see how you deal with certain problems and what you do to solve them.

4. **Group interview**. Many times companies will conduct a group interview to quickly pre-screen candidates for the job opening as well as give the candidates the chance to quickly learn about the company to see if they want to work there. Many times, a group interview will begin with a short presentation about the company. After that, they may speak to each candidate individually and ask them a few questions. One of the most important things the employer is observing during a group interview is how you interact with the other candidates. Are you emerging as a leader or are you more likely to complete tasks that are asked of you? Neither is necessarily better than the other, it just depends on what type of personality works best for the position that needs to be filled.

5. **Phone interview**. A phone interview may be for a position where the candidate is not local or for an initial pre-screening call to see if they want to invite you in for an in-person interview. You may be asked typical questions or behavioural questions. Most of the time you will schedule an appointment for a phone interview. If the interviewer calls unexpectedly, it's ok to ask them politely to schedule an appointment. In a phone interview, make sure your call waiting is turned off, you are in a quiet room and you are not eating, drinking or chewing gum.

6. **Lunch interview**. Many times lunch interviews are conducted as a second interview. The company will invite you to lunch with additional members of the team to further get to know you and see how you fit in. This is a great time to ask any questions you may have about the company or position as well, so make sure you prepare your questions in advance. Although you are being treated to a meal, the interview is not about the food. Don't order anything that is too expensive or messy to eat. Never take your leftovers home in a doggy bag either. You want to have your best table manners and be as neat as possible. You don't need to offer to pay as it is never expected for a candidate to pay at a lunch interview. Chew quietly and in small bites so you don't get caught with a mouthful of food when the recruiter asks you a question.

It is good practice to ensure that personal information and interview notes are recorded and retained following an interview. These can be useful for defending the process against any later challenge. All interviewers should be made aware that interviewees may have a right to request access to their interview notes. Hence all interviewers need to know how to store interview notes in case they are asked to provide them later.

Businesses normally make provisions for interview notes to be destroyed after a reasonable time, allowing the organisation to protect itself from any potential claims such as those for race or sex discrimination.

Retaining recruitment information

Each business should establish and adhere to retention periods for recruitment records that are based on a clear business need. Where substantial personal information has been collected about another person and is to be retained, we should ensure that there is a process in place to inform the other person of this and of how the information will be used.

If we are asking a third party, such as a previous employer, to disclose confidential personal information, the third party will need the applicant's permission before doing so. It may be easier to obtain this permission from the applicant and pass it on to the third party than for the third party to obtain permission directly.

It is important to identify clearly who in an organisation retains recruitment records (e.g. are they held centrally, at departmental level or in the line) and who has responsible for managing the records. No recruitment record should be held beyond the statutory period in which a claim arising from the recruitment process may be brought, unless there is a clear business reason for exceeding this period.

We normally consider carefully which information contained in an application form is to be transferred to the employee's employment record. It is better not to retain information that has no bearing on the on-going employment relationship.

Following the interview process for a particular vacancy, we should advise unsuccessful applicants that there is an intention to keep their names on file for future vacancies (if appropriate) and give them the opportunity to have their details removed from the files.

Employment Records

Running a business necessarily involves keeping records about workers. Such records will contain information that is personal in nature and can affect a worker's privacy. The *UK Data Protection Act* does not prevent an employer from collecting, maintaining and using records about workers but helps to strike a balance between the employer's need to keep records and the employee's right to respect for his or her private life.

Good records management practice suggests that it is necessary to distinguish between records that include 'sensitive data' and those that do not. The term 'sickness record' is therefore used to describe a record which contains details of the illness or condition responsible for a worker's absence. Similarly, an 'injury record' is a record which contains details of the injury suffered. The term 'absence record' is used to describe a record that may give the reason for absence as 'sickness' or 'accident' but does not include any reference to specific medical conditions. Many employers keep accident records. Such a record will only be an "injury record" if it includes details of the injury suffered by an identifiable worker. Sickness and injury records include information about workers' physical or mental health. The holding of sickness or injury records will therefore involve the processing of sensitive personal data. This means one of the conditions for processing sensitive personal data must be satisfied. Generally, employers are advised as far as practicable to restrict record keeping to absence records rather than sickness or injury records.

Employees have a right to gain access to information that is kept about them. This right is known as *subject access*. The right applies, for example, to sickness records, disciplinary or training records, appraisal or performance review notes, e-mails, word-processed documents, e-mail logs, audit trails, information held in general personnel files and interview notes, whether held as computerised files, or as structured paper records. A fee of up to £10 can be charged by the employer for giving access.

Responding to a subject access request involves:

- Telling the worker if the organisation keeps any personal information about him or her
- Giving the worker a description of the type of information the organisation keeps, the purposes it is used for and the types of organisations which it may be passed on to, if any
- Showing the worker all the information the organisation keeps about him or her, explaining any codes or other unintelligible terms used
- Providing this information in a hard copy or in readily readable, permanent electronic form unless providing it in that way would involve disproportionate effort or the worker agrees to receive it in some other way
- Providing the worker with any additional information the organisation has, as to the source of the information kept about him or her

Some business organisations do not process all the information they hold on workers themselves but outsource this to other organisations. Such organisations are termed 'data processors' in the Data Protection Act. In this case, the business organisation must satisfy itself that any data processor adopts appropriate security measures both in terms of the technology it uses and how it is managed.

Critically, the business organisation should have in place a written contract with any data processor it chooses that requires it to process personal information only on its instructions, and to maintain appropriate security. Where the use of a data processor would involve a transfer of information about a worker to a country outside the European Economic Area (EEA), we need to be assured that there is a proper basis for making the transfer.

Various regulations apply to employee benefits from country to country. Most countries work to a minimum or maximum benefits system. Those benefits such as paid leave, paid public holidays and parental leave should normally be included in any new employee's contract, either directly or as part of an auxiliary staff handbook (see exercises 7 and 8 at the end of this chapter).

Monitoring at Work

Figure 8.5   Closed circuit television (CCTV) technologies are ubiquitous in the workplace.

A number of the requirements of the Data Protection Act come into play whenever an employer wishes to monitor workers. The Act does not prevent an employer from monitoring workers, but such monitoring must be done in a way which is consistent with the Act. Monitoring is a recognised component of the employment relationship. Most employers will make some checks on the quantity and quality of work produced by their workers. Workers will generally expect this. Many employers carry out monitoring to safeguard workers, as well as to protect their own interests or those of their customers. For example, monitoring may take place to ensure that those in hazardous environments are not being put at risk through the adoption of unsafe working practices.

Monitoring arrangements may equally be part of the security mechanisms used to protect personal information. In other cases, for example in the context of some financial services, the employer may be under legal or regulatory obligations which it can only realistically fulfil if it undertakes some monitoring. However where monitoring goes beyond one individual simply watching another and involves the manual recording or any automated processing of personal information, it must be done in a way that is both lawful and fair to workers. Monitoring may, to varying degrees, have an adverse impact on workers. It may intrude into their private lives, undermine respect for their correspondence or interfere with the relationship of mutual trust and confidence that should exist between them and their employer. The extent to which it does this may not always be immediately obvious. It is not always easy to draw a distinction between work-place and private information. For example monitoring e-mail messages from a worker to an occupational health advisor, or messages between workers and their trade union representatives, can give rise to concern.

In broad terms, the Act requires is that any adverse impact on workers is justified by the benefits to the employer and others. This code is designed to help employers determine when this might be the case. This applies where activities that are commonly referred to as "monitoring" are taking place or are planned. This means activities that set out to collect information about workers by keeping them under some form of observation, normally with a view to checking their performance or conduct. This could be done either directly, indirectly (perhaps by examining their work output) or by electronic means.

In all but the most straightforward cases, employers are likely to find it helpful to carry out a formal or informal 'impact assessment' to decide if and how to carry out monitoring. This is the means by which employers can judge whether a monitoring arrangement is a proportionate response to the problem it seeks to address. Identifying any likely adverse impact means taking into account the consequences of monitoring, not only for workers but also for others who might be affected by it, such as customers.

Businesses need to consider:

- What intrusion, if any, will there be into the private lives of workers and others, or interference with their private e-mails, telephone calls or other correspondence? Bear in mind that the private lives of workers can, and usually will, extend into the workplace
- To what extent will workers and others know when either they, or information about them, are being monitored and then be in a position to act to limit any intrusion or other adverse impact on themselves?
- If information that is confidential, private or otherwise sensitive will be seen by those who do not have a business need to know, e.g. IT workers involved in monitoring e-mail content
- What impact, if any, will there be on the relationship of mutual trust and confidence that should exist between workers and their employer?
- What impact, if any, will there be on other legitimate relationships, e.g. between trades union members and their representatives?

An impact assessment involves:

- Identifying clearly the purpose(s) behind the monitoring arrangement and the benefits it is likely to deliver
- Identifying any likely adverse impact of the monitoring arrangement
- Considering alternatives to monitoring or different ways in which it might be carried out
- Taking into account the obligations that arise from monitoring
- Judging whether monitoring is justified.
- What impact, if any, will there be on individuals with professional obligations of confidentiality or secrecy, e.g. solicitors or doctors?
- If the monitoring will be oppressive or demeaning.

Employee Health

Data and information about workers' health is usually sensitive data and specific rules come into play whenever an employer wishes to process information about workers' health. These rules do not prevent the processing of such information but limit the circumstances in which it can take place.

It is necessary for a business to carefully address the collection and subsequent use of information about a worker's physical or mental health or condition. Collection will often be done by some form of medical examination or test, but may involve other means such as health questionnaires.

Examples of commonly-held information about workers' health include the following:

- Questionnaires completed by an employee to detect problems with their health
- Historical information about a worker's disabilities or special needs
- Results of an eye-test taken by a worker using display screens
- Records of blood tests carried out to ensure a worker has not been exposed to hazardous substances
- Results of tests carried out to check a worker's exposure to alcohol or drugs

When making a conscious decision as to whether the current or proposed collection and use of health information is justified, a manager needs to consider:

- Establishing the benefits of the collection and use of health information
- Considering any alternative method of obtaining these benefits and/or the information needed
- Weighing these benefits against the adverse impact
- Placing particular emphasis on the need to be fair to individual workers
- Ensuring that the intrusion is no more than absolutely necessary
- Bearing in mind that health information can be particularly sensitive and obtaining it can be particularly intrusive
- Taking into account the results of consultation with trade unions or other representatives, if any, or with workers themselves

Of course, a business can normally assume that a healthy workforce is also a productive workforce. Therefore good practice recommends employers to operate occupational health schemes. Providing fitness centres and gym facilities can be expensive but probably not as expensive as working days lost to ill health.

Unless told otherwise, workers are entitled to assume that information they give to a doctor, nurse or other health professional will be treated in confidence and not passed to others. So it is important to set out clearly to employees, preferably in writing, how information they supply in the context of an occupational health scheme will be used, who it might be made available to and why.

Before obtaining information through drug or alcohol testing, a business organisation should ensure that the benefits justify any adverse impact, unless the testing is required by law. The collection of information through drug and alcohol testing is unlikely to be justified unless it is for health and safety reasons. Post-incident testing, where there is a reasonable suspicion that drug or alcohol might be a factor, is more likely to be justified than random testing. Employees should normally be informed for which drugs they are being tested and, as a general rule, a written policy statement should:

- Explain the drug or alcohol policy in a staff handbook
- Explain the consequences for workers of breaching the policy
- Ensure workers are aware of the blood-alcohol level at which they may be disciplined when being tested for alcohol
- Not assume that all tests are infallible and be prepared to deal properly with disputes arising from their use.

Employee Data Analytics

Businesses and companies are increasingly turning to data analytics to gain insights into personnel trends which can aid staff recruitment, retention, development and performance. Data and the effective interpretations of what they mean are powerful tools in any industry. Just look at companies like Google, who show us that through the analysis and interpretation of data, we can create something truly massive and hugely successful! The usefulness of data is just as relevant to the human resources and talent management industries.

People analytics are the latest buzzwords to appear in human resources and talent management. But these two words shouldn't be dismissed as just another piece of management speak, as they sum up the potential for businesses to drive decisions based on the use of data, drawing on insight that has up to now been unattainable.

Data can be drawn from a variety of sources, including employee engagement surveys, absence records, training information and work scheduling. While not all businesses are using data analytics to its full extent yet, most organisations are at least engaging in some kind of analysis of their people data. See figure 7.6 for a survey of those organisations which are using analytics.

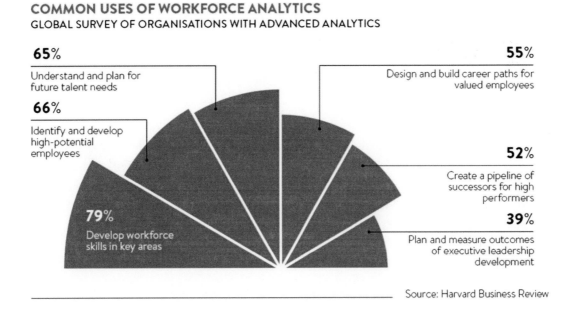

Figure 8.6 A typical employee survey of organisations using workforce analytics.

One issue slowing down the uptake of people analytics is human resources departments' lack of natural instinct for data. A useful question to pose is: what can HR learn from marketing? Marketing departments have developed analytics capabilities, including how to analyse unstructured data, how to segment their data and how to target analysis on customer needs, as well as outcome metrics to show the impact of decisions and actions.

Case Studies – Primary Data: Employees

Case Study: Asda

Asda is the UK's second largest supermarket. It was founded in 1949 under the name of Associated Dairies and Farm Group but shortened this to Asda in 1965. It is a retailer focused on selling food, clothing, electronics, toys, home furnishings and general merchandise. Asda also offers a range of additional services such as 'Asda Money' financial services.

In 1999, Asda became a subsidiary of Walmart, the largest supermarket chain in the world. This enabled Walmart to enter the UK market but also gave Asda access to the full range of expertise of the Walmart company. Walmart currently employs over 2 million colleagues worldwide in 27 countries.

In the UK, Asda is one of the largest employers with over 175,000 colleagues working across its many formats. These include a variety of roles in its Superstores, Supermarkets, Home Office, Distribution, George and Asda Living. Asda continues to expand its operations in the UK and recently acquired a number of stores from Netto to increase the number of local Asda Supermarkets.

Asda wants to be a trusted employer. Its success as a leading retailer is dependent on its trained and engaged colleagues providing excellent customer service.

This case study demonstrates how Asda's recruitment and selection processes, teamed with effective leadership and its colleague engagement strategies are helping the company to achieve its mission.

Asda's philosophy is that if your people enjoy working with you, your customers will enjoy shopping with you. Consequently it aims for all colleagues to be passionately engaged in supporting each other in a safe family environment of trust and respect. Asda has won numerous awards that recognise its commitment to its colleagues including The Sunday Times Top 100 Best Companies to Work For, The Times Top 100 Graduate Employers and Stonewall Top 100 Employers 2012.

For more information, refer to the full case study.

Questions for Discussion:

1. Explain the difference between a job description and a personal specification.
2. Describe two benefits to Asda of using online technology when recruiting new colleagues.
3. Analyse the pros and cons to Asda of aiming to recruit 70% of its leaders internally.
4. Evaluate the extent to which a commitment to training and development is effective in helping Asda's colleague retention.

Case Study: Ice Cream Deli in Mexico

Turnover (the percentage of employees leaving the organisation) is a very common problem in organisations. Managers measure turnover by the 'turnover rate' calculated by the total number of employees leaving the organisations during the month divided by the average number of employees during the month". Although achieving zero percent turnover is "neither realistic nor desirable", many academic and business specialists in the area suggest tools to reduce turnover effectively in order to lower costs and increase productivity.

In the first section of this paper, an overview is presented of some of the main causes for turnover, including the strategies to reduce it, according to three contemporary authors. A description of "Ice Cream Deli" in Cancun and Playa del Carmen is included also, as well as the interest of their Director of Operations, to maintain stability in human resources and optimise organisational productivity.

Finally, in the last section, the three methodologies applied to analyse the root causes of voluntary turnover and the main causes of organizational retention are presented in a Gallup Q-12 Survey, a Nominal Technique and an Appreciative Inquiry toward Retention.

Some of the reasons for turnover and retention in the Ice Cream Deli are expressed from the perspective of the workers and summarised in figures.

This case study focuses on a Mexican franchise (Ice Cream Deli) and its interest to reduce voluntary (avoidable) turnover in order to lower costs and increase productivity. High turnover is a common problem in many organizations in Cancun and Playa Del Carmen, Mexico. The ten "Ice Cream Deli" stores studied in this case present a high voluntary turnover, even when the job conditions in the organisation are better than the market. Arturo Mendoza, Director of Operations, is interested in analysing the root causes of the problem and providing an action plan to reduce turnover of line workers. Some of the reasons for turnover and retention are stated from the perspective of the workers.

For more information, refer to the full case study.

Questions for Discussion:

1. Review the data analysis issues in this case study.
2. Suggest other issues that you think could have been discussed.

Exercises – Primary Data: Employees

1. {multiple choice – choose the most appropriate answer (a), (b), (c) or (d)}

Criminal Records Bureau (CRB) checks for verification of prospective employee data are now called:

(a) BHS (b) CBS (c) DBS (d) EMS

2. {multiple choice – choose the most appropriate answer (a), (b), (c) or (d)}

The Act of Parliament of the United Kingdom of Great Britain and Northern Ireland which defines UK law on the processing of data on identifiable living people is the main piece of legislation that governs the protection of personal data in the UK and it is known as:

(a) APD (b) PDA (c) DPA (d) PAD

3. {multiple choice – choose the most appropriate answer (a), (b), (c) or (d)}

Personnel departments and their associated activities are also described by the acronym:

(a) RHM (b) HMR (c) HRM (d) MRH

4. {multiple choice – choose the most appropriate answer (a), (b), (c) or (d)}

Video technology used in monitoring in employees in the workplace is often referred to as:

(a) CCTV (b) VTE (c) VDU (d) HDMI

5. {multiple choice – choose the most appropriate answer (a), (b), (c) or (d)}

The potential for businesses to drive employment decisions, based on the use of data, is sometimes known as:

(a) Employee Retention
(b) Recruitment tools
(c) People analytics
(d) Vetting procedures

6. <u>Employment contracts.</u> There are several different types of employment contracts available to employers. Research and briefly summarise (one paragraph) the following (highlighting key points and differences):

    (i)   full-time and part-time contracts
    (ii)   fixed-term contracts
    (iii) zero hour contracts
    (iv) agency staff contracts

7. <u>Employment in Europe.</u> Paid annual leave for a selection of European countries is shown in the figure below (courtesy of <u>www.glassdoor.co.uk</u>).

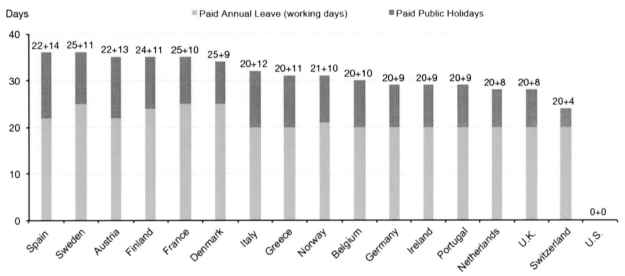

Total paid annual leave
(statutory minimum leave plus public holidays)

Notes: Statutory minimum leave is normalised in accordance to a five-day-working week. Paid public holidays exclude those that fall on Sundays, but include those that fall on Saturdays. In the U.S., there is no legal requirement for private businesses to grant paid holidays to their employees.

Source(s): International Labour Organisation, Conditions of work and employment programme (2012); Eures, Living and working conditions; and Ray, Rebecca; Schmitt, John. "No-vacation nation USA — in OECD countries" (PDF). European Economic and Employment Policy Brief (No. 3 -- 2007).

According to the 2016 data, briefly summarise the following:

    (i)   The three countries with the <u>highest</u> entitlement of statutory minimum leave
    (ii)   Countries with the <u>lowest</u> entitlement of statutory minimum leave (20 days)
    (iii) The country with the <u>most</u> paid public holidays
    (iv) The main reason for the US paid annual leave showing as zero

8. <u>Employment in Europe.</u> European paid leave and unemployment benefits are shown in the figure below (courtesy of <u>www.glassdoor.co.uk</u>).

European Paid Leave and Unemployment Benefits

Indicator	Denmark	France	Spain	Netherlands	Sweden	Finland	Italy	Norway	Austria	Belgium	Germany	U.K.	Switzerland	Ireland	U.S.
Unemployment benefits															
Period covered															
Pay															
Maternity-related entitlements															
Period covered															
Pay															
Paternity-related entitlements															
Period covered															
Pay															
Parental-related entitlements															
Period covered															
Pay															
Annual leave															
Period covered															
Public holidays															
Sick pay															
Period covered															
Pay															
Aggregate score	7.8	7.2	6.4	6.2	5.9	5.8	5.6	5.6	5.4	5.1	4.7	2.9	2.3	2.3	0.3

Legend: Most Generous, Second Most Generous, Third Most Generous, Least Generous, Second Least Generous, Third Least Generous, Tied

According to the 2016 data, briefly summarise the following:

(i)   The most and least generous countries in which to be out of work
(ii)   The most and least generous countries in which to be off work sick
(iii) The most and least generous countries for maternity leave
(iv)   The most and least generous countries for paternal leave

9. Crossword

Asda

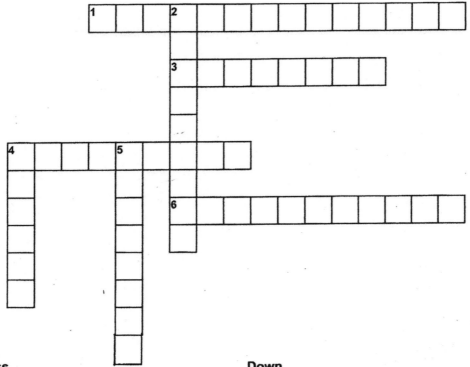

Across

1 The business function responsible for looking after employees needs

3 Workforce _____ establishes an organisation's workforce needs both now and in the future

4 Decide who to interview and hire

6 Applicants apply through CV or _____ form

Down

2 A time to discuss performance and development opportunities

4 Used to find out people thoughts and opinions

5 An organisation's _____ defines how colleagues behave

Possible answers:

application, appraisal, human resources, protocol, shortlist, survey, teamwork

10.   Wordsearch

Primary Data: Employees

```
S  I  O  C  K  N  E  S  S  R  E  C  O  R  D  S  S  S  D  M  L  O  W
M  T  H  U  N  J  P  O  J  L  M  N  T  U  W  X  P  K  D  E  G  G  U
Z  P  U  Y  S  E  C  R  U  O  S  E  R  N  A  M  U  H  R  T  D  N  F
W  F  Y  R  H  T  L  A  E  H  S  V  Z  R  G  V  E  R  B  W  P  I  J
J  X  T  E  L  D  B  K  O  N  Q  V  K  Z  B  A  O  E  G  C  P  R  R
R  C  I  P  E  I  T  S  I  L  T  R  O  H  S  C  L  C  G  X  M  O  N
K  N  R  H  N  S  V  S  W  E  I  V  R  E  T  N  I  R  N  O  E  T  K
A  S  U  Z  N  C  L  K  O  W  E  M  S  L  C  O  I  U  I  P  O  I  I
D  C  C  D  O  L  K  L  W  L  D  Z  I  K  E  U  W  I  T  A  Y  N  L
N  I  E  Q  S  O  T  J  P  G  T  A  U  W  P  A  U  T  T  N  K  O  V
B  T  S  U  R  S  J  L  W  H  V  D  T  W  P  X  I  M  E  E  I  M  G
Z  Y  G  H  E  U  E  V  E  P  A  Y  R  O  L  L  M  E  V  L  D  H  H
E  L  F  L  P  R  X  U  N  X  H  E  F  P  E  S  U  N  N  C  X  G  B
R  A  N  M  M  E  Z  N  O  I  T  C  E  L  E  S  S  T  Z  S  E  A  G
U  N  A  Y  Y  T  C  N  O  I  T  A  C  I  F  I  R  E  V  X  T  A  G
V  A  L  Y  S  C  K  S  W  E  N  C  Q  N  F  Z  N  L  Q  S  S  Q  A
```

Find the following words in the puzzle.
Words are hidden ↑ ↓ → ← and ↘ .

ANALYTICS
DISCLOSURE
HEALTH
HUMANRESOURCES
INTERVIEWS
MONITORING

PANEL
PAYROLL
PERSONNEL
RECORDS
RECRUITMENT
SECURITY

SELECTION
SHORTLIST
SIOCKNESS
VERIFICATION
VETTING

9. ANALYSING DATA & INFORMATION

Introduction to Quantitative Techniques

Statisticians improve data quality by developing specific experimental designs. Statistics itself also provides tools for prediction, forecasting and the use of statistical models. Statistics is indeed applicable to a wide variety of academic disciplines, including natural sciences, social sciences, and political sciences, but particularly to business and marketing research.

As we have already seen, statistical methods can summarise or describe a collection of data. This is called *descriptive statistics* and they are particularly useful in communicating the results of experiments and research. In addition, data patterns may be modelled in a way that accounts for randomness and uncertainty in the observations. These models can also be used to draw inferences about the process or population under study, a practice called *inferential statistics*. Inference is a vital element of scientific advance, since it provides a way to draw conclusions from data that are subject to random variation. To prove the propositions being investigated further, our conclusions are tested as part of the scientific method.

Mathematical Modelling

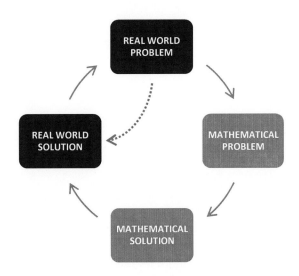

Figure 9.1   The mathematical modelling process.

Mathematical modelling is a process of representing real world problems in mathematical terms in an attempt to find solutions to the problems (see figure 9.1). If we are fortunate, it might just be possible to look at a real world problem and directly identify its solution without recourse to mathematical modelling at all (dashed line in the figure). However, real-life problems are rarely so straightforward. After all, if life were so simple, most of us would easily have most of the solutions to hand.

Of course, business problems can be complex. Choosing the right set of stocks for a portfolio, securing the optimal loan for a business start-up, hiring the best candidate for the job, etc. are easy to evaluate in hindsight but a great deal harder to determine *a priori*. A mathematical model can be considered as a simplification or abstraction of a (complex) real world problem or situation into a mathematical form, thereby converting the real world problem into a mathematical problem. The mathematical problem can then be solved using established techniques to obtain mathematical solutions. These solutions are then interpreted and translated into real world terms.

We start here with linear models that can be effective in business problems where we need to correlate variables and make forward projections.

Correlation

The concept of *correlation* is particularly noteworthy for the potential confusion it can cause. Statistical analysis of a data set often reveals that two variables (properties) of the population under consideration tend to vary together, as if they were in some ways connected. For example, a study of annual income that also looks at years of experience might find that income seems to rise with years of experience. Of course, this might make common sense but the data needs to support it because sometime we imagine two variable correlate but, in fact, they don't.

When two variables are said to be correlated, one may or may not be the cause of the other. Indeed, the correlation phenomena could be caused by a third, previously unconsidered phenomenon, called a *lurking (or confounding) variable*. For this reason, there is no obvious way to immediately infer the existence of a causal relationship between the two variables.

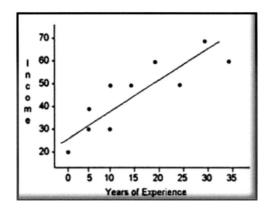

Figure 9.2 Points in a scatter diagram of income against years of experience.
Visually, there seems to be correlation between the two variables.

In the graph of figure 9.2, we can see that the ten data points of years of experience (x-axis) and the £K income (y-axis) seem 'close' to a straight line (line of *best fit*). Thankfully, we can model this situation precisely using a *linear model* and calculating how closely the data points lie to the line by calculating a *correlation coefficient* and drawing a *regression line*. In practical terms, a correlation coefficient R value between 0.7 and 1.0 is said to represent 'strong' x-y correlation, whereas R valued between 0.4 and 0.7 represents 'moderate' correlation. Otherwise (0.0 < R < 0.4), we conclude that there is no clear correlation between x and y.

Example

Suppose that a software company has launched six packages to market, one each year for the past six years, and in the year preceding launch, the company recorded the number of full weeks in which testing was carried out by the Quality Control Department. The data relating to pre-launch testing weeks and complaints about the packages in post-launch year were as follows:

Pre-launch year Tests (weeks)	23	25	17	21	29	19
Number of Complaints (Post-launch year)	59	44	89	55	25	71

Represent the information in the form of a scatter diagram showing the correlation coefficient squared R^2 and the equation of the regression line. Hence, draw your own conclusions with regard to any correlation between the variables. According to a linear model, predict the number of complaints associated with thirty five tests.

Solution

{Using Excel tools: 'insert' *scattterplot*, 'choose' *trendline*, 'option' *linear*, 'show' *equation*, 'show' R^2 *value*; other spreadsheet software tools vary}

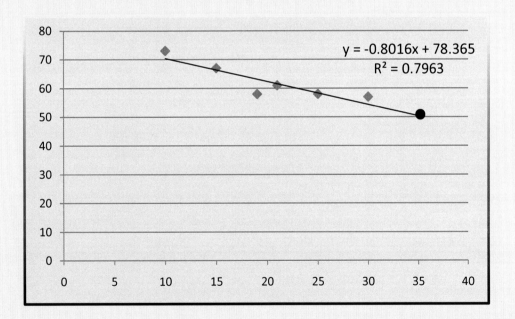

$y = -0.8016x + 78.365$
$R^2 = 0.7963$

Since $R^2 = 0.7963$, we know that $R = 0.9$ (to 1 decimal place). Since $R \in (0.7, 1.0)$, this represents strong correlation. We draw the conclusion that more pre-launch testing should associate with fewer post-launch complaints.

According to a linear model, we can 'extrapolate' the line to conclude there would be approximately fifty complaints associated with thirty five tests (represented by the black dot in the above figure. Note that reading values on the line between the end data points is called 'interpolation'.

Correlations can be positive or negative depending on the slope of the regression line.

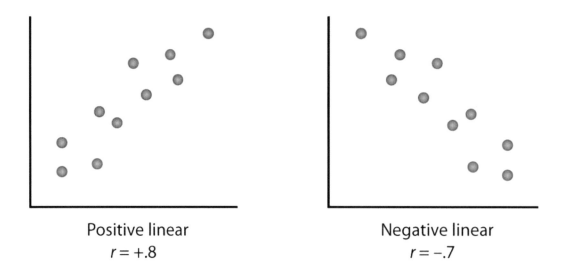

Positive linear	Negative linear
$r = +.8$	$r = -.7$

Interesting X-Y correlations in real business situations include:

- X = Commodity supply, Y = Commodity demand (negative)
- X = Customer approval rating, Y = Percentage of the operating budget spent on CSR (positive)
- X = Money in a guaranteed savings account (£), Y = Perceived financially security (positive)
- X = Number of hours of sunshine daily, Y = Ice cream cone sales daily (£) (positive)
- X = Number of times cars are recalled with problems, Y = Customer satisfaction rating (negative)
- X = Pay cheque size (£), Y = Number of hours worked by an employee (positive)
- X = Time spent marketing a business (hours per week), Y = Number of new customers (positive)
- X = Used car price (£), Y = Number of miles on the clock (negative)

We should note that correlation does not imply *causality*. In other words X does not cause Y or vice versa. A high correlation coefficient (say, 0.8) implies an apparent association between the variables and this could be the result of many intermediate variables between the two.

Sometimes apparent correlation is simply pure coincidence (see figure 9.3).

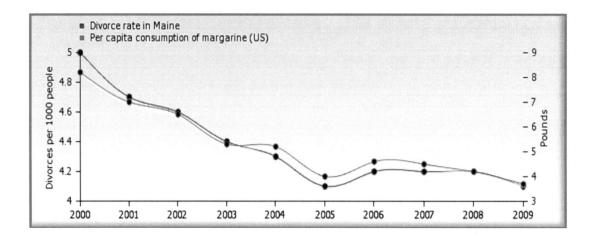

Figure 9.3   Apparent correlation between divorce and margarine consumption (Vigen, 2014).

While linear models are the simplest form of modelling, it may well be that our variables do correlate, not according to a straight line but according to a power of one of the variables giving us a curved line.

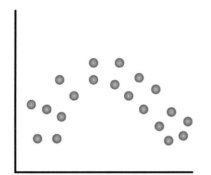 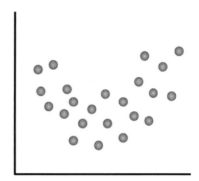

For examples, if we tried to draw a straight line through the above points, the correlation coefficient R would be very close to zero, despite the fact that we can probably see some patterns in the data. However, if we try a power model, a correlation coefficient measuring closeness of the data points to a curve (curve of best fit), will give us a meaningful result. The key here is to try the right model for the data with which we are presented.

Example

Hours of sunshine daily	1	2	3	4	5	6
Ice cream cone sales (£ hundreds)	1	4	7	15	25	35

Solution

{Using Excel tools: 'insert' *scattterplot*, 'choose' *trendline*, 'option' *power*, 'show' *equation*, 'show' R^2 *value*; other spreadsheet software tools vary}

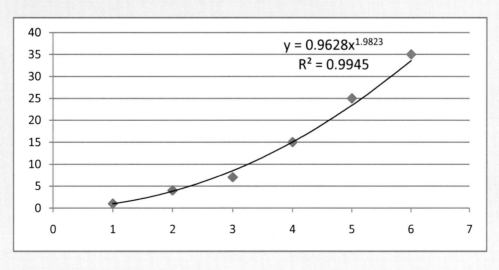

$$y = 0.9628x^{1.9823}$$
$$R^2 = 0.9945$$

Other mathematical models (all available in Excel) include *exponential, logarithmic, polynomial* and *moving average*.

Introduction to Probability Distributions

There are many probability distributions which can be used in modelling. These include:

- the Binomial distribution
- the Poisson distribution
- the Normal distribution

Each of these has their own characteristics and if we can anticipate that a particular business problem can be modelled by one of them, it makes decision making more effective and accurate.

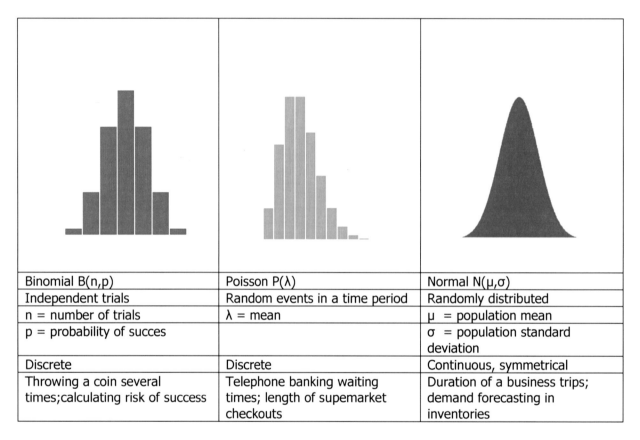

Binomial B(n,p)	Poisson P(λ)	Normal N(μ,σ)
Independent trials	Random events in a time period	Randomly distributed
n = number of trials	λ = mean	μ = population mean
p = probability of succes		σ = population standard deviation
Discrete	Discrete	Continuous, symmetrical
Throwing a coin several times;calculating risk of success	Telephone banking waiting times; length of supermarket checkouts	Duration of a business trips; demand forecasting in inventories

Other distributions that can be used in business problems (but which will not be covered in detail here) include (in alphabetical order):

- Bernoulli distribution (discrete)
- Beta distribution (continuous)
- Chi-squared distribution (continuous)
- Exponential distribution (continuous)
- Fisher distribution (discrete)
- Gamma distribution (continuous)
- Geometric distribution (discrete)
- Hypergeometric distribution (discrete)

Binomial distribution

The binomial distribution model can be used whenever there is a sequence of n independent trials that have two possible mutually exclusive outcomes (normally called success and failure) and the probability of success, p, is constant. Obviously, the probability of failure would therefore be given by (1-p). Tossing a fair coin is an example of a binomial process. Each toss is a trial with two outcomes (heads or tails) so if we consider a tail outcome as a success, p = 0.5, and the probability of failure is (1 − p), which is also 0.5. Quality control inspections give another example of a binomial process. Each inspection of a unit coming out of a production line might yield a high probability of success (say, 0.9) and a small probability of failure (say, 0.1). So for example, the binomial distribution could give us the probability of five units produced without any failures.

Probabilities can be looked up in standard tables (see Appendix D) or calculated simply in Excel using the BINOMDIST function. In the latter case we need to insert values of s, n, p, c, which are respectively the number of successes, the number of trials, the probability of success and a cumulative parameter.

Example

Suppose that the probability of finding a faulty unit coming out of a production line is known from experience to be 0.1. Assuming that FIVE units are checked independently, what is the probability that this batch will contain no faulty units?

Solution

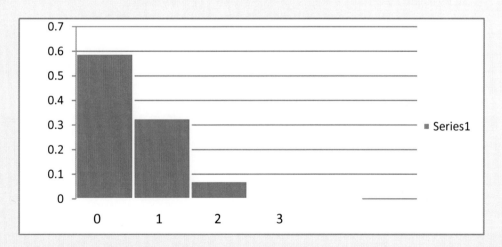

This is a case of the Binomial distribution B(n, p) when n = 5 and p = 0.1. The probability of finding zero faulty units in this batch of five units can be looked up in the tables of Appendix C, i.e. the probability P(n,r) of r 'successes' when n = 5 and r = 0, 1, 2, 3 , 4, 5, respectively can simply be read off as 0.5905, 0.3281, 0.0729, 0.0081, 0.0005 and 0.0000 (to four decimal places). So the probability we need is 0.5905 (or 0.60 to 2 decimal places or 60% as a percentage). Alternatively, we can use Excel to calculate the value of the function BINOMDIST(s, n, p, 0) when s = 0, n = 5 and p = 0.1. This would give us the same value as with tables but would also calculate to more than four decimal places if necessary.

The choice to use tables or functions is a matter of preference. In practice, the choice is usually made according to which is likely to give the answers most quickly with the least effort. It is always a good idea to use common sense in looking at our answers to see if we could have anticipated a value close to the one calculated.

Example

Suppose that a business salesperson calls customers on a weekly basis, hopefully to make new sales. She knows from experience in the long term that the probability of making a new sale when contacting a loyal customer is about 0.2, i.e. about one in every five. If she contacts six loyal customers in a given week, what will be the probability of achieving a sales target of *at least one* new sale?

Solution

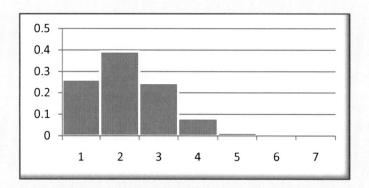

If we assume that the six calls are made independently, we can model this situation as B(n, p) when n = 6 and p = 0.2. The probability of achieving a sales target of at least one new sale is cumulative in the sense that it includes not only exactly one new sale but also two, three, four, five and six. This can be obtained using either tables or functions.

With tables, we look up in Appendix B the probability values corresponding to n = 6 and r = 1, 2, 3, 4, 5, 6, namely 0.3932, 0.2458, 0.0819, 0.0154, 0.0015, 0.0001 giving a total 0.7379. Indeed, an easier way to calculate this would be to calculate the value of (1 - 0.2621) = 0.7379 because this is equivalent to the probability of no new sales subtracted from one.

With functions, we would calculate BINOMDIST(s, n, p, 0) when s = 0, n = 6, p = 0.2 and c = 0. This gives value of the probability of no new sales as 0.262144 so subtracting from 1 gives 0.73866.

In practical business situations, we might have data or information born from experience. For examples, a marketing company might know that only five percent of calls made to potentially new customers actually result in success or that typically only ten percent of customers answer a withheld number call. This information can be very useful in deciding how many calls to make to achieve a given number of successes. Of course, in practical business situations we also know that assessing 'risk' or seeking to minimise it can also be a secret to success. Before a strategy is put in place or a new project is started, a feasibility study involving an assessment of the risks involved is normally carried out. Such activities are essential features of business plans and start-ups. Nothing can be guaranteed in practical situations, even those projects that look like 'sure things'. Probably, very few investors just before the financial crash of 2008 would have predicted the demise of major banks and other financial institutions.

Consider the music industry over the past sixty years. In the 1960s and 1970s, businesses producing and selling vinyl records experienced high volumes and high returns for their endeavours. In the 1980s and 1990s, audio cassettes and compact disks superseded vinyl records. Then in the 2000s and 2010s online downloads superseded those. Notwithstanding the fact that niche opportunities exist for older technologies, it would be a mistake to stand still too long in such a technology-dependent industry. So risk is always there and needs to be measured.

Example

	East Coast	West Coast
Risk of Failure	0.25	0.30
Probability of success	0.75	0.70

Scenario: Coffee Central Inc has hundreds of coffee shops situated mainly in East Coast and West Coast areas. Researchers have tracked the risk of failure of each of its coffee shops by measuring those failing to make a profit after two years, on the assumption that all shops behave independently. The above table shows the overall results for the East Coast and West Coast shops, respectively. The risk of failure and probability of success are complementary in the sense that they add up to one. Coffee Central is now planning to open three new West Coast shops and three new East Coast shops. Based on the above figures what is the probability that at least two shops will succeed in each case?

Solution

Given that shops behave independently, this scenario is a case of the Binomial distribution $B(n, p)$ when $n = 3$ and $p = 0.25$ or 0.30. Note that the probability of at least two succeeding is equivalent to the probability of no more than one failing.

n	r	0.25	0.30
3	0	0.4219	0.3430
3	1	0.4219	0.4410
3	2	0.1406	0.1890
3	3	0.0156	0.0270

With $r = 0.25$, the probabilities of 0, 1, failures are obtained from tables: 0.4219 and 0.4219.

So the probability of no more than one failing is 0.8438. (Notice that we could achieved a similar result using the BINOMDIST function with $p = 0.75$).

With $p = 0.30$, the probabilities of 0, 1, failures are obtained from tables as 0.3430 and 0.4410.

So the probability of no more than one failing is 0.7840. (Notice that we could achieved a similar result using the BINOMDIST function with $p = 0.05$).

Hence, the probability that at least two shops will succeed on each coast are 0.8438 and 0.7840, respectively. With both around 80%, this is likely to be good news for Coffee Central.

Practice exercise

A business owner decides to use a binomial distribution to solve one of his problems. He knows there is a 40 percent probability that he will sell one of his Red Oak floors to any customer who comes into his shop and views the wood. Out of the next three people who come into his shop, what is the probability that one person will buy a Red Oak floor?

Sometimes, we need to know the mathematical result that for a binomial distribution, the mean and variance are given by the expressions (np) and np (1-p). We do not need to derive these results here but we should be prepared to use them in practice.

Example

For a binomial distribution comprising one hundred trials with probability of success on each trial p= 0.2, calculate the mean, variance and standard deviation.

Solution

Mean = np = (100)(0.2)

Variance = np (1-p) = (100)(0.2)(0.8) = 16

Standard deviation = $\sqrt{variance}$ = $\sqrt{16}$ = 4

Practical business questions - applications of the Binomial distribution

- Auditing a series of transactions: are they in compliance with established procedures or not?
- Hiring a series of persons: how many are female or male?
- Contacting potential customers: will a certain number lead to a sale?
- Lowering prices: do sales increase or not?
- Modelling the stock market predicting a number of stocks will rise: do they or don't they?
- Dealing with an intermittent problem on a company's network: on any given day, does the problem appear or doesn't it?

Poisson distribution

The Poisson distribution is useful for solving problems in which events occur randomly. So for examples, we could use a Poisson distribution to describe the number of accidents each month in a company, the number of defects in a metre of cloth, the number of phone calls received each hour in a call centre and the number of customers entering a shop each hour.

The Poisson uses only the probability of success. It assumes that this is very small, and it looks for the few successes in a continuous background of failures. For instance, when it describes the random interruptions to a power supply it focuses on the very few times when there were disruptions, but not the large number of times when there were no disruptions. Similarly, when we consider the number of spelling mistakes in a long report, the number of faults in a pipeline or the number of accidents in a factory, we are interested only in the small number of successes and not concerned with the large number of failures.

When we have a binomial distribution in which the number of trials, n, is large (say greater than twenty) and the probability of success, p, is small, we can approximate it by a Poisson distribution because the distributions are very similar. The Poisson distribution $P(\lambda)$ requires only the value of λ to calculate it, where λ is the mean number of events per interval. As with the Binomial, a Poisson probability can be found used tables (see Appendix D) or using the Excel function POISSON.

Example

Suppose that on a North Sea oil rig there have been twenty five accidents that were serious enough to report in the past fifty weeks. In what proportion of weeks would you expect none, one, two and more than two accidents?

Solution

A small number of accidents occur, presumably at random, over time. We are not interested in the number of accidents that did not occur, so we have a Poisson process, with a mean number of accidents per week $\lambda = 25/50 = 0.50$. The Poisson tables in Appendix D give probabilities of 0, 1, 2, 3, 4 ... accidents as 0.6065, 0.3033, 0.0758, 0.0126, 0.0016 ... Further probabilities are very small as always happens for this type of distribution as r grows larger.

So $P(r = 0) = 0.6065$; $P(r = 1) = 0.3033$; $P(r = 2) = 0.0758$

Because $P(r > 2)$ would involve adding an infinite number of very small probabilities, it is better here to calculate using: $P(r > 2) = (1 - P(r \leq 2)) = (1 - 0.9856) = 0.0144$. We could alternatively use the POISSON function in Excel to calculate POISSON(0,0.5,0), POISSON(1,0.5,0), POISSON(2,0.5,0).

Often in quality assurance situations, we are dealing with very large values of trials. For instance, in monitoring boxes of cereal for weight or checking invoices for correct information, a large proportion are fine and contain no errors. Nevertheless, we might need to assess the probabilities (or risks) involved.

Example

An accounts department sends out 10,000 invoices a month and has an average of two returned with an error per month? What is the probability that exactly three invoices will be returned in a given month?

Solution

Strictly speaking, assuming errors occur independently, we should use the Binomial distribution for this problem but n is very large. So a better approach is to use the Poisson distribution to approximate it.

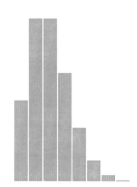

Since the mean of any Binomial distribution can be shown to be given by the value of (np), we here use:

$$n = 10000$$
$$p = 2/10000$$
$$np = 2$$
$$\lambda = 2$$

We can then solve this problem using either tables or functions.

Using Tables:

Looking up the vales in the Poisson tables we find probabilities for 0, 1, 2, 3, 4, 5 6 successes as
0.1353, 0.2707, 0.2707, 0.1804, 0.0902, 0.0361, 0.0120.
(the answer we need is shown in green highlight)

Using Excel:

Calculating POISSON(x, λ, c) with x = 3, λ = 2, c = 0 gives the value 0.1804.

Hence, the probability of exactly three invoices returned in a given month is 0.1804, i.e. 0.18 (to 2 d.p.) or 18% (to 2 s.f.).

Practical business applications of the Poisson distribution include:

- The number of bankruptcies that are filed in a month
- The number of arrivals at a car wash in one hour
- The number of network failures per day
- The number of file server virus infections at a data centre during a 24-hour period
- The number of Airbus aircraft engine shutdowns per 100,000 flight hours
- The number of work-related accidents over a given production time
- The number of customers complaining about a service problem per month
- The number of visitors to a web site per minute
- The number of calls to consumer hot line in a 5-minute period
- The number of telephone calls per minute in a small business.

Normal distribution

Both the Binomial and Poisson distributions describe discrete data, typically showing the number of 'successes'. But we often also want a probability distribution to describe continuous data, such as the volume of a dairy product in a supermarket or waiting time in a customer telephone queue. Although discrete and continuous distributions are similar in several ways, there is a key difference. With discrete probabilities we might want the probability of, say, exactly three successes, but with continuous data you cannot expect to find the probability that a measured volume is exactly 500.4564 litres. If you make the measurement precise enough, the probability of this happening is always likely to be close to zero. It would be far more useful to know the probability that the volume is 500 litres to three significant figures or lies between 400 litres and 600 litres. This is the approach of continuous probability distributions, which typically finds the probability that a value is within a specified range.

There are several continuous probability distributions, but the most widely used is the *Normal* (or *Gaussian*) distribution. This is a bell-shaped curve (illustrated in the figure below) that describes many natural features such as the heights of trees, harvest from a hectare of land, weight of sheep, flows in rivers, temperatures throughout the day, etc. It also describes many business activities, such as daily receipts, sales volumes, number of customers a week, production in a factory, and so on. The distribution is so common that a rule of thumb suggests that 'when you have a lot of observations, use the Normal distribution'.

The Normal distribution has the properties of:

- being continuous
- being symmetrical about the mean, μ
- having mean, median and mode all equal
- having a total area under the curve equal to 1
- extending to plus and minus infinity asymptotically on the x-axis

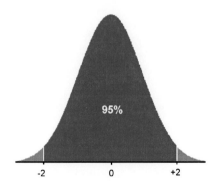

The particular case of a normal distribution with mean 0 and standard deviation 1 is called the *Standard Normal* distribution. It has the important property that 95% of its area lies within the interval -2 and +2. In fact, as we will see later, we use this property in business when we talk about 95% 'confidence intervals'. Of course, if 95% of the area lies inside the interval (-2,+2) then by the implication 5% lies outside the interval and we will also see later that this property is useful in *hypothesis tests*.

We previously looked at histograms for describing continuous data, and emphasised that the areas of the bars are important, and not just their length. Similarly with continuous data, it is the area under the curve that gives the probabilities. The height of a continuous probability distribution such as the Normal distribution does not have much practical meaning.

In the business of production, we generally make things, according to constraints on production costs and prices. Companies are generally subject to strict consumer law and best practice. Suppose a factory makes boxes of organic cereal. UK legislation sets out information for packers and importers on what they need to do to comply with the law[1]. There are three areas covered that packers and importers must comply with, providing protection for consumers on short measure:

- the contents of the packages must not be less on average than the nominal quantity
- the proportion of packages which are short of the stated quantity by more than a defined amount (the 'tolerable negative error') should be less than a specified level
- no package should be short by twice the tolerable negative error

Suppose therefore that a factory produces cereal boxes bearing a stated weight of 270g. There are always small variations in the weight of each box, and if the factory makes a large number of boxes, the weights can reasonably be expected to follow a Normal distribution. Managers in the factory are not too interested in the number of boxes that weigh, say, precisely 270g but they are more interested in complying with legislation. Financial penalties for failure to comply can be very high. So from experience, they aim for an average production weight of 280g and assume a standard deviation of 5g and a tolerable negative error of 10g, as shown in the figure below. Additionally, the Quality Assurance Department regularly checks that the probability of any box chosen at random having a weight less than 270g should not exceed 0.025 (i.e. 1 in forty).

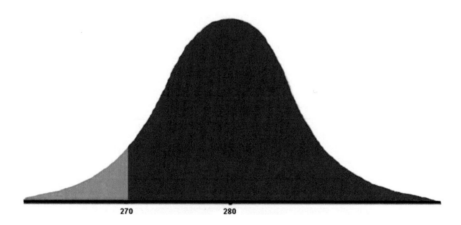

Using the function NORMDIST(270,280,5,1) in Excel gives us the probability of a chosen box weighing less than 270g to be 0.023 (which is indeed fractional less than the target 0.025). Quality control would also like to be reassured that the probability of a weight falling below twice the tolerable negative error must be very small. Calculating this using NORMDIST(270,280,5,1) gives us a value 0.00003 (i.e. 3 in 10000).

---

[1] see https://www.gov.uk/guidance/packaged-goods-weights-and-measures-regulations

It is worth noting that the Standard Normal distribution tables could also have been used to derive the values above. First, our normal variable X with mean, μ = 280g and standard deviation, σ = 5g is converted to a standard normal variable Z with mean 0 and standard deviation 1 according to the formula:

$$z = \frac{x - \mu}{\sigma}$$

Then, we look up the probability of z being less than $(\frac{270 - 280}{5})$, i.e. $P(z < -2.0) = 0.023$.

As before, we can say that the choice of a calculating a function or standard tables is a matter of preference, although the tables only yield values to four decimal places, whereas the accuracy of functions can be much higher. Since the notation z is used for the variable, standard normal distribution tables are also called 'z-tables' in various text books.

Practice exercises

Given a standard Normal distribution, find the three probability values of $P(z < 1)$, $P(z > 2.5)$ and $P(1 < z < 2.5)$ using two methods of evaluation, each of which should give a similar result to four decimal places:

> (i) Looking up the values in z-tables
> (ii) Using the NORMDIST function in Excel

Inventory management is an important part of the daily activities of retail companies. Holding too much stock costs money (e.g. extra storage space, running over sell-by-date, etc.). On the other hand running out of stock costs money (e.g. lost potential sales, customer dissatisfaction, etc.).   So consider the example below of a primarily fresh produce supermarket.

Example

Scenario: A fresh food supermarket sells, on average, 500 litres of milk a day with a standard deviation of 50 litres. This information has been built over many weeks. At the start of a certain day, the manager of the supermarket needs to know the answers to the following problem in order to make the necessary decisions about stock control. What is the probability that demand will be between 450 and 600 litres today?

Solution using functions

P(450 litres < u < 600 litres)   = NORMALDIST(600, 500, 50, 1) − NORMALDIST(450, 500, 50, 1)

= 0.97725 − 0.15866

= 0.81859 (to 5 d.p.)

Solution using tables

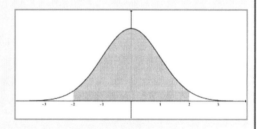

$z = \frac{x-\mu}{\sigma}$ = (600 − 500)/50 = 2.0 and P(z < 2.0) = 0.9772.

$z = \frac{x-\mu}{\sigma}$ = (400 − 500)/50 = -2.0 and P(z < -2.0) = 0.1587. So P(z > 2.0) = 0.0228

So P(-2.0 < z < 2.0) = 0.8185 (to 4 d.p.)

Example

Cover-me Insurance specialises motor insurance policies which cover only drivers with a low risk of accidents. The business model for Cover-me Insurance relies heavily on their ability to keep premiums lower because fewer of their policy holders have accidents. In a certain area near Barnes, London, experience has shown that for every one hundred drivers resident locally, Cover-me can expect an average of 0.2 accidents each a year. What is the probability that fewer than 15 out of one hundred drivers will have accidents in one year?

Solution

We have already seen that for a Binomial distribution with n trials and probability of success p the following statistics apply:

$$\text{Mean} = np = 100.(0.2) = 20$$

$$\text{Variance} = np\,(1\text{-}p) = 100.(0.2).(0.8) = 16$$

$$\text{Standard deviation} = \sqrt{variance} = \sqrt{16} = 4$$

So we can model this problem as a Normal distribution with mean 20 and standard deviation 4 giving us a probability of less than 15 accidents of NORMDIST(15,20,4,1) = 0.11.

Note that BINOMDIST(14,100,0.2,1) would have given us a probability of less than 15 accidents of 0.08. Both probabilities are close to each other (both being 0.1 to 1 d.p.) and this is one reason why we would in practice not use too many decimal places in the approximated values.

We observed earlier in this section on the Standard Normal distribution that 95% of its area lies between -2 and +2. In fact, we can use functions (or tables) to generalise this idea to say that 68% of a Normal distribution lies in the interval (-1,+1) and 99% lies in the interval (-2.57, +2.57). We will see later, we use these properties when we talk about 95% and 99% 'confidence intervals'. Of course, if 95% of the area lies inside the interval (-2,+2) then by the same token 5% lies outside.

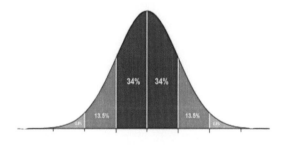

Practical business applications of the Normal distribution

The Normal Distribution has many business applications, including:

- In operations management: results of many processes are normally distributed
- In human resources management: resource professionals often use the normal distribution to describe employee performance
- In investment management: a diversified portfolio will typically have returns that are normally distributed
- In demand forecasting: the normal distribution is used to analyze customer demand

Hypothesis Tests

Hypothesis testing starts with a statement describing some aspect of a population. Then we examine a sample (or samples) from the population to see if there is evidence to support the hypothesis. In this section, we will assume that our sample size is at least thirty, so that the Normal distribution can be applied with confidence. This would be the case for example, if we had collected a batch of completed questionnaires with answers relating to quantitative data, such as money spent (£), frequency of visits, time spent (minutes), age of respondent (years) and so on.

General procedure for hypothesis testing

- **State the null and alternative hypotheses,**
- **Specify the significance level (usually 5%),**
- **Calculate the acceptance range for the variable tested,**
- **Find the actual value for the variable tested,**
- **Decide whether or not to reject the null hypothesis,**
- **State the conclusion.**

Tests about the mean – one population

Now we can use an important result in statistics that, when we take large random samples from a population, the means of the samples are normally distributed with mean µ (the same mean as the population) and standard error) $\sigma/\sqrt{n}$.

For a given value **µ₀** , two hypotheses we usually test are **H₀** and **H₁** :

$$H_0 : \mu = \mu_0 \text{ (usually called the null hypothesis)}$$
$$H_1 : \mu \neq \mu_0 \text{ (usually called the alternative hypothesis),}$$

Then we normally either accept the null hypothesis or reject it and accept the alternative. We assume a 5% significance level.

Suppose we have a population of shop-floor employee salaries in a large supermarket firm, which are assumed by the company to be normally distributed with mean £10,000 and standard deviation £1,800. In the course of a questionnaire distributed to employees, we have collected primary data and recorded the salaries of a thirty six employees. If the mean of our sample is £10,700, do we accept the company's assumption of a £10,000 mean (or not)?

Here, we can test the hypotheses:
$$H_0 : \mu = £10,000$$
$$H_1: \mu \neq £10,000$$

The mean is normally distributed with mean £10,000; standard error $1800/\sqrt{36}$ = £300.

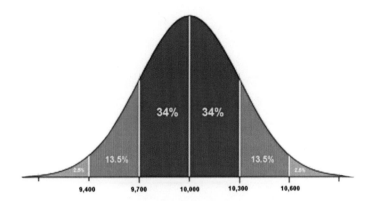

Since 95% of the samples means should lie within £9,400 and £10,600, the probability of taking a sample with mean £10,700 would be less than 5%. In other words, the sample mean of £10,700 is significantly different from the population mean and we reject H_0, so accept H_1.

In practice, we usually assume calculations at 95% (in which case we talk about a 5% significance level) or to 99% (i.e. a 1% significance level).

Example

Donald Duque owns a small stationery business in France and Donald believes that the mean value of orders received by his firm is about €250. Since he receives hundreds of orders each month there is insufficient time to check every one. He decides on a strategy of randomly selecting a sample of 50 accounts and finds a sample mean of €241 and sample standard deviation of €42. Does this evidence support his belief?

Solution

The null hypothesis is that the mean value of accounts is €250, and the alternative hypothesis is
that the mean is not €250 (it could be larger or smaller).

$$H_0 : \mu = €250$$
$$H_1 : \mu \neq €250$$

Assume a 5% significance level. We do not know the population standard deviation, but can estimate it from the sample standard deviation s = €42. Since the sample is large enough (greater than thirty) this is reasonable.

Hence, standard error = $\frac{s}{\sqrt{n}} = \frac{42}{\sqrt{50}} = \frac{42}{7.07} = 5.94$ (to 2 d.p.) = 6 (to 1 s.f.)

So we can reasonably expect that 95% of randomly-sampled means would lie within the interval (238,262).

Since Donald's value of 241 does indeed lie in this interval, accept $H_0 : \mu = €250$.

Conclusion: The mean value of orders received by the firm is indeed about €250.

In a Standard Normal distribution N(0,1) where the mean is 0 and the variance is 1, the critical value for which 5% of the area lies to the left is -1.65 (instead of the two-tailed critical value of -2.0). In figure 7.4, we can see that in a so-called 'one-tailed test' we would look to see if our test statistic lies to the right of -1.65 (in which case accept H_0) or lies to the left (in which case accept H_1).

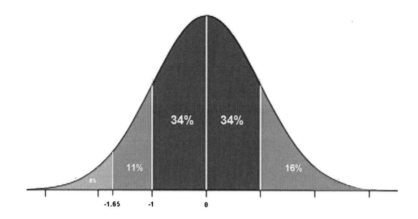

<u>Figure 8.4</u>   In a standard Normal distribution, for a one-tailed test we see that 95% of the area lies to the right of z = -1.65, so by implication 5% lies to the left, i.e. in the tail.

Hence in the previous example, where we accepted H_0 in a two-tailed test, we can rework the hypothesis test but this time as one-tailed:

$$H_0 : \mu = €250$$
$$H_1 : \mu < €250$$

The critical value in which we are interested is 1.65 standard errors to the left of the mean 250, i.e. $250 - 1.65.(6) = 250 - 9.9 = 240.1$ and the simple question is whether our sample statistic (241) lies to the left (in which case reject H_0) or to the right (in which case accept H_0).

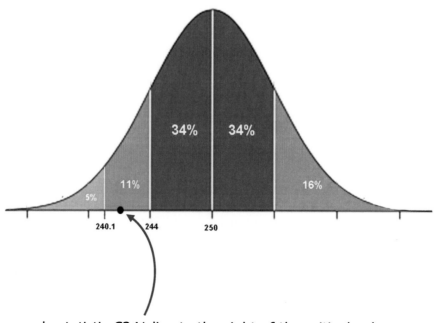

In fact, since the sample statistic €241 lies to the right of the critical value, so accept H_0.

Example

Scenario: Suppose that you have decided to embark upon a research project about the amount spent by customers in a particular age group on video games at a large Oxford Street Games Store. Secondary data prepared by the Store's marketing department (based upon the past five year's sales for this age group) indicate an average spending per customer of £49.50.

To gauge this year's spending you have decided to collect primary data in the form of one hundred well-designed questionnaires distributed randomly in the Store's coffee shop. Fifty five of those questionnaires were filled out by the particular age group of concern.

Your sample statistics for the fifty five questionnaires calculated the mean spending to be £50.68, with a standard deviation of £3.37, so you have decided to carry out two hypothesis tests (both at 5% significance level), where μ is the mean spending on video games:

  (i) two-tailed test

$$H_0 : \mu = £49.50$$
$$H_1 : \mu \neq £49.50$$

  (ii) one-tailed test

$$H_0 : \mu = £49.50$$
$$H_1 : \mu > £49.50$$

Show the results of your tests and what you would suggest to the Store based on this year's data.

Solution

The standard error $= \dfrac{3.37}{\sqrt{55}} = \dfrac{3.372}{\sqrt{55}} = 0.45$ (to 2 d.p.)

  (i) For the two-tailed test, we can reasonably expect that 95% of randomly-sampled means lie within twice the standard error, i.e. between the values 49.5 ± 0.9 which corresponds to an interval (48.6, 50.40). Clearly, £50.68 lies outside this interval and so we accept H_1 (and reject H_0).
  (ii) For the one-tailed test, we have a critical value $= 49.50 + 1.65.(0.45) = £50.24$. Clearly, £50.68 is more than £50.24. Accept H_1.

Therefore, both tests suggest we accept the alternatives H_1.

Recommendation to the Store: The average spending for this age group this year is significantly more than previous years.

Note: If we were able to extract individual year data from those five years provided by the marketing department, we could try to:

  • test for correlation between Spending (£) and Time (years)
  • model Spending (£) against Time (years) in a scatter diagram and regression line
  • predict next year's spending by extrapolation

Tests about the means – two populations

Managers sometimes want to compare two populations, to see if there are significant differences. For example, a manager of two retail shops might want to know whether each has the similar profitability (or not), or an advertising manager might want to check sales data before and after an extensive advertising campaign. We can use hypothesis testing to see if the means of two populations are the same.

For this we take a sample from each population, and if the sample means are close we can assume that the population means are the same, but if there is a significant difference in the sample means we have to assume that the population means are different. So the procedure is to take the means of two samples, $\bar{x}_1$ and $\bar{x}_2$ respectively, and find the difference $(\bar{x}_1 - \bar{x}_2)$. Then we use a standard result (which will not be proved here) that for large samples, the sampling distribution of $(\bar{x}_1 - \bar{x}_2)$ is normal with

$$\text{mean} = 0$$

$$\text{standard error} = \sqrt{\left(\frac{s_1{}^2}{n_1}\right) + \left(\frac{s_2{}^2}{n_2}\right)}$$

where: n_1 = sample size from population 1
n_2 = sample size from population 2
s_1 = standard deviation of sample 1
s_2 = standard deviation of sample 2.

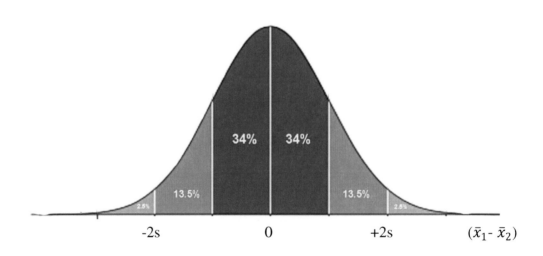

As observed previously, 95% of our $(\bar{x}_1 - \bar{x}_2)$ values will lie in the interval $(-2s, +2s)$

Example

Cheapaschips owns two retail shops offering discounted computer hardware products. Both shops have been running for several months and *Cheapaschips'* owner now wants to compare performance and profitability. A sample of 40 net daily takings from the first shop has a mean £77 and a standard deviation of £20. A sample of 40 net daily takings from the second shop has a mean of £90 and a standard deviation of £40. Are the shops net takings comparable or different?

Solution

The null hypothesis is that the mean values for each shop are the same. The alternative hypothesis is that they are not the same.

$$H_0 : \mu_1 = \mu_2$$
$$H_1 : \mu_1 \neq \mu_2$$

Our sample values are $n_1 = 40$; $n_2 = 40$; $s_1 = 20$; $s_2 = 40$

Hence, standard error s = $\sqrt{\left(\frac{20^2}{40}\right) + \left(\frac{40^2}{40}\right)}$ = $\sqrt{10 + 40}$ = $\sqrt{50}$ = 7 (to 1 s.f.)

So we now know that 95% of our $(\bar{x}_1 - \bar{x}_2)$ values should lie within the interval (-14, +14).

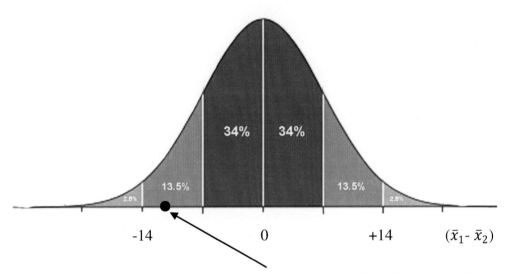

Since the actual value is $(\bar{x}_1 - \bar{x}_2)$ = £77 - £90 = -£13 and lies within the interval (-14, +14), we accept **H₀**.

Conclusion. The mean takings for each shop are comparable.

(Note that any value for $(\bar{x}_1 - \bar{x}_2)$ between -14 and +14 would have resulted in accepting **H₀** and any value for $(\bar{x}_1 - \bar{x}_2)$ outside -14 and +14 would have resulted in accepting **H₁**)

Working from a null and alternative hypothesis, two basic forms of **error** are recognized:

- Type I errors where the null hypothesis is falsely rejected giving a "false positive".
- Type II errors where the null hypothesis fails to be rejected and an actual difference between populations is missed giving a *false negative*.

After all, doctors cannot always diagnose a patient's illness perfectly in just the same way that business executives cannot always spot 'talent' at an interview.

Case Studies – Analysing Business Data & Information

Case Study: The Bakery

This large case study comprises three cases related to *The Bakery*.

The first case deals with descriptive statistics where students are asked to create different types of tables and graphs, calculate numerical measures for grouped and ungrouped data, discuss the type of relationship between two variables, and to provide observations and recommendations.

The second case focuses on the binomial, the Poisson, and normal probability distributions.

Finally, the third case focuses on statistical inference where students are asked to construct confidence intervals, run different types of hypothesis tests, and to provide observations and recommendations.

For more information, refer to the full case studies.

Questions for Discussion:

1. Complete answers to questions on pages 417/418 of the full case study.
2. Complete answers to questions on pages 418/419 of the full case study.
3. Complete answers to questions on page 420 of the full case study.

Exercises – Analysing Business Data & Information

1. {multiple choice – choose the most appropriate answer (a), (b), (c) or (d)}

Suppose that a business researcher has found good correlation between two variables (x,y) and a regression line of
$$y = 0.8016\,x - 13.5772.$$

Based on this linear model, what value of y (to one decimal place) can the researcher expect for a value x = 17.

    (a) 0   (b) 0.5   (c) 0.1   (d) 0.2

2. {multiple choice – choose the most appropriate answer (a), (b), (c) or (d)}

The average number of calls received by an international call centre for a well-known insurance company is one call per minute. Assuming a Poisson distribution, what is the percentage probability that in a randomly selected minute of the working day, more than one call will be received?

    (a) 1%   (b) 26%   (c) 74%   (d) 99%

3. {multiple choice – choose the most appropriate answer (a), (b), (c) or (d)}

In a Binomial experiment of n trials where p is the probability of success, the probability of n successes is p^n. The probability of n failures is therefore

    (a) $1 - p^n$ (b) $(1 - p)^n$ (c) $(1 - np)$ (d) p^n

4. {multiple choice – choose the most appropriate answer (a), (b), (c) or (d)}

Which of the following random variables would you most expect to be <u>normally</u> distributed?

    (a)   The number of times a die is rolled before a six is observed
    (b)   The number of accidents that occur at a busy road junction
    (c)   The number of people in the queue waiting to be served at a bank
    (d)   The weight of a box of cereal selected from a production line.

5. {multiple choice – choose the most appropriate answer (a), (b), (c) or (d)}

Which one of the following probabilities is represented by the shaded area in the figure below?

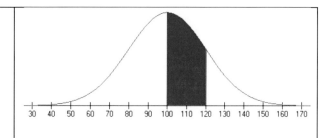

(a) Pr (Z > 120)
(b) 0.5 – Pr (Z > 120)
(c) Pr (Z < 120)
(d) Pr (Z < 120) + 0.5.

6. Binomial distribution. According to *Financial Executive* (July/August 1993), disability causes 48% of all mortgage repossessions. Given that twenty mortgage repossessions are (randomly) audited in a given year by a large lending institution, what is the probability (calculated to 3 d.p.) that less than <u>eight</u> of these are due to a disability?

7. Binomial distribution. A tree planting landscaping business knows from experience that a large proportion of newly-planted trees survive. So they work on the supposition that ninety percent of the trees planted will probably survive and make one return visit a year later to replace the ten percent which probably will not. What is the probability (to 3 d.p.) that of the next ten trees planted?

    (i)   exactly nine trees will survive
    (ii)   at most eight will survive
    (iii) exactly ten will survive.

8. Binomial distribution. A machine produces parts of which 0.5% is defective. If a random sample of thirty parts produced by this machine contains more than one defective part, the machine is shut down for repairs. Find the percentage probability that the machine will be shut down for repairs based on this sampling plan.

9. Binomial distribution. Suppose that you take a twenty-five question multiple-choice test by guessing. Each question has possible answers a, b, c, d and only one is correct. Each correction question is worth 4 marks. Assume each incorrect answer to be worth zero marks.
    In order to PASS the test, at least ten correct questions worth a total of 40 marks are required.
    What is the probability that you will pass the test?

10. Poisson distribution. The number of bankruptcies filed in a month in a small town is recorded and the average calculated per day. Bankruptcies are dated according to the day and date of process. In the past two months (assume thirty one days in each) there were 15 and 16 bankruptcies, respectively. Based on this information, estimate the percentage probability that in a given day chosen randomly, there will be no bankruptcies filed.

11. Poisson distribution. The number of network failures per day in a company's network is logged by the IT Department. The estimated average number of failures is calculated and updated daily and as a policy, the IT Department will overhaul the network operating system if the probability of two or more failures on a given day exceeds five per cent. Today's estimated average has increased to 0.40. Should IT overhaul the network operating system today?

12. Poisson distribution. The number of customers complaining daily about service at a large fashion store is recorded by the Quality Assurance Department. On average, two customers complain per day. What is the probability that two customers will complain today?

13. <u>Normal distribution.</u> A large group of university undergraduate students took a test in Business Management and the final grades had a mean of 60 and a standard deviation of 10. If we assume that we can approximate the distribution of these grades by a normal distribution, what percent of the students:

      (i)   Achieved a first-class honours grade (grade ≥ 70)?
      (ii)   achieved a second class upper grade (60 ≤ grade < 70)?
      (iii) failed the test (grade < 40)?

14. <u>Poisson distribution.</u> The purchasing preferences of visitors to an e-commerce web site are stored in encrypted 'digital profiles'. One customer's anonymised decrypted profile shows the following information for the past nine days:-

Customer ID	Purchases Day 01	Purchases Day 02	Purchases Day 03	Purchases Day 04	Purchases Day 05	Purchases Day 06	Purchases Day 07	Purchases Day 08
0133	2	0	1	0	2	2	1	2

Based on this information, calculate the mean number of purchases for this customer and estimate the percentage probability that the customer will make three (or more) purchases on day in the near future chosen randomly.

15. <u>Normal distribution.</u> The annual salaries of employees in a large company are approximately normally distributed with a mean of $50,000 and a standard deviation of $20,000.

      (i)   What percent of people earn less than $40,000?
      (ii)   What percent of people earn between $45,000 and $65,000?
      (iii) What percent of people earn more than $70,000?

16. <u>Normal distribution.</u> A large group of executive MBA students took a test in Marketing Management and the final grades had a mean of 70 and a standard deviation of 10. If we can approximate the distribution of these grades by a normal distribution, what percent of the students

      (i)   Achieved a 'distinction' by scoring higher than 80?
      (ii)   Should 'pass' the test with grades ≥ 60?
      (iii) Should 'fail' the test with grades < 60?

17. <u>Hypothesis Test (one population).</u> The manager of a small stationery business in Germany believes that the mean value of orders received by the firm is about €250. Since she receives hundreds of orders each month there is insufficient time to check every one. She decides on a strategy of randomly selecting a sample of fifty accounts and finds a sample mean of €257 and sample standard deviation of €42. Does this evidence support her belief?

18.   <u>Hypothesis Test (one population).</u> Suppose that you have decided to embark upon a research project about the amount spent by customers in a particular age group on video games at a large Oxford Street Games Store. Secondary data prepared by the Store's marketing department (based upon the past five year's sales for this age group) indicate an average spending per customer of £49.50.

To gauge this year's spending you have decided to collect primary data in the form of one hundred well-designed questionnaires distributed randomly in the Store's coffee shop. Fifty five of those questionnaires were filled out by the particular age group of concern.Your sample statistics for the fifty five questionnaires calculated the mean spending to be £50.40 with a standard deviation of £3.37, so you have decided to carry out a one-tailed hypothesis test (at 5% significance level), where μ is the mean spending on video games:

$$H_0 : \mu = £49.50$$
$$H_1 : \mu > £49.50$$

Show the results of your tests and what you would suggest to the Games Store based on this year's data.

19.   <u>Hypothesis Test (two populations).</u> *Eco-fone* owns two retail shops offering discounted mobile phones and accessories. Both shops have been running for several months and *Eco-fone's* owner now wants to compare the net taking from both shops. A sample of 40 net daily takings from the first shop has a mean £77 and a standard deviation of £20. A sample of 40 net daily takings from the second shop has a mean of £90 and a standard deviation of £40. Are the two shops net takings the same?

20.   <u>Hypothesis Test (two populations).</u> *Pecan Peanut* makes packets of nuts in its factory in Delhi and uses two machines to fill the packets. A sample of 30 packets from the first machine has a mean weight of 180 g and a standard deviation of 40 g. A sample of 40 packets from the second machine has a mean weight of 170 g and a standard deviation of 10 g. State the six point procedure for hypothesis testing and test if the two machines are comparable in terms of putting the same amount in packets?

10. FINANCIAL DATA

Financial data provides the fundamental building blocks for sound business analysis and decisions. Financial data might be used by management, investors and regulators in analysing a company or by individuals managing household budgets and savings.

People and organisations outside of a business will also use financial data reported by the business to judge its credit worthiness, decide whether to invest in the business and determine whether the business is complying with government regulations.

Business finance questions include:

- Can we afford to have discounts for certain customers?
- How can we discover what our customers want?
- How do we cost our products?
- How do we forecast sales?
- How is a payroll constructed?
- How much should we spend on R&D?
- What do we charge our customers in order to make a profit?
- What does a good invoice look like?
- What information is needed in a good business plan?
- What is VAT and how does it work in business?

Personal finance questions include:

- Which is my best bank account?
- Where will I achieve the best savings rate?
- Will changing interest rates affect my mortgage?
- Should I be considering a short-term personal loan?
- Why are my gas/electricity bills so confusing?
- Why is so much of my salary deducted each month?
- How much should I pay into a private pension?
- How much will it cost to send my children to university?

To obtain good answers to the above questions requires good financial data resources in order to make informed decisions. Of course, there will no doubt be many financial 'advisors' ready and willing to help but it is important to think carefully about such advice. Over the past years, we have seen advisors recommending financial products which are now generally accepted as tainted. These include:

- Endowment policies which would never be able to pay off the capital of a mortgage
- PPI financial products which would later be discredited
- Stock market 'sure things' which would eventually be worthless (e.g. dot com companies)

In the following sections, we consider financial statements, financial data management, financial data vendors and financial functions in Excel.

Personal Finance

Personal finance is the financial management which an individual or a family unit performs to budget, save, and spend monetary resources over time, taking into account various financial risks and future life events. When planning personal finances, the individual would consider the suitability to his or her needs of a range of banking products (checking, savings accounts, credit cards and consumer loans) or investment in private equity (stock market, bonds, mutual funds) and insurance (life insurance, health insurance, disability insurance) products or participation and monitoring of individual or employer sponsored retirement plans and income tax management. Maintaining a monthly budget spreadsheet is a good way to manage personal finances.

A key component of personal finance is financial planning, which is a dynamic process that requires regular monitoring and re-evaluation. In general, it involves five steps of assessment, goal setting, plan creation, execution and monitoring/reassessment.

Assessment: A person's financial situation is assessed by compiling simplified versions of financial statements including balance sheets and income statements. A personal balance sheet lists the values of personal assets (e.g. car, house, clothes, stocks, bank account), along with personal liabilities (e.g. credit card debt, bank loan, mortgage).

Goal setting: Having multiple goals is common, including a mix of short-term and long-term goals. For example, a long-term goal might be to 'retire at age 65 with a personal net worth of £1m' while a short-term goal might be to "save for a new car next year." Setting financial goals helps us to direct financial planning. Goal setting is carried out with an objective to meet specific financial requirements.

Plan creation: The financial plan details how to accomplish our personal financial goals. It could include, for example, reducing unnecessary expenses, increasing the employment income or investing in the stock market.

Execution: Execution of a financial plan often requires discipline and perseverance. Many people obtain assistance from professionals such as accountants, financial planners, investment advisers and lawyers.

Monitoring and reassessment: As time passes, any financial plan needs to be monitored for possible adjustments or reassessments. Typical goals that most of us might have can vary significantly over time (e.g. paying off credit cards, mortgage payments with variable interest rates etc.). Keeping a close eye on the detail can enable us to make manageable changes to keep on track.

Business Financial Statements

A set of business financial statements is comprised of several key statements usually contained in a balance sheet. These are *assets*, *liabilities* and *equity*.

Assets

An asset is an item that the business owns, with the expectation that it will yield future financial benefit. This benefit may be achieved through enhanced purchasing power (i.e. decreased expenses), revenue generation or cash receipts.

Current assets are those assets that we expect to either convert to cash or to use within one year, or one operating cycle (whichever is longer). Examples of current assets include cash, accounts receivable and inventory (e.g. raw materials, work in progress, finished goods).

Long-term assets are those that we use in the operation of the business and that will continue to offer benefit beyond a single year or operating cycle. Examples of long-term assets include buildings, machinery and equipment (also known as fixed or capital assets). Many long-term assets are gradually written off over time (amortised) as they are used. Assets can also be intangible, such as trade secrets, industry know-how, patents or copyrights. Intangible assets are expected to produce value simply through the rights and privileges conferred by owning them. Generally Accepted Accounting Principles (GAAP) often requires that assets be recorded based on certain criteria.

Assets are generally defined as items that:

- are controlled by the corporation
- are the result of a past transaction
- will result in a future benefit to the corporation

This definition is fairly intuitive and usually agrees with a company's internal analysis of their assets. However, a company's analysis and GAAP may differ over the values. This is particularly true for intangible assets and assets that are developed internally. GAAP requires assets to be valued using a specific method (which may be cost or fair market value).

Additionally, accounting is traditionally conservative. As a result, items are often required to be declared as expenses if certain criteria cannot be met that prove there will likely be a future benefit to the corporation. Notes to the financial statements can be very helpful in understanding the values that have been given to an asset and why it might differ from your expected valuation.

Liabilities

A complement to assets is liabilities. Liabilities are amounts that the company owes and will have to settle in the future. Current liabilities are those that are expected to be settled within one year, or one operating cycle (whichever is longer). Examples of current liabilities include accounts payable, demand loans and current portions of long-term liabilities. Current liabilities are often compared to current assets as a measure of liquidity. Long-term liabilities include ongoing commitments such as loans, mortgages, debentures, finance leases and other long-term financing arrangements.

Liabilities are generally defined as items that:

- are a present obligation of the corporation
- are the result of a past transaction
- will result in a future cost to the corporation

Like assets, many liabilities are intuitive. However, there may be some instances where a liability needs to be recorded, although the company may not have perceived it as one. An example of this would be finance leasing where there is no present obligation to pay the future lease payments. However, because we have essentially agreed to take on substantially all of the benefits of ownership of the asset, GAAP requires us to record a liability. Another example is where preferred shares may essentially have the qualities of debt financing and must be recorded, at least in part, as a long-term liability rather than as equity.

As with assets, there will be some instances where the valuation may also vary from what we expect.

Equity

Equity is made up of two main components: equity instruments and retained earnings. Equity instruments include capital stock, which is the amount that has been received in relation to the business' sale of shares. Other equity instruments include options or warrants. Contributed surplus is also recorded in the equity portion of the balance sheet for earnings that are not profits.

Some of the key types of financial data that are of the most importance to internal management and outside stakeholders include everything that a business owns and also all personal property, real property, intangible and tangible property. Real property is real estate and anything that is attached to it. Personal property is any property that is not real property. Tangible property is any physical property such as equipment, furniture, tools, or inventory. Intangible property is non-physical property such as a patent or goodwill.

Financial data management

Financial data management (FDM) is a process and policy, usually assisted by specialised software, which allows a business or institution to consolidate its financial information, maintain compliance with accounting rules/laws and produce detailed financial reports.

For a corporation or other large entity, the term 'financial data' refers to information on performance in terms of income, expenses, and profits, usually over the course of a full fiscal year. For an individual or small business, the term 'financial data' refers to bank account information, debts, assets and credit ratings.

A well-designed FDM program can help an organisation to develop and maintain its own set of accounting procedures, streamline its internal workflow processes to minimise overhead and expense while maximising efficiency and profit, consolidate data from among various departments and generate custom financial reports and documents for a diverse set of suppliers and clients.

Financial data vendors

A financial data vendor provides market data to financial firms, traders and investors. The data distributed is collected from sources such as stock exchange feeds, brokers and dealer desks or regulatory filings. Financial data vendors have been in existence as long as financial data has been available. Financial data includes 'pre-trade' data such as bid/ask data necessary to price a financial instrument and post-trade data such as the last trade price and other transaction data.

Because of the financial investment needed to provide data services, the industry has become increasingly consolidated.

There are many different types of instruments (including stocks, bonds, funds, options, futures and currencies) and hundreds of different markets for investment, leading to an extremely large and hard to define universe of data. The types of data offered vary by vendor and most typically cover information about entities (companies) and instruments (shares and bonds) which companies might issue.

Typically, pricing data is sold separately from other related data, such as corporate actions and events, valuation information, fundamental data including company performance and reference data on the entities and instruments themselves.

In addition to market price data, there are data known as market reference data, such as a ticker name, which describe securities, commodities and transactions.

Many vendors began as local companies, serving their own local markets. However, through merger and acquisition and in response to the increasing globalisation of world markets, vendors now describe themselves as global. The industry is largely a hidden one - both to the general public and even to some extent to its users. To begin to overcome this in 2010, *The Software and Information Industry Association* introduced Professional Certification Qualification through its Financial Services Division. Most vendors have passed the examination required to receive certification.

A list of well known financial data vendors includes:

- Bloomberg L.P.
- Cbonds
- CQG
- Dealogic
- FactSet
- Fidessa
- Fitch Finance
- I-Net Bridge
- Interactive Data Corporation
- Markit
- Mergermarket
- Money.Net
- Moody's Analytics
- Morningstar, Inc.
- NYSE Technologies
- Preqin
- Quandl
- S&P Capital IQ
- SIX Financial Information
- SunGard
- Symphony Communication
- Thomson Reuters
- Xignite

Financial functions in Excel

Businesses and individuals processing financial data usually do so in Excel or some equivalent spreadsheet package, using standard financial functions. For example, to calculate the accrued interest for a security that pays a periodic interest, we use the ACCRINT function. This function and other financial functions are shown in figure 9.1. More functions are given in the appendix.

Function	Description
ACCRINT	Returns the accrued interest for a security that pays periodic interest
COUPDAYS	Returns the number of days in the coupon period that contains the settlement date
CUMPRINC	Returns the cumulative principal paid on a loan between two periods
DB	Returns the depreciation of an asset for a specified period using the fixed–declining balance method
DISC	Returns the discount rate for a security
DURATION	Returns the annual duration of a security with periodic interest payments
EFFECT	Returns the effective annual interest rate
FV	Returns the future value of an investment
FVSCHEDULE	Returns the future value of an initial principal after applying a series of compound interest rates
INTRATE	Returns the interest rate for a fully invested security
IPMT	Returns the interest payment for an investment for a given period
IRR	Returns the internal rate of return for a series of cash flows
ISPMT	Calculates the interest paid during a specific period of an investment
MDURATION	Returns the MacAulay modified duration for a security with an assumed par value of $100
MIRR	Returns the internal rate of return where positive and negative cash flows are financed at different rates
NOMINAL	Returns the annual nominal interest rate
NPER	Returns the number of periods for an investment
NPV	Returns the net present value of an investment based on a series of periodic cash flows & discount rate
XIRR	Returns the internal rate of return for a schedule of cash flows that is not necessarily periodic
XNPV	Returns the net present value for a schedule of cash flows that is not necessarily periodic
YIELD	Returns the yield on a security that pays periodic interest
YIELDDISC	Returns the annual yield for a discounted security; for example, a Treasury bill
YIELDMAT	Returns the annual yield of a security that pays interest at maturity

Figure 10.1 A selection of financial functions in Excel (see Appendix A for more functions).

Example – the ACCRINT function

The following spreadsheet shows an example of the Excel ACCRINT function, used to calculate the accrued interest of a security that pays periodic interest. The security's issue date is 01-Jan-2012, the first interest date is 01-Apr-2012, the settlement date is 31-Dec-2013 and the annual coupon rate is 8%. The security's par value is $10,000, payments are made quarterly, and a US (NASD) 30/360 day count basis is used.

	A	B	C	D
				Accrued interest on a security with an issue date of 01-Jan-2012, a first interest date of 01-Apr-2012 and a settlement date of 31-Dec-2013. The annual coupon rate is 8%, the par value of the security is $10,000 and payments are made
1	issue date:	01-Jan-2012		quarterly, on a US (NASD) 30 / 360 basis:
2	first interest date:	01-Apr-2012		=ACCRINT(B1, B2, B3, 8%, 10000, 4)
3	settlement date:	31-Dec-2013		

Figure 10.2 A selection of financial functions in Excel (see the appendix for more functions).

The above function gives the result $1,600.

Big Data

Big data is a term for data sets that are so large or complex that traditional data processing applications are inadequate. Challenges include analysing, capturing, searching, sharing, storing, transferring, visualising, querying and updating. The term often refers simply to the use of predictive analytics or certain other advanced data analytics methods that extract value from data, and seldom to a particular size of data set. Accuracy in big data may lead to more confident decision making, and better decisions can result in greater operational efficiency, cost reduction and reduced risk.

Analysis of data sets can find new correlations to spot business trends, prevent diseases, combat crime and so on. Business executives and practitioners of advertising regularly meet difficulties with large data sets in areas including Internet search, finance and business informatics.

Data sets are growing rapidly in part because they are increasingly gathered by cheap and numerous information-sensing mobile devices, aerial (remote sensing), software logs, cameras, microphones, radio-frequency identification (RFID) readers and wireless sensor networks. The world's technological per-capita capacity to store information has roughly doubled every 40 months since the 1980s. It has been estimated that every day three Exabytes (3×10^{18}) units of data are created. One question for large enterprises is determining who should own big data initiatives that affect the entire organisation.

Relational database management systems and desktop statistics and visualisation packages often have difficulty handling big data. The work instead requires massively parallel software running on tens, hundreds, or even thousands of servers. What is considered big data varies depending on the capabilities of the users and their tools. Expanding capabilities make big data a moving target.

Case Studies – Financial Data

Case Study: Intelligent Finance: Leading a Revolution in Banking

Changes in society, markets and economies has intensified the need for most organisations to be more and more innovative with the products that they offer, in order to attract new customers and increase product holdings. New products and services can provide the mechanisms through which further market growth can be achieved. Increasing competition, which often stems from new products and services, means that innovation in new product development is no longer an option but a necessity.

In today's technology-driven, modern world, most organisations operate in highly competitive markets; this is particularly true of the financial services sector. Technology has been one of the key drivers of change within this market and most retail banks now offer on-line banking services. Until recently, most banks operated from the traditional high street branches, offering very similar products and services to their customers. A product can be defined as anything that can be offered for sale, this could be something tangible that can be owned or it may be a service that is performed for the buyer. Most products contain both a tangible and a service element. If an organisation identifies a group of customers who require a combination of either goods and or services which is not currently offered, it will have discovered a 'gap' in the market.

This case study examines how technology has enabled Intelligent Finance to revolutionise banking, by creating not just a new bank but a totally new way of banking. Intelligent Finance's objective is to be the consumer's champion by placing the needs of customers at the heart of its marketing activity

For more information, refer to the full case study.

Questions for Discussion:

1. Carry out market research amongst a small sample (five) of other students to find out what they see as being essential features of a banking service.
2. What makes the banking industry so competitive?
3. Carry out an analysis on a product or service of your choice. Try to identify by using a product positioning framework, if there is a gap in the market.
4. How has the development of Intelligent Finance impacted on the personal banking market?
5. Why is it so important for Intelligent Finance to build its brand?

Case Study: *Saving for the future: Don't leave it too late!*

Issues relating to personal finance appear both in the national news and in academic journals. The monthly announcement of the Bank of England base rates, consumer debt, house repossessions and pensions regularly hit the headlines.

One of the most important financial decisions facing young adults is planning for the future. Yet research conducted by Aegon UK, a provider of life insurance and pension products found that about ten million people in the United Kingdom have no long-term savings plan or provision for a pension.

In a textbook, you will find the saving ratio defined as the proportion of disposable income that is not consumed. If you delve into national accounts, you will find that the saving ratio is calculated as the proportion of household resources not consumed.

There is a 'reality gap' between what people expect later in life and what they are actually saving for. Of course, part of the reason for the 'reality gap' is that the future is exactly that, the future! However, it is probably true that many people are unable to perform basic financial calculations. Yet, it is possible to do the relevant calculations using an inexpensive scientific calculator in seconds. If one uses basic numerical properties, it is a relatively easy task to make informed financial decisions. This is the objective of this paper.

For more information, refer to the full case study.

Questions for Discussion:

Assume an individual saves £500 per year continuously for 30 years at an interest rate of 7.5%.

1. What is the final value of the plan?
2. How much must the individual save each year in an equivalent plan of 20 years so that it has the same final value?
3. Compare the total payments made in the 30 and 20 year plans.

Exercises – Financial Data

1. {multiple choice – choose the most appropriate answer (a), (b), (c) or (d)}

A set of business financial statements is comprised of several key statements usually contained in a balance sheet. These are *assets*, *liabilities* and ...

   (a) equity   (b) equality   (c) egalite   (d) equary

2. {multiple choice – choose the most appropriate answer (a), (b), (c) or (d)}

A process and policy, usually assisted by specialised software, which allows a business or institution to consolidate its financial information, maintain compliance with accounting rules/laws and produce detailed financial reports, is described by the acronym:

   (a) ATM   (b) FTE   (c) FDM   (d) BBC

3. {multiple choice – choose the most appropriate answer (a), (b), (c) or (d)}

Which of the following is NOT a well known financial data vendor?

   (a) Bloomberg   (b) Moody's   (c) S&P Capital   (d) Skysports

4. {multiple choice – choose the most appropriate answer (a), (b), (c) or (d)}

Which Excel function returns the net present value of an investment based on a series of periodic cash flows & discount rate?

   (a) MVP   (b) NPV   (c) PVI   (d) VAL

5. {multiple choice – choose the most appropriate answer (a), (b), (c) or (d)}

Maintaining which one of the following is a good way to manage personal finances?

     (a)   Daily Sense of Humour Review
     (b)   Weekly Optimism Assessment
     (c)   Monthly Budget Preparation
     (d)   Annual Suspension of Disbelief

6.   <u>Financial Functions.</u> Consider the ACCRINT function calculation for a security with the following parameters:

- The security's issue date is 01-Jan-2012,
- The first interest date is 01-Apr-2012,
- The settlement date is 31-Dec-2013
- The annual coupon rate is 7%.
- The security's par value is $150,000,
- Payments are made quarterly,
- A US (NASD) 30/360 day count basis is used.

What is the ACCRINT value with these parameters?

7.   <u>Personal Budget.</u> Create your own Excel version of the personal budget sheet shown below and enter your own estimates for each cell. Does your income exceed your outgoings?

Income (weekly/monthly)

Wages/salary	£	
Wages/salary (partner)	£	
Benefits	£	
Money from other people	£	
Other	£	
	£	
Total income	£	

Outgoings (weekly/monthly)

Mortgage/rent	£	
Second mortgage/secured loan	£	
Ground rent/service charges	£	
Buildings/contents insurance	£	
Life insurance/endowment	£	
Council tax	£	
Gas	£	
Electricity	£	
Water	£	
Food/housekeeping	£	
Travel	£	
Telephone	£	
TV licence/rental	£	
Clothing/emergencies	£	
Prescriptions/health costs	£	
Other	£	
Total outgoings	£	

My total income is £ ....

My total outgoings are £....................

8.   <u>Mortgages.</u> Most of us don't have hundreds of thousands of pounds in savings. So to make a large purchase, such as a home, we need a mortgage. When choosing a mortgage, we don't just focus on the interest rate and fees that are charged. We also consider what type of mortgage we want.

There are two main types:

- Fixed rate – the interest charged stays the same for a number of years, typically between two to five years
- Variable rate – the interest charged can change at any time and the Standard variable rate (SVR) changes after a rise or fall in the base rate set by the Bank of England.

Research some of the advantages and disadvantages of the two types.

9.   <u>Business Plans.</u> The website www.bplans.co.uk offers several sample business plans to use as a starting point for preparing your own business plan (see a typical list selection below).

- Airline and Aviation (7 free plans)
- Bar and Nightclub (11 free plans)
- Beauty Salon and Day Spa (10 free plans)
- Bed and Breakfast and Hotel (10 free plans)
- Car Wash and Automotive (29 free plans)
- Coffee Shop and Internet Cafe (8 free plans)

(i) Choose any one business plan to analyse the various types of data contained in the *executive summary, objectives* and *mission* .

(ii) Create your own business plan *executive summary, objectives* and *mission* for an original idea of your own.

10.   <u>Wordsearch.</u>

Financial Data

```
B  J  A  J  S  H  S  L  Q  F  F  K  S  Q  K  V  F  H  F  R  L  D  P
G  F  S  Q  O  Q  S  J  V  M  I  R  O  T  F  A  H  L  X  D  V  K  E
L  B  S  G  X  Z  F  X  W  N  Q  L  A  I  C  N  A  N  I  F  G  W  N
I  A  E  A  S  Q  P  J  F  V  G  D  B  V  K  M  T  S  B  A  T  D  S
M  L  S  I  K  S  T  N  E  M  T  S  E  V  N  I  L  E  Z  S  K  O  I
M  A  S  Y  O  M  I  M  C  T  K  M  U  G  O  A  L  I  L  G  M  Y  O
T  N  M  X  J  Z  O  B  F  Y  T  Y  R  C  K  F  Y  T  D  N  L  H  N
E  C  E  D  Q  T  V  N  S  I  F  Y  T  D  S  P  T  I  M  I  N  D  S
G  E  N  L  M  Z  G  O  I  L  R  T  C  Z  T  E  I  L  E  V  E  K  A
D  U  T  N  L  N  A  O  L  T  I  S  M  Q  E  T  U  I  P  A  G  E  D
U  J  C  B  Y  I  Y  V  O  Y  O  E  I  S  S  Q  Q  B  D  S  A  A  S
B  L  T  D  O  G  F  P  S  I  G  R  V  M  S  H  E  A  W  B  G  A  G
U  T  M  D  J  N  Z  R  L  H  Y  E  I  R  A  I  K  I  W  A  T  L  R
X  S  L  J  Z  F  D  S  X  A  I  T  Z  N  Q  F  R  L  N  S  R  V  U
M  T  V  F  P  I  V  S  N  Q  N  N  O  X  G  Y  H  P  A  I  O  Q  T
L  G  O  E  L  A  I  G  T  H  X  I  C  I  X  W  J  J  Y  D  M  T  C
```

Find the following words in the puzzle.
Words are hidden ↑ ↓ → ← and ↘ .

ASSESSMENT	FINANCIAL	MONITORING
ASSETS	GOAL	MORTGAGE
BALANCE	INTEREST	PENSIONS
BONDS	INVESTMENTS	PLAN
BUDGET	LIABILITIES	SAVINGS
EQUITY	LOAN	

11. APPENDICES

Appendix A: Tables of Functions in Business Software

Database functions

Function	Description
DAVERAGE	Returns the average of selected database entries
DCOUNT	Counts the cells that contain numbers in a database
DCOUNTA	Counts nonblank cells in a database
DGET	Extracts from a database a single record that matches the specified criteria
DMAX	Returns the maximum value from selected database entries
DMIN	Returns the minimum value from selected database entries
DPRODUCT	Multiplies the values in a particular field of records that match the criteria in a database
DSTDEV	Estimates the standard deviation based on a sample of selected database entries
DSTDEVP	Calculates the standard deviation based on the entire population of selected database entries
DSUM	Adds the numbers in the field column of records in the database that match the criteria
DVAR	Estimates variance based on a sample from selected database entries
DVARP	Calculates variance based on the entire population of selected database entries

Date and time functions

Function	Description
DATE	Returns the serial number of a particular date
DATEVALUE	Converts a date in the form of text to a serial number
DAY	Converts a serial number to a day of the month
DAYS360	Calculates the number of days between two dates based on a 360−day year
EDATE	Returns the serial number of the date, i.e. the indicated number of months before or after the start date
EOMONTH	Returns the serial number of the last day of the month before or after a specified number of months
HOUR	Converts a serial number to an hour
MINUTE	Converts a serial number to a minute
MONTH	Converts a serial number to a month
NETWORKDAYS	Returns the number of whole workdays between two dates
NOW	Returns the serial number of the current date and time
SECOND	Converts a serial number to a second
TIME	Returns the serial number of a particular time
TIMEVALUE	Converts a time in the form of text to a serial number
TODAY	Returns the serial number of today's date
WEEKDAY	Converts a serial number to a day of the week
WEEKNUM	Converts a serial number to a number representing where the week falls numerically with a year
WORKDAY	Returns the serial number of the date before or after a specified number of workdays
YEAR	Converts a serial number to a year
YEARFRAC	Returns the year fraction representing the number of whole days between start_date and end_date

Financial functions

Function	Description
ACCRINT	Returns the accrued interest for a security that pays periodic interest
ACCRINTM	Returns the accrued interest for a security that pays interest at maturity
AMORDEGRC	Returns the depreciation for each accounting period by using a depreciation coefficient
AMORLINC	Returns the depreciation for each accounting period
COUPDAYBS	Returns the number of days from the beginning of the coupon period to the settlement date
COUPDAYS	Returns the number of days in the coupon period that contains the settlement date
COUPDAYSNC	Returns the number of days from the settlement date to the next coupon date
COUPNCD	Returns the next coupon date after the settlement date
COUPNUM	Returns the number of coupons payable between the settlement date and maturity date
COUPPCD	Returns the previous coupon date before the settlement date
CUMIPMT	Returns the cumulative interest paid between two periods
CUMPRINC	Returns the cumulative principal paid on a loan between two periods
DB	Returns the depreciation of an asset for a specified period using the fixed–declining balance method
DDB	Returns the depreciation of an asset for a specified period using the double–declining balance method
DISC	Returns the discount rate for a security
DOLLARDE	Converts a dollar price, expressed as a fraction, into a dollar price, expressed as a decimal number
DOLLARFR	Converts a dollar price, expressed as a decimal number, into a dollar price, expressed as a fraction
DURATION	Returns the annual duration of a security with periodic interest payments
EFFECT	Returns the effective annual interest rate
FV	Returns the future value of an investment
FVSCHEDULE	Returns the future value of an initial principal after applying a series of compound interest rates
INTRATE	Returns the interest rate for a fully invested security
IPMT	Returns the interest payment for an investment for a given period
IRR	Returns the internal rate of return for a series of cash flows
ISPMT	Calculates the interest paid during a specific period of an investment
MDURATION	Returns the MacAulay modified duration for a security with an assumed par value of $100
MIRR	Returns the internal rate of return where positive and negative cash flows are financed at different rates
NOMINAL	Returns the annual nominal interest rate
NPER	Returns the number of periods for an investment
NPV	Returns the net present value of an investment based on a series of periodic cash flows &discount rate
ODDFPRICE	Returns the price per $100 face value of a security with an odd first period
ODDFYIELD	Returns the yield of a security with an odd first period
ODDLPRICE	Returns the price per $100 face value of a security with an odd last period
ODDLYIELD	Returns the yield of a security with an odd last period
PMT	Returns the periodic payment for an annuity
PPMT	Returns the payment on the principal for an investment for a given period
PRICE	Returns the price per $100 face value of a security that pays periodic interest
PRICEDISC	Returns the price per $100 face value of a discounted security
PRICEMAT	Returns the price per $100 face value of a security that pays interest at maturity
PV	Returns the present value of an investment
RATE	Returns the interest rate per period of an annuity
RECEIVED	Returns the amount received at maturity for a fully invested security
SLN	Returns the straight–line depreciation of an asset for one period
SYD	Returns the sum–of–years' digits depreciation of an asset for a specified period
TBILLEQ	Returns the bond–equivalent yield for a Treasury bill
TBILLPRICE	Returns the price per $100 face value for a Treasury bill
TBILLYIELD	Returns the yield for a Treasury bill
VDB	Returns the depreciation of an asset for a specified or partial period using a declining balance method
XIRR	Returns the internal rate of return for a schedule of cash flows that is not necessarily periodic
XNPV	Returns the net present value for a schedule of cash flows that is not necessarily periodic
YIELD	Returns the yield on a security that pays periodic interest
YIELDDISC	Returns the annual yield for a discounted security; for example, a Treasury bill
YIELDMAT	Returns the annual yield of a security that pays interest at maturity

Information functions

Function	Description
CELL	Returns information about the formatting, location, or contents of a cell
ERROR.TYPE	Returns a number corresponding to an error type
INFO	Returns information about the current operating environment
ISBLANK	Returns TRUE if the value is blank
ISERR	Returns TRUE if the value is any error value except #N/A
ISERROR	Returns TRUE if the value is any error value
ISEVEN	Returns TRUE if the number is even
ISLOGICAL	Returns TRUE if the value is a logical value
ISNA	Returns TRUE if the value is the #N/A error value
ISNONTEXT	Returns TRUE if the value is not text
ISNUMBER	Returns TRUE if the value is a number
ISODD	Returns TRUE if the number is odd
ISREF	Returns TRUE if the value is a reference
ISTEXT	Returns TRUE if the value is text
N	Returns a value converted to a number
NA	Returns the error value #N/A
TYPE	Returns a number indicating the data type of a value

Logical functions

Function	Description
AND	Returns TRUE if all of its arguments are TRUE
FALSE	Returns the logical value FALSE
IF	Specifies a logical test to perform
NOT	Reverses the logic of its argument
OR	Returns TRUE if any argument is TRUE
TRUE	Returns the logical value TRUE

Lookup and reference functions

Function	Description
ADDRESS	Returns a reference as text to a single cell in a worksheet
AREAS	Returns the number of areas in a reference
CHOOSE	Chooses a value from a list of values
COLUMN	Returns the column number of a reference
COLUMNS	Returns the number of columns in a reference
GETPIVOTDATA	Returns data stored in a PivotTable
HLOOKUP	Looks in the top row of an array and returns the value of the indicated cell
HYPERLINK	Creates a shortcut or jump that opens a document stored on a network server, an intranet, or the Internet
INDEX	Uses an index to choose a value from a reference or array
INDIRECT	Returns a reference indicated by a text value
LOOKUP	Looks up values in a vector or array
MATCH	Looks up values in a reference or array
OFFSET	Returns a reference offset from a given reference
ROW	Returns the row number of a reference
ROWS	Returns the number of rows in a reference
RTD	Retrieves real-time data from a program that supports COM automation
TRANSPOSE	Returns the transpose of an array
VLOOKUP	Looks in the first column of an array and moves across the row to return the value of a cell

Mathematical and trigonometry functions

Function	Description
ABS	Returns the absolute value of a number
ACOS	Returns the arccosine of a number
ACOSH	Returns the inverse hyperbolic cosine of a number
ASIN	Returns the arcsine of a number
ASINH	Returns the inverse hyperbolic sine of a number
ATAN	Returns the arctangent of a number
ATAN2	Returns the arctangent from x– and y–coordinates
ATANH	Returns the inverse hyperbolic tangent of a number
CEILING	Rounds a number to the nearest integer or to the nearest multiple of significance
COMBIN	Returns the number of combinations for a given number of objects
COS	Returns the cosine of a number
COSH	Returns the hyperbolic cosine of a number
DEGREES	Converts radians to degrees
EVEN	Rounds a number up to the nearest even integer
EXP	Returns e raised to the power of a given number
FACT	Returns the factorial of a number
FACTDOUBLE	Returns the double factorial of a number
FLOOR	Rounds a number down, toward zero
GCD	Returns the greatest common divisor
INT	Rounds a number down to the nearest integer
LCM	Returns the least common multiple
LN	Returns the natural logarithm of a number
LOG	Returns the logarithm of a number to a specified base
LOG10	Returns the base–10 logarithm of a number
MDETERM	Returns the matrix determinant of an array
MINVERSE	Returns the matrix inverse of an array
MMULT	Returns the matrix product of two arrays
MOD	Returns the remainder from division
MROUND	Returns a number rounded to the desired multiple
MULTINOMIAL	Returns the multinomial of a set of numbers
ODD	Rounds a number up to the nearest odd integer
PI	Returns the value of pi
POWER	Returns the result of a number raised to a power
PRODUCT	Multiplies its arguments
QUOTIENT	Returns the integer portion of a division
RADIANS	Converts degrees to radians
RAND	Returns a random number between 0 and 1
RANDBETWEEN	Returns a random number between the numbers you specify
ROMAN	Converts an Arabic numeral to Roman, as text
ROUND	Rounds a number to a specified number of digits
ROUNDDOWN	Rounds a number down, toward zero
ROUNDUP	Rounds a number up, away from zero
SERIESSUM	Returns the sum of a power series based on the formula
SIGN	Returns the sign of a number
SIN	Returns the sine of the given angle
SINH	Returns the hyperbolic sine of a number
SQRT	Returns a positive square root
SQRTPI	Returns the square root of (number * pi)
SUBTOTAL	Returns a subtotal in a list or database
SUM	Adds its arguments
SUMIF	Adds the cells specified by a given criteria
SUMPRODUCT	Returns the sum of the products of corresponding array components
SUMSQ	Returns the sum of the squares of the arguments
SUMX2MY2	Returns the sum of the difference of squares of corresponding values in two arrays
TAN	Returns the tangent of a number
TANH	Returns the hyperbolic tangent of a number
TRUNC	Truncates a number to an integer

Statistical functions

Function	Description
AVEDEV	Returns the average of the absolute deviations of data points from their mean
AVERAGE	Returns the average of its arguments
AVERAGEA	Returns the average of its arguments, including numbers, text, and logical values
BETADIST	Returns the beta cumulative distribution function
BETAINV	Returns the inverse of the cumulative distribution function for a specified beta distribution
BINOMDIST	Returns the individual term binomial distribution probability
CHIDIST	Returns the one-tailed probability of the chi-squared distribution
CHIINV	Returns the inverse of the one-tailed probability of the chi-squared distribution
CHITEST	Returns the test for independence
CONFIDENCE	Returns the confidence interval for a population mean
CORREL	Returns the correlation coefficient between two data sets
COUNT	Counts how many numbers are in the list of arguments
COUNTA	Counts how many values are in the list of arguments
COUNTBLANK	Counts the number of blank cells within a range
COUNTIF	Counts the number of nonblank cells within a range that meet the given criteria
COVAR	Returns covariance, the average of the products of paired deviations
CRITBINOM	Returns the smallest value for which the cumulative binomial distribution is less than a value
DEVSQ	Returns the sum of squares of deviations
EXPONDIST	Returns the exponential distribution
FDIST	Returns the F probability distribution
FINV	Returns the inverse of the F probability distribution
FISHER	Returns the Fisher transformation
FISHERINV	Returns the inverse of the Fisher transformation
FORECAST	Returns a value along a linear trend
FREQUENCY	Returns a frequency distribution as a vertical array
FTEST	Returns the result of an F-test
GAMMADIST	Returns the gamma distribution
GAMMAINV	Returns the inverse of the gamma cumulative distribution
GAMMALN	Returns the natural logarithm of the gamma function, $\Gamma(x)$
GEOMEAN	Returns the geometric mean
GROWTH	Returns values along an exponential trend
HARMEAN	Returns the harmonic mean
HYPGEOMDIST	Returns the hypergeometric distribution
INTERCEPT	Returns the intercept of the linear regression line
KURT	Returns the kurtosis of a data set
LARGE	Returns the k-th largest value in a data set
LINEST	Returns the parameters of a linear trend
LOGEST	Returns the parameters of an exponential trend
LOGINV	Returns the inverse of the lognormal distribution
LOGNORMDIST	Returns the cumulative lognormal distribution
MAX	Returns the maximum value in a list of arguments
MAXA	Returns the maximum value in a list of arguments, including numbers, text, and logical values
MEDIAN	Returns the median of the given numbers
MIN	Returns the minimum value in a list of arguments
MINA	Returns the smallest value in a list of arguments, including numbers, text, and logical values
MODE	Returns the most common value in a data set
NEGBINOMDIST	Returns the negative binomial distribution
NORMDIST	Returns the normal cumulative distribution
NORMINV	Returns the inverse of the normal cumulative distribution
NORMSDIST	Returns the standard normal cumulative distribution
NORMSINV	Returns the inverse of the standard normal cumulative distribution
PEARSON	Returns the Pearson product moment correlation coefficient
PERCENTILE	Returns the k-th percentile of values in a range
PERCENTRANK	Returns the percentage rank of a value in a data set
PERMUT	Returns the number of permutations for a given number of objects
POISSON	Returns the Poisson distribution
PROB	Returns the probability that values in a range are between two limits

QUARTILE	Returns the quartile of a data set
RANK	Returns the rank of a number in a list of numbers
RSQ	Returns the square of the Pearson product moment correlation coefficient
SKEW	Returns the skewness of a distribution
SLOPE	Returns the slope of the linear regression line
SMALL	Returns the k−th smallest value in a data set
STANDARDIZE	Returns a normalized value
STDEV	Estimates standard deviation based on a sample
STDEVA	Estimates standard deviation based on a sample, including numbers, text, and logical values
STDEVP	Calculates standard deviation based on the entire population
STDEVPA	Calculates standard deviation based on the entire population, including numbers, text values
STEYX	Returns the standard error of the predicted y−value for each x in the regression
TDIST	Returns the Student's t−distribution
TINV	Returns the inverse of the Student's t−distribution
TREND	Returns values along a linear trend
TRIMMEAN	Returns the mean of the interior of a data set
TTEST	Returns the probability associated with a Student's t−test
VAR	Estimates variance based on a sample
VARA	Estimates variance based on a sample, including numbers, text, and logical values
VARP	Calculates variance based on the entire population
VARPA	Calculates variance based on the entire population, including numbers, text, and logical values
WEIBULL	Returns the Weibull distribution
ZTEST	Returns the one−tailed probability−value of a z−test

Text functions

Function	Description
ASC	Changes full−width (double−byte) English letters to half−width (single−byte) characters
BAHTTEXT	Converts a number to text, using the ß (baht) currency format
CHAR	Returns the character specified by the code number
CLEAN	Removes all nonprintable characters from text
CODE	Returns a numeric code for the first character in a text string
CONCATENATE	Joins several text items into one text item
DOLLAR	Converts a number to text, using the $ (dollar) currency format
EXACT	Checks to see if two text values are identical
FIND, FINDB	Finds one text value within another (case−sensitive)
FIXED	Formats a number as text with a fixed number of decimals
JIS	Changes half−width (single−byte) English letters to full−width (double−byte) characters
LEFT, LEFTB	Returns the leftmost characters from a text value
LEN, LENB	Returns the number of characters in a text string
LOWER	Converts text to lowercase
MID, MIDB	Returns a specific number of characters from a text string starting at the position you specify
PHONETIC	Extracts the phonetic (furigana) characters from a text string
PROPER	Capitalizes the first letter in each word of a text value
REPLACE, REPLACEB	Replaces characters within text
REPT	Repeats text a given number of times
RIGHT, RIGHTB	Returns the rightmost characters from a text value
SEARCH, SEARCHB	Finds one text value within another (not case−sensitive)
SUBSTITUTE	Substitutes new text for old text in a text string
T	Converts its arguments to text
TEXT	Formats a number and converts it to text
TRIM	Removes spaces from text
UPPER	Converts text to uppercase
VALUE	Converts a text argument to a number

Appendix B: Probability Distributions – Binomial Distribution

The probability P(n,r) of r successes in n independent trials, where p is the probability of success on each trial e.g. if p = 0.5 (fair coin) then P(3,2) = 0.375 ; P(6,3) = 0.3125

							p					
n	r	0.00	0.05	0.10	0.15	0.20	0.25	0.30	0.35	0.40	0.45	0.50
2	0	1.0000	0.9025	0.8100	0.7225	0.6400	0.5625	0.4900	0.4225	0.3600	0.3025	0.2500
2	1	0.0000	0.0950	0.1800	0.2550	0.3200	0.3750	0.4200	0.4550	0.4800	0.4950	0.5000
2	2	0.0000	0.0025	0.0100	0.0225	0.0400	0.0625	0.0900	0.1225	0.1600	0.2025	0.2500
3	0	1.0000	0.8574	0.7290	0.6141	0.5120	0.4219	0.3430	0.2746	0.2160	0.1664	0.1250
3	1	0.0000	0.1354	0.2430	0.3251	0.3840	0.4219	0.4410	0.4436	0.4320	0.4084	0.3750
3	2	0.0000	0.0071	0.0270	0.0574	0.0960	0.1406	0.1890	0.2389	0.2880	0.3341	0.3750
3	3	0.0000	0.0001	0.0010	0.0034	0.0080	0.0156	0.0270	0.0429	0.0640	0.0911	0.1250
4	0	1.0000	0.8145	0.6561	0.5220	0.4096	0.3164	0.2401	0.1785	0.1296	0.0915	0.0625
4	1	0.0000	0.1715	0.2916	0.3685	0.4096	0.4219	0.4116	0.3845	0.3456	0.2995	0.2500
4	2	0.0000	0.0135	0.0486	0.0975	0.1536	0.2109	0.2646	0.3105	0.3456	0.3675	0.3750
4	3	0.0000	0.0005	0.0036	0.0115	0.0256	0.0469	0.0756	0.1115	0.1536	0.2005	0.2500
4	4	0.0000	0.0000	0.0001	0.0005	0.0016	0.0039	0.0081	0.0150	0.0256	0.0410	0.0625
5	0	1.0000	0.7738	0.5905	0.4437	0.3277	0.2373	0.1681	0.1160	0.0778	0.0503	0.0313
5	1	0.0000	0.2036	0.3281	0.3915	0.4096	0.3955	0.3602	0.3124	0.2592	0.2059	0.1563
5	2	0.0000	0.0214	0.0729	0.1382	0.2048	0.2637	0.3087	0.3364	0.3456	0.3369	0.3125
5	3	0.0000	0.0011	0.0081	0.0244	0.0512	0.0879	0.1323	0.1811	0.2304	0.2757	0.3125
5	4	0.0000	0.0000	0.0005	0.0022	0.0064	0.0146	0.0284	0.0488	0.0768	0.1128	0.1563
5	5	0.0000	0.0000	0.0000	0.0001	0.0003	0.0010	0.0024	0.0053	0.0102	0.0185	0.0313
6	0	1.0000	0.7351	0.5314	0.3771	0.2621	0.1780	0.1176	0.0754	0.0467	0.0277	0.0156
6	1	0.0000	0.2321	0.3543	0.3993	0.3932	0.3560	0.3025	0.2437	0.1866	0.1359	0.0938
6	2	0.0000	0.0305	0.0984	0.1762	0.2458	0.2966	0.3241	0.3280	0.3110	0.2780	0.2344
6	3	0.0000	0.0021	0.0146	0.0415	0.0819	0.1318	0.1852	0.2355	0.2765	0.3032	0.3125
6	4	0.0000	0.0001	0.0012	0.0055	0.0154	0.0330	0.0595	0.0951	0.1382	0.1861	0.2344
6	5	0.0000	0.0000	0.0001	0.0004	0.0015	0.0044	0.0102	0.0205	0.0369	0.0609	0.0938
6	6	0.0000	0.0000	0.0000	0.0000	0.0001	0.0002	0.0007	0.0018	0.0041	0.0083	0.0156

Appendix C: Probability Distributions – Poisson distribution

POISSON

The probability P(r) of r successes in an interval, where λ is the mean number of events per interval

e.g. If $\lambda = 0.5$ for the number of online sales per minute in a website then P(1) = **0.3033** and P(3) = 0.0126

r	λ 0.10	0.20	0.30	0.40	0.50	0.60	0.70	0.80	0.90	1.00
0	0.9048	0.8187	0.7408	0.6703	0.6065	0.5488	0.4966	0.4493	0.4066	0.3679
1	0.0905	0.1637	0.2222	0.2681	0.3033	0.3293	0.3476	0.3595	0.3659	0.3679
2	0.0045	0.0164	0.0333	0.0536	0.0758	0.0988	0.1217	0.1438	0.1647	0.1839
3	0.0002	0.0011	0.0033	0.0072	0.0126	0.0198	0.0284	0.0383	0.0494	0.0613
4	0.0000	0.0001	0.0003	0.0007	0.0016	0.0030	0.0050	0.0077	0.0111	0.0153
5	0.0000	0.0000	0.0000	0.0001	0.0002	0.0004	0.0007	0.0012	0.0020	0.0031
6	0.0000	0.0000	0.0000	0.0000	0.0000	0.0000	0.0001	0.0002	0.0003	0.0005
7	0.0000	0.0000	0.0000	0.0000	0.0000	0.0000	0.0000	0.0000	0.0000	0.0001

r	λ 1.10	1.20	1.30	1.40	1.50	1.60	1.70	1.80	1.90	2.00
0	0.3329	0.3012	0.2725	0.2466	0.2231	0.2019	0.1827	0.1653	0.1496	0.1353
1	0.3662	0.3614	0.3543	0.3452	0.3347	0.3230	0.3106	0.2975	0.2842	0.2707
2	0.2014	0.2169	0.2303	0.2417	0.2510	0.2584	0.2640	0.2678	0.2700	0.2707
3	0.0738	0.0867	0.0998	0.1128	0.1255	0.1378	0.1496	0.1607	0.1710	0.1804
4	0.0203	0.0260	0.0324	0.0395	0.0471	0.0551	0.0636	0.0723	0.0812	0.0902
5	0.0045	0.0062	0.0084	0.0111	0.0141	0.0176	0.0216	0.0260	0.0309	0.0361
6	0.0008	0.0012	0.0018	0.0026	0.0035	0.0047	0.0061	0.0078	0.0098	0.0120
7	0.0001	0.0002	0.0003	0.0005	0.0008	0.0011	0.0015	0.0020	0.0027	0.0034
8	0.0000	0.0000	0.0001	0.0001	0.0001	0.0002	0.0003	0.0005	0.0006	0.0009
9	0.0000	0.0000	0.0000	0.0000	0.0000	0.0000	0.0001	0.0001	0.0001	0.0002

r	λ 2.10	2.20	2.30	2.40	2.50	2.60	2.70	2.80	2.90	3.00
0	0.1225	0.1108	0.1003	0.0907	0.0821	0.0743	0.0672	0.0608	0.0550	0.0498
1	0.2572	0.2438	0.2306	0.2177	0.2052	0.1931	0.1815	0.1703	0.1596	0.1494
2	0.2700	0.2681	0.2652	0.2613	0.2565	0.2510	0.2450	0.2384	0.2314	0.2240
3	0.1890	0.1966	0.2033	0.2090	0.2138	0.2176	0.2205	0.2225	0.2237	0.2240
4	0.0992	0.1082	0.1169	0.1254	0.1336	0.1414	0.1488	0.1557	0.1622	0.1680
5	0.0417	0.0476	0.0538	0.0602	0.0668	0.0735	0.0804	0.0872	0.0940	0.1008
6	0.0146	0.0174	0.0206	0.0241	0.0278	0.0319	0.0362	0.0407	0.0455	0.0504
7	0.0044	0.0055	0.0068	0.0083	0.0099	0.0118	0.0139	0.0163	0.0188	0.0216
8	0.0011	0.0015	0.0019	0.0025	0.0031	0.0038	0.0047	0.0057	0.0068	0.0081
9	0.0003	0.0004	0.0005	0.0007	0.0009	0.0011	0.0014	0.0018	0.0022	0.0027
10	0.0001	0.0001	0.0001	0.0002	0.0002	0.0003	0.0004	0.0005	0.0006	0.0008
11	0.0000	0.0000	0.0000	0.0000	0.0000	0.0001	0.0001	0.0001	0.0002	0.0002
12	0.0000	0.0000	0.0000	0.0000	0.0000	0.0000	0.0000	0.0000	0.0000	0.0001

Appendix D: Probability Distributions – Standard Normal distribution

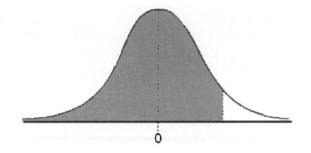

The probability P(Z < z) in the Normal distribution N(μ,σ), where mean μ = 0 and standard deviation σ = 1									
e.g. If z = 1.0 then P(Z < 1) = 0.8413 and if z = 2.0 then P(Z < 2) = 0.9772									
	λ								
z	0.00	0.01	0.02	0.03	0.04	0.05	0.06	0.07	0.08	0.09
0.00	0.5000	0.5040	0.5080	0.5120	0.5160	0.5199	0.5239	0.5279	0.5319	0.5359
0.10	0.5398	0.5438	0.5478	0.5517	0.5557	0.5596	0.5636	0.5675	0.5714	0.5753
0.20	0.5793	0.5832	0.5871	0.5910	0.5948	0.5987	0.6026	0.6064	0.6103	0.6141
0.30	0.6179	0.6217	0.6255	0.6293	0.6331	0.6368	0.6406	0.6443	0.6480	0.6517
0.40	0.6554	0.6591	0.6628	0.6664	0.6700	0.6736	0.6772	0.6808	0.6844	0.6879
0.50	0.6915	0.6950	0.6985	0.7019	0.7054	0.7088	0.7123	0.7157	0.7190	0.7224
0.60	0.7257	0.7291	0.7324	0.7357	0.7389	0.7422	0.7454	0.7486	0.7517	0.7549
0.70	0.7580	0.7611	0.7642	0.7673	0.7704	0.7734	0.7764	0.7794	0.7823	0.7852
0.80	0.7881	0.7910	0.7939	0.7967	0.7995	0.8023	0.8051	0.8078	0.8106	0.8133
0.90	0.8159	0.8186	0.8212	0.8238	0.8264	0.8289	0.8315	0.8340	0.8365	0.8389
1.00	0.8413	0.8438	0.8461	0.8485	0.8508	0.8531	0.8554	0.8577	0.8599	0.8621
1.10	0.8643	0.8665	0.8686	0.8708	0.8729	0.8749	0.8770	0.8790	0.8810	0.8830
1.20	0.8849	0.8869	0.8888	0.8907	0.8925	0.8944	0.8962	0.8980	0.8997	0.9015
1.30	0.9032	0.9049	0.9066	0.9082	0.9099	0.9115	0.9131	0.9147	0.9162	0.9177
1.40	0.9192	0.9207	0.9222	0.9236	0.9251	0.9265	0.9279	0.9292	0.9306	0.9319
1.50	0.9332	0.9345	0.9357	0.9370	0.9382	0.9394	0.9406	0.9418	0.9429	0.9441
1.60	0.9452	0.9463	0.9474	0.9484	0.9495	0.9505	0.9515	0.9525	0.9535	0.9545
1.70	0.9554	0.9564	0.9573	0.9582	0.9591	0.9599	0.9608	0.9616	0.9625	0.9633
1.80	0.9641	0.9649	0.9656	0.9664	0.9671	0.9678	0.9686	0.9693	0.9699	0.9706
1.90	0.9713	0.9719	0.9726	0.9732	0.9738	0.9744	0.9750	0.9756	0.9761	0.9767
2.00	0.9772	0.9778	0.9783	0.9788	0.9793	0.9798	0.9803	0.9808	0.9812	0.9817
2.10	0.9821	0.9826	0.9830	0.9834	0.9838	0.9842	0.9846	0.9850	0.9854	0.9857
2.20	0.9861	0.9864	0.9868	0.9871	0.9875	0.9878	0.9881	0.9884	0.9887	0.9890
2.30	0.9893	0.9896	0.9898	0.9901	0.9904	0.9906	0.9909	0.9911	0.9913	0.9916
2.40	0.9918	0.9920	0.9922	0.9925	0.9927	0.9929	0.9931	0.9932	0.9934	0.9936
2.50	0.9938	0.9940	0.9941	0.9943	0.9945	0.9946	0.9948	0.9949	0.9951	0.9952
2.60	0.9953	0.9955	0.9956	0.9957	0.9959	0.9960	0.9961	0.9962	0.9963	0.9964
2.70	0.9965	0.9966	0.9967	0.9968	0.9969	0.9970	0.9971	0.9972	0.9973	0.9974
2.80	0.9974	0.9975	0.9976	0.9977	0.9977	0.9978	0.9979	0.9979	0.9980	0.9981
2.90	0.9981	0.9982	0.9982	0.9983	0.9984	0.9984	0.9985	0.9985	0.9986	0.9986
3.00	0.9987	0.9987	0.9987	0.9988	0.9988	0.9989	0.9989	0.9989	0.9990	0.9990

Appendix E: Supplementary Materials

Basic supplementary materials are available on the publisher's website:

http://www.algana.com/ABDI/

Recommended web references used in this book include:-

http://www.legislation.gov.uk/ukpga/1998/29/contents

http://education.iseek.com

http://www.refseek.com/

http://www.bpubs.com/

http://www.inomics.com

http://www.statista.com/statistics

www.marketingcharts.com

http://www.thecompleteuniversityguide.co.uk/league-tables

www.surveymonkey.co.uk/

www.lse.co.uk

http://www.algana.com/publishing/

Appendix F: Sketch Solutions to Exercises

Exercises – Section 2

1. A visual way of representing the difference between data and information is called the:

    (a) KIWD pyramid   (b) KIW triangle   (c) IWD tetrahedron   (d) KIWD circle

2. Data that has not yet been processed into useful business information is called:

    (a) Clean data   (b) Raw data   (c) Unformatted data   (d) Metadata

3. Collecting data based upon a specific customer with regard to personal details and spending habits is called:

    (a) Profiling   (b) Tracking   (c) Marketing   (d) Selling

4. Managing relationships between businesses and customers can be assisted by which type of business software?

    (a) B2B software   (b) Unix software   (c) CRM software   (d) Spyware

5. What is the name of the loyalty card currently used by Tesco supermarket?

    (a) Nectar card   (b) Tastecard   (c) Pluscard   (d) Clubcard

6. Information from Data

    (i)   B2BB2C – Business to Business; Business to Consumer
    (ii)   SUSANJONES19ECONSW155SL201607794675555

    Example Data
    SUSANJONES19ECONSW155SL201607794675555

    Example Information
    Name: Susan Jones
    Age: 19
    Degree: Economics
    Address:
    University of Roehampton
    LONDON
    SW15 5SL
    Year of entry: 2016
    Phone: 07794675555

    (iii)   RBSLLOYBARC – Royal Bank of Scotland; Lloyds; Barclays (Banks)
    (iv)   INCVATCGT – Income Tax; Value-added Tax; Capital Gains Tax (Taxes)

7. Types of Files

    (i)   xls – Excel spreadsheets
    (ii)   dbs – Access databases
    (iii)   docx – Word documents
    (iv)   sav – SPSS data files
    (v)   ppt – PowerPoint slides

8. Breaches of the UK Data

Nationwide Building Society (2006)

The moment date breaches entered consciousness in the UK, the Nationwide incident involved an unencrypted laptop stolen from a company employee that put at risk the personal data of 11 million savers. The UK's poor disclosure regulations made it difficult for outsiders to get information on what had occurred. The Financial Services Authority (FSA) eventually fined Nationwide £980,000, still the largest sum ever imposed for data loss in the UK, seen at the time as a warning shot for other firms that might have similar incidents. Not everyone noticed.

HM Revenue & Customs (2007)

Probably the most infamous large data breach ever to occur in the UK, two CDs containing the records of 25 million child benefit claimant in the UK (including every child in the country) went missing in the post. There was never any indication that these password-protected discs had fallen into the wrong hands but the incident underlined how valuable data was being handled by poorly-trained junior employees.

T-Mobile (2009)

Sales staff were caught selling customer records to brokers who used the information to market them as their contracts were coming to an end. It was never clear how many records were involved in this murky insider trade but it was believed to run from half a million to millions. Initially the ICO refused to name the firm but was forced to after rival networks said they were not involved, leaving only one name. In 2011, the two employees involved were fined £73,000 by the courts.

Brighton and Sussex University Hospitals NHS Trust (2010)

The Information Commissioner (ICO) ended up imposing a fine of £325,000 after sensitive patient data of thousands of people was discovered on hard drives sold on eBay. An investigation found that at least 232 de-commissioned drives that should have been deep cleaned and destroyed by a contractor ended up being sold second hand.

Sony PlayStation Network (2011)

The largest data breach in history at the time, Sony's disastrous 2011 breach saw hackers make off with the customer records of 77 million people relating to its PlayStation Network, including a small number revealing credit card numbers. Apart from downing the company's systems for an extraordinary 23 days, the breach crossed national frontiers, affecting people from all over the world, including the UK. Britain's ICO eventually issued a £250,000 fine for what will go down as the first big data breach to affect people across the globe.

Morrison's supermarket (2014)

An unusual example of the insider attack, the attacker published details of the firm's entire workforce database online, 100,000 employees in all. An employee was eventually arrested for the incident and will presumably come to court at some point which could reveal more details of how the firm's security was bypassed. Inside events are rare but particularly feared because they abuse privileged access that is hard to lock down. Some employees later launched legal action.

Staffordshire University (2014)

A re-run on the lost laptop theme that people assumed had been consigned to history, this time involving 125,000 students and applicants on a computer stolen from a car. However, the files had been password-protected said the University, plaintively. That wouldn't have been much of a barrier to the name, address, telephone number and email data. Included this incident as a reminder that just because times have moved on doesn't mean the old problem go away.

Mumsnet (2014)

A direct victim of the infamous and widespread Heartbleed SSL software flaw, the compromise allowed hackers to access anything up to 1.5 million user accounts on the hugely popular site, its owners revealed. Although the data inside these accounts was less sensitive than for some of the other accounts, the hack revealed both the potency of big but undiscovered software issues affecting multiple sites and that even big brands could be affected.

Think W3 Limited (2014)

A serious attack in which a hacker was able to get his or her hands on 1,163,996 credit and debit card records from online holiday firm Think W3 by using an SQL injection attack to exploit a weakness on its website. The ICO described the incident as a "staggering lapse" and fined it £150,000.

Moonpig (2015)

Another biggie, a software flaw in the business' Android app let a researcher access the records of any Moonpig account holder he tried, in theory compromising a total of three million people. The researcher reported the issue to the firm 18 months before going public in early 2015, after receiving an inadequate response. This was significant partly because it involved a mobile app rather than the more common website breach.

TalkTalk (2014/2015)

Publicised in October 2015, TalkTalk initially struggled to confirm how many of its four million customers were affected after hackers exploited a reported weakness in the firm's website. TalkTalk CEO Baroness Dido Harding sounded disquietingly vague about the attack's scale when interviewed on TV, and it later transpired that a 'mere' 157,000 personal records had been compromised. Shockingly, the incident was the second (and possibly third) data breach affecting the company in under a year, which could mark it as the moment when dissatisfaction over the rising number of breaches becomes both political and mainstream in the UK.

9. Wordsearch

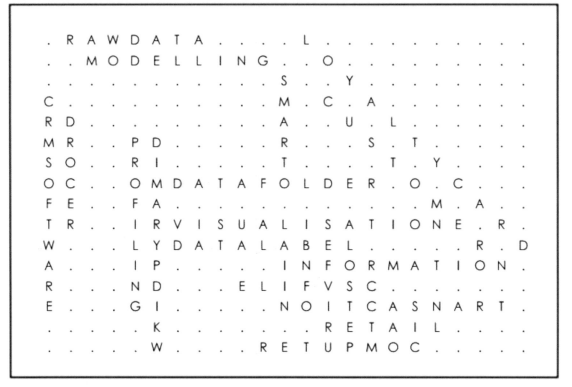

```
 .  R  A  W  D  A  T  A  .  .  .  .  L  .  .  .  .  .  .  .  .  .
 .  .  M  O  D  E  L  L  I  N  G  .  .  O  .  .  .  .  .  .  .  .
 .  .  .  .  .  .  .  .  .  .  S  .  .  Y  .  .  .  .  .  .  .  .
 C  .  .  .  .  .  .  .  .  M  .  C  .  A  .  .  .  .  .  .  .  .
 R  D  .  .  .  .  .  .  .  A  .  .  U  .  L  .  .  .  .  .  .  .
 M  R  .  .  P  D  .  .  .  .  R  .  .  .  S  .  T  .  .  .  .  .
 S  O  .  .  R  I  .  .  .  .  T  .  .  .  .  T  .  Y  .  .  .  .
 O  C  .  .  O  M  D  A  T  A  F  O  L  D  E  R  .  O  .  C  .  .
 F  E  .  .  F  A  .  .  .  .  .  .  .  .  .  .  .  M  .  A  .  .
 T  R  .  .  I  R  V  I  S  U  A  L  I  S  A  T  I  O  N  E  .  R  .
 W  .  .  .  L  Y  D  A  T  A  L  A  B  E  L  .  .  .  .  .  R  .  D
 A  .  .  .  I  P  .  .  .  .  .  I  N  F  O  R  M  A  T  I  O  N  .
 R  .  .  .  N  D  .  .  .  E  L  I  F  V  S  C  .  .  .  .  .  .
 E  .  .  .  G  I  .  .  .  .  .  N  O  I  T  C  A  S  N  A  R  T  .
 .  .  .  .  .  K  .  .  .  .  .  .  .  R  E  T  A  I  L  .  .  .
 .  .  .  .  .  W  .  .  .  .  R  E  T  U  P  M  O  C  .  .  .  .
```

Word directions and start points are formatted: (Direction, X, Y)

COMPUTER (W,18,16)
CRMSOFTWARE (S,1,4)
CSVFILE (W,16,13)
CUSTOMER (SE,14,4)
DATAFOLDER (E,7,8)
DATALABEL (E,7,11)

INFORMATION (E,12,12)
LOYALTYCARD (SE,13,1)
MODELLING (E,3,2)
PROFILING (S,5,6)
RAWDATA (E,2,1)
RECORD (N,2,10)

RETAIL (E,14,15)
SMART (S,12,3)
TRANSACTION (W,22,14)
VISUALISATION (E,7,10)
WKIDPYRAMID (N,6,16)

Exercises – Section 3

1. A structure of organisation that can respond to rapidly changing environments, consisting of large groups of specialists organised into multidisciplinary teams is called:

    (a) Totalitarianism   (b) Adhocracy   (c) Entrepreneurial   (d) Consultancy

2. Ethical behaviour of a business organisation is often referred to using the acronym:

    (a) EB   (b) CSR   (c) ETH   (d) MORAL

3. The patent for the *PageRank* algorithm, a method for ranking web pages in terms of popularity, is currently owned by:

    (a) Microsoft Corp.   (b) Alta Vista   (c) Google   (d) LinkedIn

4. In PEST analysis for business organisations, the "S" stands for:

    (a) Scientific   (b) Solving   (c) Spreadsheet   (d) Social

5. Which of the following activities has had the most a significant negative impact on Royal Mail revenues in the UK?

    (a) Emailing   (b) Phoning   (c) Texting   (d) Faxing

6. Information Systems

TPS – low level processing of the main data such as daily processes within an organisation, used to support the activities and managed at supervisory level.

Data warehouse systems are consolidated organisational database systems, used for high level analysis through data mining and on-line analytical processes (OLAP), pattern recognising, historical/retro detail, forecasting etc.

KBS – are systems built on expert knowledge used for example in medical diagnosis, they are able to help predict trends, diagnostics etc.

DSS – support the decision making process within an organisation, usually by providing aggregated/consolidated information often in the form of reports and graphs for middle and top management.

7. Business Functions

Purchasing is the process of buying goods, raw materials and services from suppliers. It includes invoicing, payment and debt collection.

Marketing is the mechanism used to promote the goods or services of an organisation. It includes the production of advertising material in many forms; e.g. printing and publishing in many forms, the media and the internet.

HRM manages the human resources; i.e. the staff. Dealing with problems and issues, unions, disputes, recruitment and dismissals related to the staff.

Stock control ensures the presence of the correct material being available at the right time within the budget. Records of the movement of stock are kept and the theory of stock control.

8. Unethical Business Practices

Adidas used kangaroo skin to make some types of football boots. Adidas phased out the use of kangaroo leather by 98 per cent over 12 months but still use small amounts of it. Therefore, ethical rights groups have called for a boycott.

Apple relied on child slave labour working in dangerous conditions, for ten hours each day while being exposed to cancerous vapours. The conditions at the manufacturing plant Foxconn were are bad enough that they had to install "anti-suicide nets." The workers live in horrible conditions and experience unreasonable workloads and humiliating discipline. Apple has reduced some of their work with Foxconn, but they still rely primarily on them.

Barrick Gold Corporation was accused of torching 300 houses in Papua New Guinea to expand their mining operations. The torching occurred without warning or time to get possessions and included physical attacks on those who resisted. Other accusations against Barrick Corporation include manipulating Chilean and Australian land titles and dumping toxic waste in Tanzania.

BP created one of the worst environmental disasters ever to befall the United states, the Deepwater Horizon oil spill in the Gulf of Mexico.

Toyota ignored information about safety and delayed investigating possible recalls. In 2009, they learned about sticking pedals and faulty brakes; instead of addressing the issue, they added side airbags. In some cases, Toyota faced accusations of hiding evidence for hundreds of cases involving death and rollovers, putting their drivers and passengers at risk.

9. Wordsearch

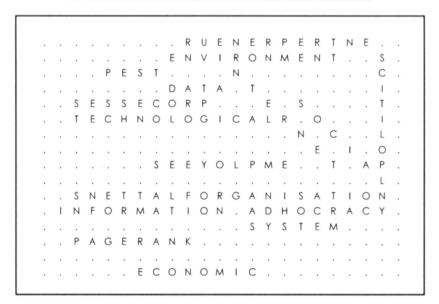

SOLUTION

BUSINESS ORGANISATIONS & IS

Word directions and start points are formatted: (Direction, X, Y)

ADHOCRACY (E,14,12)	FLATTENS (W,10,11)	POLITICS (N,22,9)
DATA (E,9,4)	INFORMATION (E,2,12)	PROCESSES (W,11,5)
ECONOMIC (E,7,16)	INTERNET (SE,12,2)	SOCIAL (SE,17,5)
EMPLOYEES (W,16,9)	ORGANISATION (E,11,11)	SYSTEM (E,14,13)
ENTREPRENEUR (W,21,1)	PAGERANK (E,3,14)	TECHNOLOGICAL (E,3,6)
ENVIRONMENT (E,9,2)	PEST (E,5,3)	

Exercises – Section 4

1. A business researcher has found good reliable secondary data about customer preference in car buying and hopes to look for differences between female and male customer preferences but mistakenly collects and represents data as a single (female and male combined) customer group: This is called

    (a) Under-aggregation   (b) Dis-aggregation   (c) Aggregation   d) Over-aggregation

2. A company has found good reliable secondary data about customers who pay invoices on time and those who do not. This type of data is called:

    (a) Cardinal   (b) Categorical   (c) Ordinal   (d) Binomial

3. Based on "How Americans Spend Their Money" (pie chart, figure 4.9), the fraction NOT spent on housing in 2013 was approximately:

    (a) $1/3$ (b) $1/2$ (c) $2/3$ (d) $3/4$

4. If you were searching for good, reliable secondary data on trade and business publication, which of these websites would you be most likely to use?

    (a) www.lse.co.uk   (b) www.bpubs.com   (c) www.aeaweb.org   (d) www.inomics.com

5. Based on Apple revenue shown in the histogram of figure 4.11, revenue for the entire year 2013 was approximately:

    (a) $575 billion   (b) $625 billion   (c) $675 billion   (d) $725 billion

6. Data for ten new London universities

    (i)   Mayfield University Consultants- probably independent
    (ii) Place the table into a suitable business software package.
    (iii) Sort the table according to overall score (highest first, lowest last).

CUG Rank		University Name	Entry Standards		Overall Score	
2016	2015					
66	93	Roehampton	284	▮	625	▮▮▮
89	94	Middlesex	271	▮	565	▮▮
100	96	Westminster	309	▮▮	525	▮▮
104	107	Kingston	297	▮▮	511	▮
107	99	Greenwich	309	▮▮	505	▮
108	110	West London	257	▮	492	▮
109	-	St Mary's, Twickenham	287	▮	486	▮
119	120	London South Bank	244	▮	429	▮
124	122	East London	273	▮	406	▮
126	123	London Metropolitan	220	▮	327	▮

    (iv) Present the data in (ii) in the form of a mixed histogram with improving universities shown in green and the others shown in red.

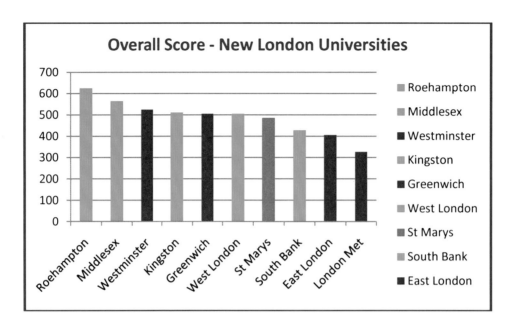

7. Unemployment Data

TOTAL UNEMPLOYED	350	600	850	800	700	600	500
CALENDAR YEAR	2008	2009	2010	2011	2012	2013	2014

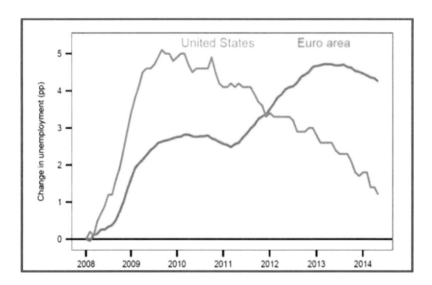

http://econintersect.com/b2evolution/blog1.php/2014/09/22/what-we-read-today-22-september-2014

8. Gantt Chart

No.	Task	Duration	Start date	Finish date	Predecessors
1	Learn Qual basics	5 weeks			
2	Learn NVivo, examples	4 weeks			
3	Prepare report (deadline Wk 10)	5 weeks			1,2
4	Learn Excel or SPSS	4 weeks			
5	Learn quants basics	4 weeks			
6	Learn tests, hypothesis and correlations	2weeks			4,5
7	Prepare for on-line test (deadline Wk12)	4 weeks			

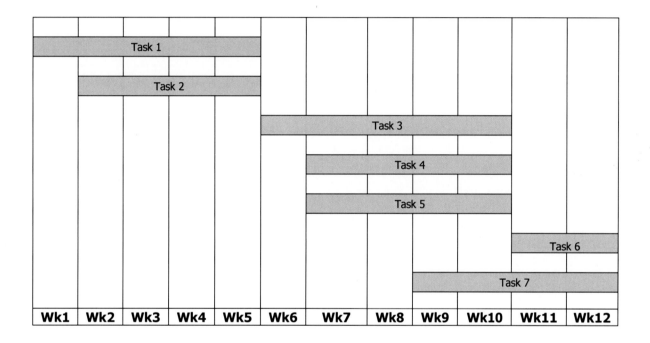

9. Approximate values:

DAY	11 Jan	12 Jan	13 Jan	14 Jan	15 Jan
Daily S.P. average	635	630	627	624	628
Absolute inc from previous day	N/A	-5	-3	-3	+4
% increase from previous day	N/A	-0.8	-0.5	-0.5	+0.6

10.

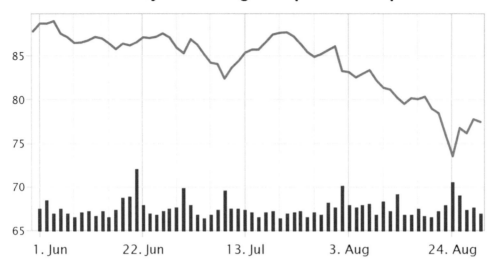

3 Month Lloyds Banking Group Share Graph

11. <u>Wordsearch</u>

Secondary Data

```
E  K  V  L  T  F  Q  W  J  X  O  R  D  I  N  A  L  M  G  Z  F  X  B
N  A  Y  R  A  D  N  O  C  E  S  X  D  R  U  D  T  U  H  F  N  W  T
T  E  S  N  O  M  I  N  A  L  Q  B  F  A  D  T  H  Q  R  Z  O  I  T
Q  C  C  T  T  N  A  G  C  P  R  L  E  H  B  I  L  O  M  K  I  O  S
Y  N  A  A  J  H  S  G  R  T  R  A  H  C  E  N  I  L  L  C  T  D  U
N  E  T  G  P  I  P  A  Y  E  F  P  H  I  I  A  K  N  V  I  A  P  U
O  R  T  M  D  S  C  G  S  T  A  B  L  E  Y  U  S  Q  N  T  S  A  V
S  E  E  O  E  T  X  C  A  R  D  I  N  A  L  Y  Q  C  C  S  I  N  Z
P  F  R  Y  T  O  D  I  S  A  G  G  R  E  G  A  T  E  D  E  N  A  O
C  E  P  R  A  G  Z  E  L  O  R  A  J  T  Q  M  O  R  E  L  A  M  E
B  R  L  L  G  R  N  L  N  P  B  W  W  X  F  O  M  C  I  D  G  B  Z
A  G  O  I  E  A  W  J  T  C  H  A  R  T  Q  G  L  F  G  N  R  T  P
O  H  T  Q  R  M  J  C  Y  O  H  L  H  Y  R  V  S  I  N  A  O  O  B
V  A  G  Q  G  F  P  V  F  Y  T  R  A  H  C  E  I  P  F  C  Z  Q  S
G  O  H  Z  G  J  X  B  H  M  U  B  L  E  Y  L  G  N  E  T  X  M  C
S  B  M  H  A  O  T  R  A  H  C  D  E  X  I  M  P  C  L  P  O  P  M
```

Find the following words in the puzzle.
Words are hidden ↑ ↓ → ← and ↘ .

AGGREGATED	HISTOGRAM	PIECHART
CANDLESTICK	LINECHART	REFERENCE
CARDINAL	MIXEDCHART	SCATTERPLOT
CHART	NOMINAL	SECONDARY
DISAGGREGATED	ORDINAL	TABLE
GANTT	ORGANISATION	

Exercises – Section 5

1. A specific market focus which enables a business to serve a narrow target market better than its competitors is called:

   (a) Market variety   (b) Market niche   (c) Market value   (d) Market share

2. Using information systems to achieve the lowest operational costs and the lowest prices has enabled several successful businesses in the UK. They have been able to keep prices low and shelves well stocked using an efficient inventory replenishment system. Which of the following businesses would fall in that category?

   (a) Boots   (b) H. Samuel   (c) W.H. Smith   (d) Poundland

3. Which of the following industries has been most negatively affected by e-commerce and the Internet?

   (a) Car Dealers   (b) Travel Agents   (c) Supermarkets   (d) Banks

4. What is the name given to the well-known model of competitive forces?

   (a) Peter   (b) Porter   (c) Pater   (d) Pellegrini

5. The ability to offer individually tailored products or services using the same production resources as mass production is called mass ....?

   (a) Customisation   (b) Custom   (c) Customer   (d) Conte

6. Strategic Transitions

YouTube, which started up in February 2005, quickly became the most popular video-sharing Web site in the world. Even though YouTube's original mission was to provide an outlet for amateur filmmakers, clips of copyrighted Hollywood movies and television shows soon proliferated on the YouTube Web site. It is difficult to gauge how much proprietary content from TV shows winds up on YouTube without the studios' permission. YouTube has also implemented Video ID filtering and digital fingerprinting technology that allows copyright owners to compare the digital fingerprints of their videos with material on YouTube and then flag infringing material. Using this technology, it is able to filter many unauthorised videos before they appear on the YouTube Website.

7. Resource-based view on strategy

(i)   Is your resource valuable? If a resource is valuable, that's a good thing. But it's not enough to claim that a firm possesses something valuable. All businesses have access to electricity, which is valuable. It doesn't create advantage.

(ii) Is it rare? If access to this resource is limited, and your business has it, we begin to see the seeds of competitive advantage. But trouble may still be lurking.

(iii) Is it inimitable? Once your competitor realizes you have this stuff, can they imitate or copy it? Many of us remember that Dell Computers was once the company to beat in the PC business because they practically invented the web-based supply chain system. Now, most PC manufacturers have matched that capability. Since the web-based supply chain could be copied, it wasn't infinitely sustainable.

(iv) Is it non-substitutable? If your business has superior delivery speed and accuracy using a truck-based delivery system, and your competition can meet or beat your capabilities using rail as a substitute, then this is not the basis of sustainable competitive advantage.

(v)   Is it operationalisable? This refers to your business' ability to put your resource to good use. A good example of a business that had a tremendous resource but not the supporting capabilities, is Xerox's invention of the Alto computer. The Xerox Alto computer had a bitmapped screen and a graphical user interface; it was the predecessor of the Apple Macintosh and Microsoft Windows operating systems. But Xerox lacked the market capabilities to exploit such an asset and it never saw commercial success.

8. Sustained competitive advantage

(i) Strong research and Innovation. The technology industry is one of the leading industries with respect to strong research and innovation. And when it comes to setting the pace using innovation as leverage; Apple and Sony are the two companies that have held their leadership position using innovation as a competitive advantage.

(ii) Brand Popularity. Being recognized all over the world as a respected brand is a sustained competitive advantage that companies such as Virgin, Apple and Coca cola have used as leverage to hold the market sway for years. Virgin is a company that has used its brand name as leverage to break into new markets in completely new territories.

(iii) Corporate reputation. Corporate reputation is a form of sustained competitive advantage that companies such as Price Waterhouse and Berkshire Hathaway have leveraged to become world class entities.

(iv) Strategic assets. Holding strategic assets such as patents is a strong source of sustained competitive advantage and General Electric has stood the test of time because of the several patents held. Mind you that possession of these strategic assets has made General Electric one of the most powerful companies in the world.

(v) Access to working Capital. Generally, public liability companies (quoted companies) have a sustained competitive advantage over private companies because of their infinite capacity to raise capital from the public. Take a look at how Oracle acquired 57 companies in a space of five years and Reliance Industries investing a billion dollars in a single swoop to open a chain of retail stores.

(vi) Barriers to Entry. Barriers to entry due to government restrictions and regulations have been the source of sustained competitive advantage for companies such as Telmex and Chevron.

(vii) Superior Product or customer support. IKEA has become a market leader in the furniture industry because of its ability to provide superior product at an affordable rate; backed by a strong customer support system.

8. Wordsearch

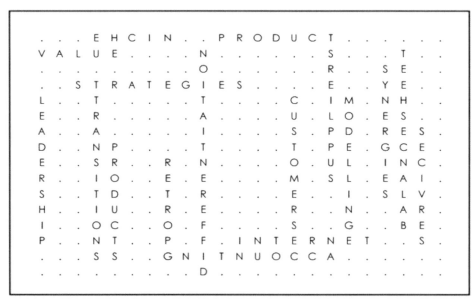

Word directions and start points are formatted: (Direction, X, Y)

ACCOUNTING (W,17,15) MODELLING (S,18,5) STRATEGIES (E,3,4)
BALANCESHEET (N,21,13) NICHE (W,8,1) SUPPLIERS (N,17,10)
CUSTOMERS (S,15,5) PORTER (N,8,14) SYNERGIES (S,20,3)
DIFFERENTIATION (N,10,16) PRODUCT (E,11,1) TRANSITIONS (S,4,5)
INTERNET (E,12,14) PRODUCTS (S,5,8) VALUE (E,1,2)
LEADERSHIP (S,1,5) SERVICES (N,22,14)

Exercises – Section 6

1.   Which of the following questions is the most likely odd one out in relation to frequent problems relating to our customers?

        (a)   Why don't they buy our products?
        (b)   What is the colour theme of their website?
        (c)   Are they receiving our goods on time?
        (d)   What do they think of the quality of our services and goods?

2.   Which of the following questions is the most likely odd one out in relation to frequent problems relating to our employees?

        (a)   Are they happy and productive in our organisation?
        (b)   Do we offer them a rewarding working environment?
        (c)   Do we operate effective marketing campaigns?
        (d)   Are we promoting our highest achievers?

3.   Which of the following questions is the most likely odd one out in relation to frequent problems relating to our product development?

        (a) Do we invest appropriately in product development?
        (b) Do we understand the life-cycle of our products?
        (c) Are we located in a purpose-built building?
        (d) What is a realistic product stream that will lead to commercial success?

4.   Research the following books on "negotiations" and identify which you would recommend to a friend:

        (a) *Getting to Yes* by Roger Fisher and William Ury
        (b) *How to Win Friends and Influence People* by Dale Carnegie
        (c) *Negotiation Genius* by Deepak Malhotra
        (d) *Influence: the Psychology of Persuasion* by Robert B. Cialdini.

        Various answers but *Getting to Yes* is the best seller.

5.   To whom is the following quote attributable: "We cannot negotiate with people who say what's mine is mine and what's yours is negotiable."?

   (a) John F Kennedy   (b) Bill Gates   (c) Taylor Swift   (d) Richard Branson

6.   Negotiation.

The discussion of the advantages and disadvantages of a 'Win-Lose' approach to negotiation might start with an introduction to the terminology (i.e. one party wins, the other loses). There is a place for win-lose approaches to negotiations where the 'win' in the issue or outcome is deemed more important than the relationship.
Advantages include:
   •   Win-lose can bring more competitive advantage as the negotiator is targeted with obtaining their objectives to the detriment of the other party's
   •   Very focused
   •   Win-lose more appropriate for certain types of purchases i.e. transactional
   •   Win-lose often perceived as a powerful perspective/position.
Disadvantages include:
   •   Win-lose could damage the buyer-supplier relationship, (not taking account of the other person's perspective). May leave the 'losing' party feeling resentful
   •   Seen as a dominant/aggressive position
   •   Too much focus on achieving own objectives, could mean missing an opportunity
   •   Less flexible.

7.   <u>Decision Making.</u> Various solutions possible

Should I continue for a Masters Degree (MBA) after graduating?			
Pros	**Score/10**	**Cons**	**Score/10**
Increased job opportunities		**Cost of fees**	
Better promotion prospects		**Restricts income**	
More useful to an employer		**Delays start of work**	
Develops business knowledge		**Need to pay rent**	
Total Pros		Total Cons	
Average Pros		**Average Cons**	

8.   <u>Negotiation.</u> This is a past exam question of CIPS 2013.

The scenario poses an ultimatum and an impasse situation. There is also an element of an unreasonable deadline too (on offer today only). The buyer has a range of questions that he can ask to avoid walking away and keep the negotiations open. He will want to understand if there is an opportunity to extend the deadline and what lies behind the fixed stance on price and payment terms. The buyer can use questions to keep the negotiation going, try to regain control, to refocus the negotiation towards a more integrative approach/outcome and create options to find something to bargain with to improve the price and payment terms. Candidates can draw from sources such as Gerard Nierenberg (Fundamentals of negotiations) or Steele, Murphy and Russell (It's a Deal).

Answers could provide THREE question types from the following or other valid questions if justified:
- Open ended – requires more than yes/no answer and elicits more information to keep the discussions progressing and potentially new options. For examples:
    Why are you taking such a firm position on your payment terms?
    What else could either of us do to close the gap between our positions?
    Why can't we negotiate on this deadline?
- Probing – asks for more detail, clarification or explanation to gain further understanding of why there is no room for negotiation and no alternatives to offer. For examples:
    Are you feeling pressure to bring the negotiations to a close?
    What is your reasoning behind not wanting to negotiate further?
    Why is it important to conclude negotiation?
- Hypothetical – opens up options. The buyer could put forward some options regarding price and payment terms or could offer other variables to trade to see if they are more valuable to the supplier that the price level and payment terms the supplier has offered. For examples:
    If it was 2 weeks from now and we were looking back at this negotiation, what might we wish we had brought to the table?
    If we can come up with an alternative, would you still want me to 'take or leave' your offer?
    If I were able to look at increasing volumes would you be able to discuss discounting prices?
- Multiple – covers more than one issue, puts the other party under pressure and potentially introduces other options to consider. For examples:
    How can we extend the deadline and how would this affect the price and terms you can offer?
    What is different tomorrow that would remove this offer or prevent you improving your offer and including a discussion on volume?

9. <u>Decision Making.</u> Various solutions possible

Should I invest in the UK stock market at the moment or not?			
Pros	**Score/10**	**Cons**	**Score/10**
Possibility of high returns		Volatility too high	
Stocks look at present		Nervous buyers (Brexit)	
Alternatives (property) poor		High risk	
Stock market on upward trend		Possible low returns	
Total Pros		**Total Cons**	
Average Pros		**Average Cons**	

10. <u>Negotiation.</u> Solution should recognise that there are a number of factors to consider when entering into a negotiation. Topics that could be covered are:

   - Power and authority of those to attend the negotiation
   - Size of the supply organisation relative to the buying organisation
   - The ability and cost to switch suppliers (number of potential suppliers, substitutes, level of differentiation of product)
   - Attractiveness of the buying account to the supplier (reputation, prompt payer, ethical dealings, supplier development)
   - Urgency of demand
   - Knowledge/information about the supplier and its negotiating position
   - The importance of each party's resources to the other party
   - Amount of existing business with the supplier (if any)
   - Market position of the supplier e.g. market leader or contender
   - Personal relationships/reciprocity
   - Business relationships (if any)
   - Future goals and objectives e.g. consolidation/acquisition.

11.   <u>Wordsearch</u>

<u>SOLUTION</u>

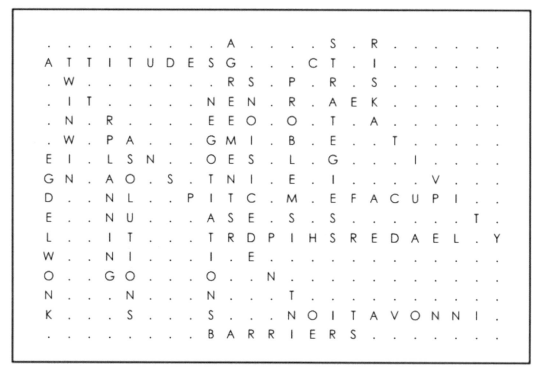

Word directions and start points are formatted: (Direction, X, Y)

AGREEMENTS (S,10,1)   INNOVATION (W,22,15)   RISK (S,17,1)
ATTITUDES (E,1,2)   KNOWLEDGE (N,1,15)   SOLUTIONS (S,5,7)
BARRIERS (E,9,16)   LEADERSHIP (W,21,11)   STRATEGIES (S,15,1)
CREATIVITY (SE,14,2)   NEGOTIATIONS (S,9,4)   TRANSPARENT (SE,3,4)
DECISIONS (N,11,11)   PLANNING (S,4,6)   WINWIN (S,2,3)
FACUP (E,16,9)   PROBLEMS (S,13,3)

Exercises – Section 7

1. A researcher analysing a small used car business knows that the number of employees in the three fundamental departments (salesroom, marketing and accounts) are split more or less evenly (one third of employees in each). Unfortunately, the first sample chosen to gauge overall employee preferences, although obtained randomly, surprisingly contained no-one from accounts. On balance, what is her best sampling option now?

    (a) Cluster   (b) Stratified   (c) Give up   (d) Random (again)

    Guarantees a third from each department.

2. A researcher decides to use multi-stage sampling technique for his research methodology. This involves randomly selecting seven streets from each and every borough of Greater Manchester then randomly choosing three residents in each street. Approximately, how many people will he have in the whole sample?

    (a) 20   (b) 200   (c) 2000   (d) 20000

    The Metropolitan Boroughs of Greater Manchester are (in alphabetical order) Bolton, Bury, City of Manchester, Oldham, Rochdale, City of Salford, Stockport, Tameside, Trafford and Wigan (ten in total). So the total in his sample is $10 \times 7 \times 3 = 210$ individuals (approximately 200).

3. Of 100 randomly selected people in the area of Roehampton in London, twenty had the last name "Smith" and twenty had the first name "John". Which of the following sentences is descriptive but not inferential?

    (a) 20% of the people of Greater London have "Smith" as the last name
    (b) 20% of these people of Roehampton have "Smith" as the last name
    (c) 20% of the people of London have "John" as the first name
    (d) 20% of the people in the UK have "John" as the first name

4. In her answer to a question in a questionnaire, a respondent lied about her age, claiming to be ten years younger than she actually was. Which compound term best describes the bias created by the claim?

    (a) Accidental, interviewer-induced,
    (b) Interviewer-induced, deliberate,
    (c) Deliberate, respondent-induced
    (d) Interviewer-induced, deliberate

5. Generally, which of the following would you expect to lead to a higher response rate?

    (a) Postal surveying,
    (b) Text surveying
    (c) Email surveying
    (d) Questionnaire distribution

    Generally, people do not often reply to postal or email questionnaires (perhaps 5%). Short text questions, perhaps 20%. Questionnaires distributed by hand and collected in perhaps 70%.

6. <u>Over-complication.</u>

Uncommon	Common
Consider	Think
Effectuate	Cause
Elucidate	Explain
Employ	Use
Initiate	Begin/Start
Major	Important/Main
Perform	Do
Quantify	Measure
Require	Want/Need
Reside	Live
State	Say
Sufficient	Enough
Terminate	End
Ultimate	Last
Utilize	Use
Assist	Help

7.   <u>Airline Data files.</u>

Use sorting on the gender column to create each file (do NOT type values)

airline_male.xls

ID	GENDER	AGE_GP	INFLT_RT	TRVL_FREQ
2	1	4	1	5
4	1	5	2	11
6	1	6	4	11
7	1	6	4	14
8	1	3	1	5
12	1	6	4	14
13	1	3	1	14
14	1	4	1	10
16	1	5	2	10
18	1	3	2	11
19	1	2	1	14

airline_female.xls

ID	GENDER	AGE_GP	INFLT_RT	TRVL_FREQ
1	2	2	2	2
3	2	3	2	5
5	2	6	2	11
9	2	4	2	5
10	2	3	3	6
11	2	5	1	9
15	2	3	4	5
17	2	6	5	7
20	2	3	1	5

Looks likely – men double figures, women single figures.

8. Bad design

This questionnaire is designed to support research on "business banking". Your answers will be completely anonymous and the data provided will be used for any purpose.

Comment [J1]: "NOT be"

Cheers!

Comment [J2]: Too colloquial

NAME: AGE:

Comment [J3]: Never ask for a name in anonymous questionnaires

1. Are you?

    Female   Male   Other

Comment [J4]: Unexpected option

2. What is your UK bank?

    HSBC   Santander   Lloyds   RBS   Halifax

Comment [J5]: Incomplete bank list, perhaps respondent banks with Co-op Bank?

3. Using a scale 1-3, how would you rate customer service at your bank?

    3   2   1

Comment [J6]: Too narrow for a rating scale

Comment [J7]: Which is highest, 1 or 3?

4. Aproximately, how much do you pay over the counter (£) each year?

    0-50   51-500   501-1000   1001-10000   >10001

Comment [J8]: Grammatical error

Comment [J9]: Almost impossible for anyone to answer

Comment [J10]: Irregular intervals

5. Do you think your bank is the best bank of those in question 3?

    Yes   No

Comment [J11]: Best according to which criteria – too open-ended

Comment [J12]: He means question 2

215

9.   <u>Wordsearch</u>

<u>**SOLUTION**</u>

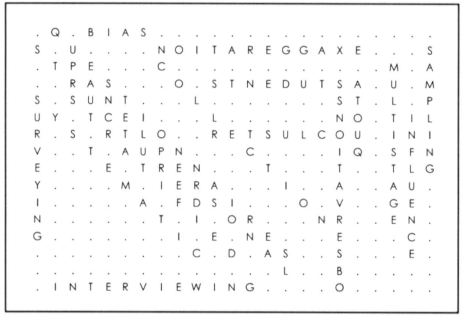

Word directions and start points are formatted: (Direction, X, Y)

BIAS (E,9,1)
CLUSTER (W,22,2)
COLLECTION (N,17,15)
EXAGGERATION (E,8,8)
INFLUENCE (S,21,6)
INTERVIEWING (S,3,4)

MULTISTAGE (E,7,16)
OBSERVATIONS (W,18,4)
QUESTIONNAIRES (SE,1,3)
PANEL PERSONAL (W,21,5)
QUOTA (E,11,12)
SAMPLING (S,2,6)

STRATIFIED (E,6,2)
STRUCTURED (N,23,14)
STUDENTS (SE,5,8)
SURVEYING (E,6,7)
SYSTEMATIC (E,13,3)

Exercises – Section 8

1. Criminal Records Bureau (CRB) checks for verification of prospective employee data are now called:

    (a) BHS   (b) CBS   (c) DBS   (d) EMS

2. The Act of Parliament of the United Kingdom of Great Britain and Northern Ireland which defines UK law on the processing of data on identifiable living people is the main piece of legislation that governs the protection of personal data in the UK and it is known as:

    (a) APD   (b) PDA   (c) DPA   (d) PAD

3. Personnel departments and their associated activities are also described by the acronym:

    (a) RHM   (b) HMR   (c) HRM   (d) MRH

4. Video technology used in monitoring in employees in the workplace using is often referred to as:

    (a) CCTV   (b) VTE   (c) VDU   (d) HDMI

5. The potential for businesses to drive employment decisions, based on the use of data, is sometimes known as:

    (a) Employee Retention
    (b) Recruitment tools
    (c) People analytics
    (d) Vetting procedures

6. Employment contracts.

Full-time and part-time contracts must give employees:

- a written statement of employment or contract
- the statutory minimum level of paid holiday
- a payslip showing all deductions, eg National Insurance contributions (NICs)
- the statutory minimum length of rest breaks
- Statutory Sick Pay (SSP)
- maternity, paternity and adoption pay and leave

Fixed-term contracts:

- last for a certain length of time
- are set in advance
- end when a specific task is completed
- end when a specific event takes place
- Fixed-term employees must receive the same treatment as full-time permanent staff

Zero hour contracts are also known as casual contracts:

- are usually for 'piece work' or 'on call' work, eg interpreters
- employees are on call to work when you need them
- employers don't have to give employees work
- employees don't have to do work when asked
- workers are entitled to statutory annual leave Minimum Wage, the same as regular workers
- employers cannot stop a zero hours worker from getting work elsewhere

Agency staff:

- Employers pay the agency, including the employee's National Insurance contributions (NICs) and Statutory Sick Pay (SSP)
- the agency has responsibility to make sure workers get their rights under working time regulations
- after 12 weeks' continuous employment in the same role, agency workers get the same terms and conditions as permanent employees, including pay, working time, rest periods, night work, breaks and annual leave
- employers must allow agency workers to use any shared facilities (eg a staff canteen or childcare) and give them information about job vacancies from the first day they work there
- employers are still responsible for their health and safety

7.   Employment in Europe.

Paid Annual Leave. Sweden, France and Denmark all offer 25 working days a year as minimum —the highest entitlement. The UK is bunched towards the bottom again with the likes of Italy, Greece, Germany, Portugal and Switzerland – all offering the minimum 20 days. Spain is a great place for public holidays with 14 offered to those based there, whereas the UK and the Netherlands each provide eight days as standard. Annual leave is paid time off work granted by employers to employees to be used for whatever the employee wishes. Depending on the employer's policies, differing number of days may be offered, and the employee may be required to give a certain amount of advance notice, may have to coordinate with the employer to be sure that staffing is adequately covered during the employee's absence, and other requirements may have to be met. The vast majority of countries today mandate a minimum amount of paid annual leave by law, though the United States is a notable exception in mandating no minimum paid leave and treating it as a perk rather than a right.

8.   Employment in Europe.

'Best' Country To Be Out Of Work. It's never good to be out of work, but Denmark is the 'best' place in Europe to be unemployed with residents receiving 90 percent of previous earnings granted for up to 104 weeks. The UK, by contrast, offers a least generous flat rate of €66 or €84 per week, for up to 26 weeks. Ireland too is one of the least generous, providing a flat-rate of €188 per week for between 22 and 33 weeks, depending on contributions. As a benchmark, the U.S. offers between 40 percent and 50 percent of earnings for up to 26 weeks, depending on the individual state.

Sick Pay Won't Go Far In Britain. UK is again at the bottom of this list in terms of sick pay – the allowance in the UK is 28 weeks, paid at a flat rate of around £88 per week. Paid sick leave is most generous in the Netherlands, where workers can be absent for up to 104 weeks and receive 70 percent of their salary for the whole period!

New Mothers Get Lots Of Time Off In The UK. The most generous amount of leave by some considerable margin is here in the UK with Ireland a close second at 52 and 42 weeks respectively. In terms of pay however, in Austria, Denmark, France, Germany, the Netherlands and Spain mothers get 100 percent of previous earnings for the entire period. In the UK, 39 of the 52 weeks are paid, the first six weeks at 90 percent of earnings, and the remainder at up to £140-odd per week.

British Fathers Only Get Ten Days Off. This policy is not regulated by the EU, so entitlements vary. However new fathers in Finland receive a massive 45 working days off, leading the pack by some considerable margin. UK dads get just 10 working days off.

9.   Across: human resources, planning, shortlist, application
      Down: appraisal, survey,

10.   Wordsearch

SOLUTION

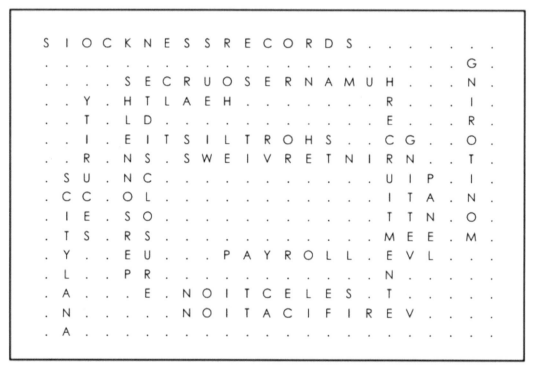

Primary Data: Employees

```
S I O C K N E S S R E C O R D S . . . . .   . .
. . . . . . . . . . . . . . . . . . . . G .
. . . . S E C R U O S E R N A M U H . . . N .
. . Y . H T L A E H . . . . . . . R . . . I .
. . T . L D . . . . . . . . . . . E . . . R .
. . I . E I T S I L T R O H S . . C G . . O .
. . R . N S . S W E I V R E T N I R N . . T .
. S U . N C . . . . . . . . . . U I P . I .
. C C . O L . . . . . . . . . . I T A . N .
. I E . S O . . . . . . . . . . T T N . O .
. T S . R S . . . . . . . . . M E E . M .
. Y . . E U . . . P A Y R O L L . E V L . . . .
. L . . P R . . . . . . . . . . N . . . .
. A . . . E . N O I T C E L E S . T . . . . .
. N . . . . . N O I T A C I F I R E V . . . .
. A . . . . . . . . . . . . . . . . . . .
```

Word directions and start points are formatted: (Direction, X, Y)

ANALYTICS (N,2,16)   PANEL (S,20,8)   SELECTION (W,16,14)
DISCLOSURE (S,6,5)   PAYROLL (E,10,12)   SHORTLIST (W,15,6)
HEALTH (W,10,4)   PERSONNEL (N,5,13)   SIOCKNESS (E,1,1)
HUMANRESOURCES (W,18,3) RECORDS (E,10,1)   VERIFICATION (W,19,15)
INTERVIEWS (W,17,7)   RECRUITMENT (S,18,4)   VETTING (N,19,12)
MONITORING (N,22,11)   SECURITY (N,3,11)

Exercises – Section 9

1. Suppose that a business researcher has found good correlation between two variables (x,y) and a regression line of y = 0.8016 x − 13.5772. Based on this linear model, what value of y (to one decimal place) can the researcher expect for a value x = 17.

    (a) 0   (b) 0.5   (c) 0.1   (d) 0.2

2. The average number of calls received by an international call centre for a well-known insurance company is one call per minute. Assuming a Poisson distribution, what is the percentage probability that in a randomly selected minute of the working day, more than one call will be received?

    (a) 1%   (b) 26%   (c) 74%   (d) 99%

3. In a Binomial experiment of n trials where p is the probability of success, the probability of n successes is p^n. The probability of n failures is therefore

    (a) $1 - p^n$ (b) $(1 - p)^n$ (c) $(1 - np)$ (d) p^n

4. Which of the following random variables would you most expect to be <u>normally</u> distributed?

    (a) The number of times a die is rolled before a six is observed
    (b) The number of accidents that occur at a busy road junction
    (c) The number of people in the queue waiting to be served at a bank
    (d) The weight of a box of cereal selected from a production line.

5. Which one of the following probabilities is represented by the shaded area in the figure below?

(a) Pr(Z > 120)
(b) 0.5 - Pr(Z > 120)
(c) Pr(Z < 120)
(d) Pr(Z <120) + 0.5.

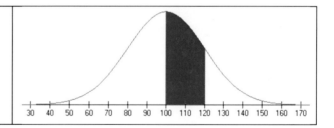

6. <u>Binomial distribution.</u>

    P(x ≤ 7) = BINOMDIST(7,20,0.48,1) = 0.173921 = 0.174(to 3 d.p)

7. <u>Binomial distribution.</u>

    (i)   P(x = 9) = BINOMDIST(9,10,0.9,0) = 0.38742 = 0.387
    (ii)   P(x ≤ 8) = BINOMDIST(8,10,0.9,1)= 0.263901 = 0.264
    (iii)   P(x = 10) = BINOMDIST(10,10,0.9,0) = 0.348678 = 0.349

    Note: All add up to 1 since all possibilities are included in these three cases.

8. <u>Binomial distribution.</u>

    P(x > 1) = P(x ≥ 2) = 1 − BINOMDIST(1,30,0.005,1) = 0.00991 = 1% (to 1 s.f.)

9.   Binomial distribution.

   P(x ≥ 10) = 1 - P(x ≤ 9) = 1 - BINOMDIST(9,25,0.25,1) = 1- 0.928671737 = 7% (to 1 s.f.)

13.   Poisson distribution.

   Consider last two months to calculate a daily average, λ = (15+16)/62 = 0.5
   POISSON(0,0.5,0) = 0.6065. Percentage probability 61% (to 2 s.f.)

14.   Poisson distribution.

   P(x ≥ 2) = 1 - P(x ≤ 1) = 1 - POISSON(1,0.40,1) = 1 – 0.938448 = 0.061552
   This exceeds 5%, so IT should overhaul.

15.   Poisson distribution.

   P(x = 2) = POISSON(2,2,0) = 0.270671 = 0.27 (to 2 d.p.)

13.   Normal distribution.

   (i)   P(grade ≥70) = 1-NORMDIST(69,60,10,1) = 1 – 0.81594 = 0.18406 = 18%
   (ii)   P(60≤grade<70) = NORMDIST(69,60,10,1)-NORMDIST(59,60,10,1) = 35%
   (iii)   P(grade < 40) = NORMDIST(39,60,10,1) = 0.017864 = 2%

15.   Poisson distribution.

   λ = 1.25, so P(r ≤ 2),= POISSON(2,1.25,1) = 0.868468
   So P(r ≥ 3), probability of three or more purchases = 1 - P(r ≤ 2) = 0.131532
   Percentage probability that the customer purchases three (or more) is 13% (to 2 s.f.)

15.   Normal distribution.

   Excel:

   (i)   P(grade < 40) = NORMDIST(40,50,20,1) = 0.3085 = 30.85%
   (ii)   P(45≤grade<65) = NORMDIST(65,50,20,1)- NORMDIST(45,50,20,1) = 37.21%
   (iii)   P(grade ≥70) = 1-NORMDIST(70,50,20,1) = 0.1587 = 15.87%

   Tables:

   i) For x = 40000, z = -0.5
   Area to the left (less than) of z = -0.5 is equal to 0.3085 = 30.85% earn less than $40,000.

   ii) For x = 45000 , z = -0.25 and for x = 65000, z = 0.75
   Area between z = -0.25 and z = 0.75 is equal to 0.3721 = 37.21% earn between $45,000 and $65,000.

   iii)For x = 70000, z = 1
   Area to the right (higher) of z = 1 is equal to 0.1587 = 15.87% earn more than $70,000.

16.   Normal distribution.

Tables

(i)   For x = 80, z = 1; Area to the right of z = 1 is equal to 0.1586 = 15.87% scored more than 80.
(ii)   For x = 60, z = -1 Area to the right of z = -1 is equal to 0.8413 = 84.13% should pass the test.
(iii) 100% - 84.13% = 15.87% should fail the test.

Excel

(i) $P(x > 80) = 1 - P(x \leq 80)$ =1-NORMDIST(80,70,10,1) = 0.158655 = 15.87% .
(ii) $P(x \geq 60) = 1 - P(x < 60)$ =1-NORMDIST(60,70,10,1) = 0.841345 = 84.13%.
(iii) 100% - 84.13% = 15.87% should fail the test.

17.   Hypothesis Test (one population).

The null hypothesis is that the mean value of accounts is €250, and the alternative hypothesis is that the mean is not €250 (it could be larger or smaller).

$$H_0 : \mu = €250$$
$$H_1 : \mu \neq €250$$

Assume a 5% significance level. We do not know the population standard deviation, but can estimate it from the sample standard deviation s = €42. Since the sample is large enough (greater than thirty) this is reasonable.

Hence, standard error $= {}^s/_{\sqrt{n}} = {}^{42}/_{\sqrt{50}} = {}^{42}/_{7.07} = 5.94$ (to 2 d.p.) = 6 (to 1 s.f.)
So we now know that 95% of randomly-sampled means would lie within the interval (238,262).
Since the value of 257does indeed lie in this interval, accept $H_0 : \mu = €250$.
Conclusion: The mean value of orders received by the firm is about €250

18.   Hypothesis Test (one population).

The null hypothesis is that the mean value is £49.50, and the alternative hypothesis is that the mean is greater than £49.50.

$$H_0 : \mu = \textbf{£49.50}$$
$$H_1 : \mu > \textbf{£49.50}$$

Assume a 5% significance level. We do not know the population standard deviation, but can estimate it from the sample standard deviation s = £3.37. Since the sample is large enough (greater than thirty) this is reasonable.

Hence, standard error $= {}^s/_{\sqrt{n}} = {}^{3.37}/_{\sqrt{50}} = {}^{3.37}/_{7.07} = 0.477$ (to 3 d.p.)
So we know that 95% of means lie to the left of 49.50+ (1.65).(0.477), i.e. £50.29.

49.50   50.29

Accordingly, 5% will lie to the right (see diagram) Since the value of £50.40 lies to the right of £50.29, reject H_0 and accept H_1. Suggestion to the Games Store: The mean value of orders is now more than previous year (good news!)

19.   Hypothesis Test (two populations).

The null hypothesis is that the mean values for each shop are the same. The alternative hypothesis is that they are not the same.

$$H_0 : \mu_1 = \mu_2$$
$$H_1 : \mu_1 \neq \mu_2$$

Our sample values are $n_1 = 40$; $n_2 = 40$; $s_1 = 20$; $s_2 = 40$

Hence, standard error s = $\sqrt{\left(\frac{20^2}{40}\right) + \left(\frac{40^2}{40}\right)}$ = $\sqrt{10 + 40}$ = $\sqrt{50}$ = 7 (to 1 s.f.)

So we now know that 95% of our $(\bar{x}_1 - \bar{x}_2)$ values would lie within the interval (-14,+14).

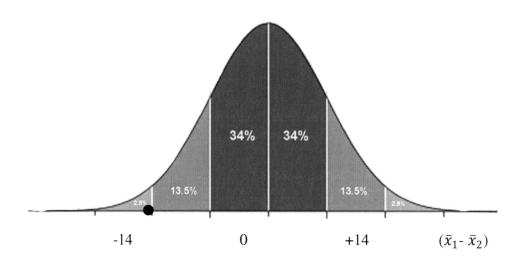

| -14 | 0 | +14 | $(\bar{x}_1 - \bar{x}_2)$ |

Since the actual value obtained from the samples is $(\bar{x}_1 - \bar{x}_2)$ = £77 - £90 = -£13, we accept **H₀.**
Conclusion. The mean takings for each shop are comparable.
(Note that any value for $(\bar{x}_1 - \bar{x}_2)$ between -14 and +14 would have resulted in accepting **H₀**)

20.   Hypothesis Test (two populations).

1 State the null and alternative hypotheses.
We want to check that the two machines are putting the same amounts in packets, so the null hypothesis is that the means from each machine are the same. The alternative hypothesis is that the means are not the same.

$$H_0 : \mu_1 = \mu_2$$
$$H_1 : \mu_1 \neq \mu_2$$

2 Specify the level of significance.
We can use the standard 5%.
3 Calculate the acceptance range for the variable tested.
We are looking at the sampling distribution of $\bar{x}_1 - \bar{x}_2$, with sample sizes $n_1 = 30$ and
$n_2 = 40$, and standard deviations $s_1 = 14$ and $s_2 = 10$. This sampling distribution is Normal with:
mean = 0

$$\text{standard error} = \sqrt{\left(\frac{s_1^2}{n_1}\right) + \left(\frac{s_2^2}{n_2}\right)} = 3.01$$

For a 5% significance level and a two-sided test, the acceptance range is within 1.96 standard deviations of the mean. This defines the interval:
$0 - 1.96 \times 3.01$ to $0 + 1.96 \times 3.01$ or $(-6,+6)$
4 Find the actual value for the variable tested.
The observed difference in samples is $\bar{x}_1 - \bar{x}_2 = 180 - 170 = 10$.
5 Decide whether or not to reject the null hypothesis.
The actual value of 10 is outside the interval (-6,6), so we reject the null hypothesis.
6 State the conclusion. The evidence from the samples does not support the view that the mean weight put into packets is the same from each machine.

Exercises – Section 10

1. A set of business financial statements is comprised of several key statements usually contained in a balance sheet. These are *assets*, *liabilities* and ....?

    (a) equity   (b) equality   (c) egalite   (d) equary

2. A process and policy, usually assisted by specialised software, which allows a business or institution to consolidate its financial information, maintain compliance with accounting rules/laws and produce detailed financial reports, is described by the acronym:

    (a) ATM   (b) FTE   (c) FDM   (d) BBC

3. Which of the following is NOT a well known financial data vendor?

    (a) Bloomberg   (b) Moody's   (c) S&P Capital   (d) Skysports

4. Which Excel function returns the net present value of an investment based on a series of periodic cash flows & discount rate?

    (a) MVP   (b) NPV   (c) PVI   (d) VAL

5. Maintaining which one of the following is a good way to manage personal finances?

    (a)   Daily Sense of Humour Review
    (b)   Weekly Optimism Assessment
    (c)   Monthly Budget Preparation
    (d)   Annual Suspension of Disbelief

6.   Financial Functions.

D3			f_x	=ACCRINT(B1,B2,B3,7%,15000,4)				
	A	B	C	D	E	F	G	H	I
1		01-Jan-12						
2		01/04/2012						
3		31/12/2013		2100				
4								

9.   <u>Personal Budget.</u> Various solutions

Income (weekly/monthly)

Wages/salary	£
Wages/salary (partner)	£
Benefits	£
Money from other people	£
Other	£
	£
Total income	£

Outgoings (weekly/monthly)

Mortgage/rent	£
Second mortgage/secured loan	£
Ground rent/service charges	£
Buildings/contents insurance	£
Life insurance/endowment	£
Council tax	£
Gas	£
Electricity	£
Water	£
Food/housekeeping	£
Travel	£
Telephone	£
TV licence/rental	£
Clothing/emergencies	£
Prescriptions/health costs	£
Other	£
Total outgoings	£

My total income is £ ....

My total outgoings are £...................

8.   <u>Mortgages.</u>

Fixed rate

Advantages
Peace of mind that your monthly payments will stay the same
Easier to help budget

Disadvantages
Fixed rate deals are usually slightly higher than variable rate mortgages. If interest rates fall, you won't benefit
Charges if you want to leave the deal early – you are tied in for the length of the fixed period – you should look for a new mortgage deal two to three months before it ends or you'll be moved automatically onto your lender's standard variable rate which is usually higher

Variable rate mortgages (SVR)

Advantages
Freedom – you can overpay or leave at any time

Disadvantages
Your rate can be changed at any time during the loan

9.   Business Plan

Arz al-Lubnan Hookah Bar

Executive Summary

Arz al-Lubnan Hookah Bar (Cedars of Lebanon) is a new hookah bar concept which will focus on a combination of Middle Eastern customers and customers over 22 years in age to offer a more adult alternative to hookah bars frequented by college-age customers. The first bar will be established in Trendytown, and managed by the business founders, Sayed and Yasmine Batroun.

The business will generate revenues through the sale of flavored tobaccos, non-alcoholic drinks, and appetizers. The business seeks angel investor funding to launch its first bar.

The business projects to become profitable in its first year with good profit from strong sales in the first year. Sales will triple by the third year of operation. Net profit of sales will be respectable due to the high margin on the products sold. Exit for investors is possible from sale of the franchise to a chain of bars looking to expand their market.

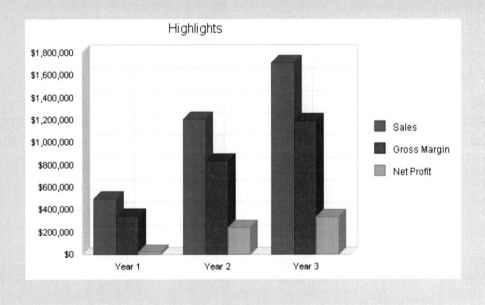

Objectives

Arz al-Lubnan Hookah Bar seeks to achieve the following objectives with the launch of its first hookah lounge:

1. To establish a community of hookah smokers who contribute programming, events, and culture ideas to Arz al-Lubnan Hookah Bar resulting in 50 events or programs held in its third year of operation.
2. To maintain a Facebook Fan page of 5,000 individuals by the end of its third year as a sign of its community.
3. To become profitable in its second year through the sale of tobacco, food and drinks.
4. To establish a franchisable model for hookah bars and initiate fundraising and planning for franchising by its fifth year of operation.

Mission

The mission of Arz al-Lubnan Hookah Bar is to provide a comfortable environment, sometimes relaxing and sometimes energetic and stimulating, around which those who love hookah smoking, as well as new converts, can come together. The environment will draw on elements of Middle Eastern culture as well as the culture of the local environment.

10. Wordsearch.

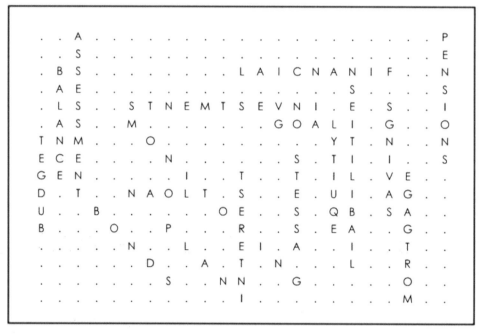

Word directions and start points are formatted: (Direction, X, Y)

ASSESSMENT (S,3,1)
ASSETS (N,15,13)
BALANCE (S,2,3)
BONDS (SE,4,11)
BUDGET (N,1,12)
EQUITY (N,17,12)

FINANCIAL (W,20,3)
GOAL (E,14,6)
INTEREST (N,12,16)
INVESTMENTS (W,16,5)
LIABILITIES (N,18,14)
LOAN (W,9,10)

MONITORING (SE,6,6)
MORTGAGE (N,21,16)
PENSIONS (S,23,1)
PLAN (SE,8,12)
SAVINGS (N,20,11)

INDEX

http://www.algana.com/ABDI/